SCANDINAVIAN
PHRASEBOOK

Scandinavian phrasebook
3rd edition – February 2001
First published – December 1992

Published by
Lonely Planet Publications Pty Ltd ABN 36 005 607 983
90 Maribyrnong St, Footscray, Victoria 3011, Australia

Lonely Planet Offices
Australia Locked Bag 1, Footscray, Victoria 3011
USA 150 Linden St, Oakland CA 94607
UK 10a Spring Place, London NW5 3BH
France 1 rue du Dahomey, 75011 Paris

Cover illustration
A horse is a horse, of course of course by Patrick Marris

ISBN 1 86450 225 8

text © Lonely Planet Publications Pty Ltd 2001
cover illustration © Lonely Planet Publications Pty Ltd 2001

10 9 8 7 6 5 4   2 1

Printed by The Bookmaker International Ltd
Printed in China

About the Authors

Birgitte Hou Olsen updated the Danish chapter, based on a chapter by Peter A. Crozier.

Bergljót av Skardi wrote the Faroese chapter. She is 50 years old and teaches Faroese and English at the high school in her home town Tórshavn in the Faroe Islands.

Gerald Porter updated the Finnish chapter, based on an original chapter by Markus Lehtipuu. He's English but has lived in Finland for many years. He is at present lecturing in the English department at the University of Vaasa.

Icelandic was updated by Margrét Eggertsdóttir, based on a chapter by Ingibjörg Árnadóttir. Margrét was born in Reykjavik in 1960. At present she is a lecturer in Icelandic language and literature at the University of Copenhagen.

The Norwegian chapter was updated by Runa Eilertsen and Daniel Cash. Daniel is Australian but has lived in Norway. He currently works for a Melbourne-based newspaper. Runa is a native-born Norwegian who lives in Oslo. This chapter was developed from an original chapter by Doekes Lulofs.

Anna Herbst updated the Swedish chapter, based on an original chapter by Pär Sörme. Anna is Swedish but has lived in Australia since 1986. She has taught English and Swedish language and literature in secondary school, adult education and university in Sweden and Australia, and English and media subjects at university in China. She has also worked in broadcasting and once made a living as a folksinger.

From the Authors

Birgitte Hou Olsen wishes to thank Karin Vidstrup Monk from Lonely Planet for a creative and fruitful working relationship during the entire process.

Bergljót av Skardi wishes to thank her colleague Guðrun Gaard for passing the phrasebook job on to her. Also a big thank you to Hans Marius Johannessen for suggestions and advice.

Gerald Porter wants to record his thanks to Sirkku Aaltonen for love and constant guidance.

Margrét Eggertsdóttir would like to thank Professor Robert Cook at the University of Iceland for his contribution to the chapter on body language, showing his clear insight into what characterises the Icelanders.

Runa Eilertsen would like to thank Daniel Cash.

Anna Herbst would like to thank Dino Bressan for being most helpful in allowing her to test the phonetic transcriptions on him.

From the Publisher
Thanks go to Christian Becker-Christensen and Jan Katlev for their invaluable linguistic advice and also to Wenche Eriksen and Natasha Sayer for their assistance on the Norwegian chapter.

Patrick Marris illustrated the book and the cover and still managed to find the time to help Yukiyoshi Kamimura lay out some of the chapters. Fabrice Rocher supervised layout. Karin Vidstrup Monk edited, proofed and oversaw the whole process. Emma Koch edited, Fleur Goding proofed and Natasha Velleley produced the map.

CONTENTS

SWEDISH 307

INTRODUCTION

Although it's not widely known outside Europe, the term 'Scandinavia' actually refers only to Denmark, Norway and Sweden while 'the Nordic countries' include Scandinavia plus Finland, Iceland and the Faroe Islands. This phrasebook covers all six languages and is thus really two in one: a Scandinavian phrasebook and a Nordic phrasebook!

To add to the confusion, five of the six languages – Danish, Swedish, Norwegian, Icelandic and Faroese – are referred to as the Scandinavian languages and they all form the northern branch of the Germanic languages tree. Finnish is the exception, being from a different family tree altogether. The Scandinavian languages have all descended from Old Norse, the language of the Vikings, while Finnish is related to Estonian and (more remotely) Hungarian.

However, luckily for English-speakers, these five languages are cousins of English and you'll be able to recognise quite a few words, eg, dør/dör for 'door' and hus/hús for 'house'. One big advantage of Danish, Swedish, Norwegian, Faroese and Icelandic being so closely related is that once you've got the hang of one language, the others should seem quite familiar.

This book provides the basics for you to get around while making the most of all the Nordic countries have to offer. English is spoken very widely (and very well!) throughout these countries but if you take the time to learn at least a few phrases in the local language you'll find that you're more than rewarded for your efforts.

INTRODUCTION

SCANDINAVIAN & NORDIC

Arctic Ocean

Faxaflói ☆ Reykjavik
ICELAND
Heimaey

FAROE ISLANDS
Tórshavn

0 — 150 — 300 km
0 — 90 — 180 mi

Shetland Islands

Orkney Islands

Bergen

Outer Hebrides

Atlantic Ocean

Stavanger

Scotland

North Sea

Northern Ireland

Isle of Man

IRELAND

BRITAIN

St George's Channel

Wales

England

Frisian Islands

NETHERLANDS

Map 11

INTRODUCTION

EUROPE

Barents Sea

Inarijärvi

Lofoten Islands

Norwegian Sea

● Oulu
Oulujärvi

FINLAND

Kemi

Kemi

Trondheim ●

Kitinen

Pyhäjoki

SWEDEN

Kallavesi

Tampere ●
Gulf of Bothnia

Saimaa

Turku ● *Päijänne*
Helsinki ☆

NORWAY

Oslo ☆

Åland

Gulf of Finland

Klarälven

Mälaren

RUSSIAN FEDERATION

Vänern

Stockholm ☆

ESTONIA

Skagerrak

Vättern

Gulf of Riga

Kattegat

Gothenburg ●

Gotland

LATVIA

Jutland

Öland

DENMARK

Helsingborg ●
Copenhagen ☆ ● Malmö

LITHUANIA

Zealand
Funen *Bornholm*

Baltic Sea

RUSSIAN FEDERATION

GERMANY

POLAND

BELARUS

INTRODUCTION

HOW TO USE THIS PHRASEBOOK
Transliterations
Simplified transliterations have been provided in blue throughout this book. Italic is used to indicate where to place stress in a word.

Polite Forms
When a language has polite and informal forms of the singular pronoun 'you', the polite form has been used in most cases. However, you'll come across the informal form of 'you' in some phrases, such as those for talking with children.

Arthur or Martha?
When there are both feminine and masculine forms of a word, it's indicated in either of two ways, with the feminine form always appearing first:

- with a slash separating the feminine form and masculine ending (which is added to the feminine form) of a word:

  hot   hait/-oor   *heit/-ur* (f/m)

- when the distinction between masculine and feminine is more complex, each word is given in full, separated with a slash:

  cold   kerld/kuhld-oor   *køld/kaldur* (f/m)

These distinctions occur mostly in Faroese and Icelandic, but you may see them pop up in the other languages from time to time.

Finally
Don't be concerned if you feel you can't memorise words. You'll find the most essential words and phrases in the Quick Reference section at the start of each chapter. You could also try tagging a few pages for other key phrases.

INTRODUCTION

ABBREVIATIONS USED IN THIS BOOK

col	colloquial	n	neuter
f	feminine	pl	plural
inf	informal	pol	polite
m	masculine	sg	singular

PRONUNCIATION GUIDE

Below is a general pronunciation guide of the sounds that are common to the languages in this book, outlining in blue our representation of each sound, used in the simplified transliterations throughout the book. In addition, each language chapter contains a section about pronunciation particular to that language. It's a good idea to have a look at this as well, as it explains any sounds that might be slightly different in that language, or not found in any of the other languages.

Vowels

ah	as the 'a' in 'father'
uh	as the 'u' in 'cut'
a	as the 'a' in 'act'
eh	as the 'e' in 'bet'
ee	as the 'ee' in 'seethe'
i	as the 'i' in 'hit'
ü	a bit like the 'e' in British English 'dew' – try pursing your lips and saying 'ee'
o	a short 'o' as in 'pot'
oh	as the 'o' in 'note'
oo	a long 'oo' as in 'cool'
u	a short 'oo' as in 'foot'
ö	as the 'e' in 'summer'
or	as the 'or' in 'for', with less emphasis on the 'r'
er	as the 'er' in 'fern' but shorter, without the 'r'

INTRODUCTION

Diphthongs

ae	as the 'ea' in 'bear'
ay	as the 'ay' in 'day'
ai	as the sound of 'eye'
oy	the 'oy' as in 'toy'
ow	as the 'ou' in 'out'

Semiconsonants

w	as in 'wet'
y	as in 'yet'

Consonants

g	always a hard 'g' as in 'get', never as in 'gentle'
s	always as in 'kiss', never as in 'treasure'
sh	as in 'ship'
ch	as in 'chew'
dj	as the 'j' in 'jaw'
th	as the 'th' in 'lather'
h	as the 'h' in 'horse'
ng	as in 'sing'
ngn	as the meeting of sounds in 'hang-nail'
rr	a trilled 'r'
rt	as the 'rt' in American English 'start'
rd	as the 'rd' in American English 'weird'
rn	as the 'rn' in American English 'earn'
rl	as the 'rl' in American English 'earl'
dn	as the 'dn' in 'hadn't'
dl	as the 'dl' in 'saddle'

All other consonants are pronounced as in English.

DANISH

DANISH

QUICK REFERENCE

Hello.	hai/ghor-*da*	Hej/Goddag. (inf/pol)
Goodbye.	hai hai/fah-*vehl*	Hej hej/Farvel. (inf/pol)
Yes./No.	ya/nai	Ja./Nej.
Excuse me.	*ān*-sgül	Undskyld.
Sorry.	*ān*-sgül/bi-*kla*-ah	Undskyld/Beklager.
Thank you.	tahg	Tak.
That's fine.	di ehŕ ee *oŕ*-dehn.	Det er i orden.
You're welcome.	sehl tahg	Selv tak.

I'd like a ...	yai vi *gehŕ*-neh ha en ...	Jeg vil gerne have en...
one-way ticket	*ehng*-gild-bi-lehd	enkeltbillet
return ticket	*ŕeh-tooŕ*-bi-lehd	returbillet

I (don't) understand.
    yai fo-*sdor* (ig)   Jeg forstår (ikke).
Do you speak English?
    ta-lah dee *ehng*-ehlsg?   Taler De engelsk? (pol)
Where is ...?
    vor ehŕ ...?   Hvor er ...?
Go straight ahead.
    gä *li*-eh ooth   Gå lige ud.
Turn left/right.
    dŕai ti *vehns-dŕah*/ *hoy*-yah.   Drej til venstre/ højre.
Do you have any rooms available?
    hah ee *lith*-ee *vehŕl*-sah?   Har I ledige værelser?
I'm looking for a public toilet.
    yai *li*-thah *ehf*-dah id *o*-fehnd-leed toy-*lehd*   Jeg leder efter et offentligt toilet.

1	in	en	6	sehgs	seks
2	tor	to	7	sü-w	syv
3	tŕeh	tre	8	ā-deh	otte
4	feeŕ	fire	9	nee	ni
5	fehm	fem	10	tee	ti

Danish belongs to the North Germanic language group, together with Swedish, Norwegian, Icelandic and Faeroese.

Consequently, written Danish bears a strong resemblance to these languages. Spoken Danish, on the other hand, has evolved in a different direction, introducing sounds and pronunciation not found elsewhere.

Danish has a polite form of address, using the personal pronouns **De** and **Dem**. The words and phrases in this chapter are mostly in the familar form using **du** and **dig**, except where it's more appropriate to use the formal form. In general, use the formal form when speaking to senior citizens and officials, and the familiar form the rest of the time.

As Danish is not broadly spoken and few visitors take the time or effort to learn it, most Danes speak English. However, an effort to learn at least the basics is well received. It's a good idea to memorise the words for 'thank you', 'goodbye', 'hello' and 'I'm sorry'. This minimum effort will be appreciated, and with an increased command of the language you'll be rewarded by gaining a greater insight into Denmark and the Danes.

The pronunciation of each word and phrase in this chapter is transcribed using a simplified phonetic system, so with not too much effort it should be possible to grasp the basic sentence structure and begin creating your own sentences.

PRIMARY STRESS

In Danish the stress is usually placed on the first syllable, or on the first letter of the word.

DANISH

PRONUNCIATION

Danish varies from island to island as well as from north to south, with each region having its distinct dialect. The translation and pronunciation presented here follows the form of Danish known as Nudansk, (literally 'Now Danish'). This is the form of Danish spoken in Copenhagen, and understood throughout the country.

Stressed syllables in multi-syllable words are printed here in italic type, and longer syllables have been split into more manageable lengths.

Danes do not necessarily pronounce what they write. The pronunciation of letters varies depending on the word, and written vowels and/or consonants will sometimes 'disappear' completely in the pronunciation. Unfortunately there are no hard and fast rules as to how any given letter is to be pronounced. In general, the best advice for good pronunciation is to listen and learn. Good luck!

Danish varies from the general pronunciation guide, given at the front of this book, in only two respects:

Vowels

DANISH	GUIDE	SOUNDS
u(n), *å, o*	ā	a long rounded 'a' as in 'walk'

Consonants

r	ŕ	rolled in the throat

PRONOUNS					
SG			**PL**		
I	yai	*jeg*	we	vee	*vi*
you	doo	*du*	you (pl)	ee	*I*
he	han	*han*	they	dee	*de*
she	hoon	*hun*			
it	dehn (di)	*den (det)*			

GREETINGS & CIVILITIES
Useful Phrases

Hello.
   hai/daow/ghor-*da*   *Hej/Dav/Goddag.* (inf/pol)
Goodbye.
   hai hai/fah-*vehl*   *Hej hej/Farvel.* (inf/pol)
Yes./No.
   ya/nai   *Ja./Nej.*
Excuse me.
   ān-sgül   *Undskyld.*
May I? Do you mind?
   mā yai? *ti*-la-thah dee?   *Må jeg? Tillader De?* (pol)
Sorry. (excuse me, forgive me)
   ān-sgül/bi-*kla*-ah   *Undskyld/Beklager.*
Thank you.
   tahg   *Tak.*
Many thanks.
   mahng-eh tahg   *Mange tak.*
That's fine. You're welcome.
   di ehŕ ee *oŕ*-dehn. sehl tahg   *Det er i orden. Selv tak.*

DANISH

Greetings

Good morning.
   gor *morn*   *God morgen.*
Good afternoon.
   gor *ehf*-dah-mi-da   *God eftermiddag.*
Good evening/night.
   gor-*ahf*-dehn/go-*nad*   *Godaften./Godnat.*
How are you?
   voŕ-*dan* gor di?   *Hvordan går det?*
Well, thanks.
   god tahg   *Godt, tak.*

Forms of Address

Madam/Mrs	fŕoo	*fru*
Sir/Mr	hehŕ	*herr (hr.)*
Miss	fŕer-gehn	*frøken*
companion	kahm-ah-ŕahd	*kammerat*
friend	vehn	*ven*

SMALL TALK
Meeting People

What is your name?
va *hi*-thah doo/dee?   *Hvad hedder du/De?* (inf/pol)

My name is ...
mid naown ehŕ ...   *Mit navn er ...*

I'd like to introduce you to ...
yai vi gehŕ-neh   *Jeg vil gerne*
pŕehsehn-ti-ah dai for ...   *præsentere dig for ...*

I'm pleased to meet you.
di ehŕ *hüg*-lid ad *tŕah*-feh   *Det er hyggeligt at træffe*
dehm/*mer*-theh dai   *Dem/møde dig.* (pol/inf)

Nationalities

Where are you from?
vor *kom*-ah doo *frah*?   *Hvor kommer du fra?*

I'm from ...	yai ehŕ ffah ...	*Jeg er fra ...*
Australia	aow-*sdŕahl*-yehn	*Australien*
Canada	*ka*-na-da	*Kanada*
Denmark	*dan*-mahg	*Danmark*
England	*ehng*-lan	*England*
Ireland	*eeŕ*-lan	*Irland*
New Zealand	nü *si*-lan	*New Zealand*
Scotland	*sgod*-lan	*Skotland*
the USA	oo ehs a	*USA*
Wales	*wa*-ehls	*Wales*

Age

How old are you?
    vor *gah*-mehl ehŕ doo?   *Hvor gammel er du?*

I'm ... years old.
    yai ehŕ ... or *gah*-mehl   *Jeg er ... år gammel.*

Occupations

What do you do?   va *la*-wah doo?   *Hvad laver du?*

I'm (a/an) ...;	yai ehŕ ...;	*Jeg er ...;*
I work as (a/an) ...	yai *ah*-bai-dah som ...	*Jeg arbejder som ...*
artist	*kānsd*-nah	*kunstner*
business person	fo-*ŕahd*-nings-dŕeeoo-neh	*forretnings-drivende*
doctor	*leh*-eh	*læge*
engineer	ing-shin-*yer*	*ingeniør*
farmer	*bā*-neh	*bonde*
journalist	shā-na-*lisd*	*journalist*
lawyer	ath-vor-*kad*	*advokat*
manual worker	*ah*-bai-dah	*arbejder*
mechanic	mi-*ka*-ni-gah	*mekaniker*
nurse	*sü*-eh-plai-yah-skeh	*sygeplejerske*
office worker	kon-*tooŕ*-ah-bai-dah	*kontorarbejder*
scientist	*fors*-gah	*forsker*
student	sdoo-*di*-ah-neh	*studerende*
teacher	*lehŕ*-ah	*lærer*
waiter	*cheh*-nah	*tjener*
writer	fo-*fa*-dah	*forfatter*

DANISH

PRETTY PLEASE

Note that there is no equivalent to the word 'please' in Danish. Politeness is most often expressed by tone of voice and/or by beginning the sentence with phrases such as 'May I ...' Må jeg ... or 'Could I ...' Kunne jeg ...

DANISH

Religion

What is your religion?
vil-kehn rehlig-*yorn*   Hvilken religion
til-her-ah doo?   tilhører du?
I'm not religious.
yai ehr ig rehlig-*yers*   Jeg er ikke religiøs.

I'm ...   yai ehr ...   Jeg er ...
  Buddhist   boo-*deesd*   buddist
  Catholic   kator-*leeg*   katolik
  Christian   *krehs*-dehn   kristen
  Hindu   *hin*-doo   hindu
  Jewish   *yer*-theh   jøde
  Muslim   moos-*leem*   muslim

Family

Are you married?   ehr doo geefd?   Er du gift?

I'm ...   yai ehr ...   Jeg er ...
  married   geefd   gift
  single   *oo*-geefd   ugift

How many children do you have?
  vor *mahng*-eh bern hah doo?   Hvor mange børn har du?
I don't have any children.
  yai hah *ing*-ehn bern   Jeg har ingen børn.
I have a daughter/a son.
  yai hah in *da*-dah/en sern   Jeg har en datter/en søn.
How many brothers/
sisters do you have?
  vor *mahng*-eh *brerth*-rah/   Hvor mange brødre/
  sers-dfah hah doo?   søstre har du?
Is your husband/wife here?
  ehr deen man/*kor*-ne hehf?   Er din mand/kone her?
Do you have a boyfriend/girlfriend?
  hah doo in *kehrs*-deh?   Har du en kæreste?

brother	*broŕ*	*bror*
children	bern	*børn*
daughter	*da*-dah	*datter*
family	fa-*meel*-yeh	*familie*
father	fah	*far*
grandfather	*behs*-deh-fah	*bedstefar*
grandmother	*behs*-deh-mooŕ	*bedstemor*
grandparents	*moŕ*-mooŕ o	*mormor og*
(maternal)	*moŕ*-fah	*morfar*
grandparents	*fah*-mooŕ o	*farmor og*
(paternal)	*fah*-fah	*farfar*
husband	man	*mand*
mother	mooŕ	*mor*
sister	*sers*-dah	*søster*
son	sern	*søn*
wife	*kor*-ne	*kone*

DANISH

Kids' Talk

How old are you?
    vor *gah*-mehl ehŕ doo?   *Hvor gammel er du?*

When's your birthday?
    vo-*nor* hah doo *fer*-sehl-sda?   *Hvornår har du fødselsdag?*

What do you do after school?
    va *la*-wah doo *ehf*-dah *skor*-leh?   *Hvad laver du efter skole?*

Do you have a pet at home?
    hah doo id *keh*-leh-düŕ?   *Har du et kæledyr?*

I have a ...	yai hah ...	*Jeg har ...*
bird	in fool	*en fugl*
budgerigar	in on-doo-*lad*	*en undulat*
canary	in ka-*nah*-yeh-fool	*en kanariefugl*
cat	in kad	*en kat*
dog	in hoon	*en hund*
frog	in fŕer	*en frø*
guinea pig	id *mah*-sveen	*et marsvin*

DANISH

Feelings

I like ...	yai ka god lee ...	*Jeg kan godt lide ...*
I don't like ...	yai ka ig lee ...	*Jeg kan ikke lide ...*
I'm in a hurry.	yai hah tŕaowld	*Jeg har travlt.*
I'm well.	yai hah di god	*Jeg har det godt.*
I'm sorry.	di ger mai ānd	*Det gør mig ondt*
(condolence)	ad *her*-ah	*at høre.*
I'm grateful.	yai ehŕ	*Jeg er*
	tahg-*nehm*-lee	*taknemlig.*

I'm ...	yai ehŕ ...	*Jeg er ...*
angry	vŕehth	*vred*
happy	glath	*glad*
hungry	*sul*-dehn	*sulten*
sad	tŕeesd	*trist*
sleepy	*serv*-nee	*søvnig*
thirsty	*ters*-dee	*tørstig*
tired (fatigued)	tŕahd	*træt*
worried	be-*kerm*-ŕerth	*bekymret*

I'm cold/hot.	yai fŕü-sah/*svith*-ah	*Jeg fryser/sveder.*
You're right.	doo hah ŕahd	*Du har ret.*

Some Useful Phrases

Sure.
    seh-*fer*-lee/di ehŕ klahd   *Selvfølgelig./Det er klart.*
Just a minute.
    id *oy*-eh-*blig*   *Et øjeblik.*
It's (not) important.
    di ehŕ (ig) *vig*-deed   *Det er (ikke) vigtigt.*
It's (not) possible.
    di ehŕ (ig) *moo*-leed   *Det er (ikke) muligt.*
Wait!
    vehnd!   *Vent!*
Good luck!
    hehl o *ler*-geh!   *Held og lykke!*

BREAKING THE LANGUAGE BARRIER

Do you speak English?
ta-lah dee *ehng*-ehlsg?   *Taler De engelsk?* (pol)

Does anyone speak English?
ehŕ dah norn dah   *Er der nogen der*
ta-lah *ehng*-ehlsg?   *taler engelsk?*

I speak a little ...
yai *ta*-lah in *smoo*-leh ...   *Jeg taler en smule ...*

I don't speak ...
yai *ta*-lah ig ...   *Jeg taler ikke ...*

I (don't) understand.
yai fo-*sdor* (ig)   *Jeg forstår (ikke).*

DANISH

Could you repeat that?
koo-neh dee *gehn*-ta di?   *Kunne De gentage det?* (pol)

Could you speak more
slowly please?
koo-neh dee *ta*-leh   *Kunne De tale*
lahng-som-ah?   *langsommere?* (pol)

How do you say ...?
vor-*dan see*-ah man ...?   *Hvordan siger man ...?*

What does ... mean?
va bi-*tüth*-ah ...?   *Hvad betyder ...?*

I speak ...	yai *ta*-lah ...	*Jeg taler ...*
English	*ehng*-ehlsg	*engelsk*
French	fŕahnsg	*fransk*
German	tüsg	*tysk*
Italian	ee-tal-*yehnsg*	*italiensk*
Spanish	sbansg	*spansk*

BODY LANGUAGE

The good old handshake is the go in Denmark! The older generation has always used it, and still do, the younger seemed to drop it for a number of years but have reintroduced it. This applies not only to men but also women.

Never shake someone's hand with the other hand in your pocket as this is considered impolite. A single kiss on the cheek (just one) – often accompanied by a hug – is used for closer friends and relatives. And don't forget that men hug in Denmark too!

To express the affirmative, Danes will sometimes pull in air abruptly while making a 'hah' sound accompanied by a slight backward tilt of the head, and a 'no' can be expressed by the usual shaking of the head.

When Danes raise their glasses to toast they will seek brief eye contact with everyone at the table before and after drinking and say Skål!. You shouldn't start eating a meal until everybody is ready and the host(ess) nods to everyone and says Værsgo (please start).

Danes have a tradition of thanking their hosts after a meal or any type of get-together by either ringing up specifically to do so or by saying Tak for sidst (lit. thanks for last) next time they meet.

DANISH

SIGNS

FORBUDT	PROHIBITED
GRATIS ADGANG	FREE ADMISSION
INDGANG	ENTRANCE
INFORMATION	INFORMATION
INGEN ADGANG	NO ENTRY
NØDUDGANG	EMERGENCY EXIT
RESERVERET	RESERVED
RYGNING FORBUDT	NO SMOKING
TELEFON	TELEPHONE
TOILET	TOILET
UDGANG	EXIT
VARM/KOLD	HOT/COLD
ÅBEN/LUKKET	OPEN/CLOSED

PAPERWORK

address	a-*dŕah*-seh	*adresse*
age	*al*-ah	*alder*
birth certificate	*fer*-sels-a-tehsd/	*fødselsattest/*
	dåbs-a-tehsd	*dåbsattest*
border	*gŕahn*-seh	*grænse*
car registration	in-*ŕeh*-gee-*sdŕeh*-ŕing	*indregistre-ring*
	(s-a-tehsd)	*(sattest)*
customs	tol	*told*
date of birth	*fer*-sehls-da-tor	*fødselsdato*
driver's licence	*ker*-koŕd	*kørekort*
identification	li-gee-tee-ma-*shorn*	*legitimation*
immigration	i-mee-*gŕah*-*shorn*	*immigration*
marital status	see-*veel*-sdan	*civilstand*
name	naown	*navn*
nationality	na-shor-na-lee-*tid*	*nationalitet*
passport	*pas*	*pas*
passport number	*pas*-nām-mah	*pasnummer*
place of birth	fer-theh-*sdehht*	*fødested*
profession	*pŕor*-feh-*shorn*	*profession*
reason for travel	*foŕ*-māl meh *ŕai*-sehn	*formål med rejsen*
religion	*ŕeh*-leeg-*yorn*	*religion*
sex	kern	*køn*
visa	*vee*-sām	*visum*

GETTING AROUND

What time does the ... leave/arrive?	vo-*nor* gor/ an-kom-ah ...	*Hvornår går/ ankommer ...*
(air)plane	*flü*-ehht	*flyet*
boat	*bā*-thehn	*båden*
bus	*boo*-sehn/ *ŕoo*-deh-bee-lehn	*bussen/ rutebilen*
train	*tā*-wehth	*toget*

DANISH

DANISH

Directions

Where is ...?
   vor ehŕ ...?   *Hvor er ...?*

How do I get to ...?
   vo-*dan* kom-ah yai ti ...?   *Hvordan kommer jeg til ...?*

Is it far from here?
   ehŕ di lahngd *hiŕ-fŕah*?   *Er det langt herfra?*

Is it near here?
   ehŕ di ee *nehŕ*-hi-thehn?   *Er det i nærheden?*

Can I walk there?
   ka yai *gā* dah-hehn?   *Kan jeg gå derhen?*

Can you show me (on the map)?
   koo-neh dee/doo vee-seh mai di   *Kunne De/du vise mig det*
   (pā *koŕd*-ehth)?   *(på kortet)?* (pol/inf)

Are there other means of getting there?
   ehŕ dehŕ *ahn*-dŕah *māth*-ah   *Er der andre måder*
   ad *kom*-eh dehŕ-*hehn* pā?   *at komme derhen på?*

I want to go to ...
   yai vi *gehŕ*-neh ti ...   *Jeg vil gerne til ...*

Go straight ahead.
   gā *li*-eh ooth   *Gå lige ud.*

It's two streets down.
   di ehŕ tor *gath*-ah   *Det er to gader*
   lehng-ah *ni*-theh   *længere nede.*

HYGGE!

Hygge is a concept close to Danish hearts. It describes many things, like being cosy and comfortable in a warm bed, or sitting in front of the fireplace with a cup of hot cocoa, or a surprise visitor with whom you stay up all night chatting. So if you're experiencing what you think is hygge, you could always try saying: Det er hyggeligt! and watch the reaction...

Turn left/	dŕai ti *vehns*-dŕah/	*Drej til venstre/*
right ...	*hoy*-yah ...	*højre ...*
at the next corner	vi *nehs*-deh *yer*-neh	*ved næste hjørne*
at the traffic lights	vi tŕah-*feeg*-lü-sehth	*ved trafiklyset*

behind	ba	*bag*
far	fyehŕn	*fjern*
near	nehŕ	*nær*
in front of	*foŕ*-an	*foran*
opposite	pā dehn	*på den*
	morth-sa-deh	*modsatte*
	see-theh a	*side af*

DANISH

Booking Tickets

Where can I buy a ticket?
    vor ka yai *ker*-beh in bi-*lehd?*   *Hvor kan jeg købe en billet?*

I want to go to ...
    yai vi *gehŕ*-neh ti ...   *Jeg vil gerne til ...*

Do I need to book?
    ehŕ di nerth-*vehn*-deed   *Er det nødvendigt*
    ad bi-sdi-leh plas?   *at bestille plads?*

I'd like to book a seat to ...
    yai vi *gehŕ*-neh   *Jeg vil gerne*
    bi-sdi-leh plas ti ...   *bestille plads til ...*

It's full.
    di ehŕ *ful*-d *book*-ehth   *Det er fuldt booket.*

Are there no seats available at all?
    ehŕ dah slehd *ing*-ehn   *Er der slet ingen*
    le-thee plas-ah?   *ledige pladser?*

Can I get a stand-by ticket?
    ka yai mās-gi *ker*-beh   *Kan jeg måske købe*
    in stan-*bai* bi-*lehd?*   *en stand-by billet?*

I'd like ...	yai vi *gehŕ*-neh ha ...	*Jeg vil gerne have ...*
a one-way ticket	en *ehng*-gild-bi-lehd	*en enkeltbillet*
a return ticket	en *ŕeh-tooŕ*-bi-lehd	*en returbillet*
two tickets	tor bi-*lehd*-ah	*to billetter*
tickets for all of us	bi-*lehd*-ah ti os *al*-eh	*billetter til os alle*
a student discount	sdoo-*dehn*-dah-ŕah-bad	*studenterrabat*
a child's fare	in *ber*-neh-bi-lehd	*en børnebillet*
a pensioner's fare	in pahng-sho-*neesd*-bi-lehd	*en pensionist-billet*
1st class	*fers*-deh *klas*-eh	*første klasse*
2nd class	*an*-ehn *klas*-eh	*anden klasse*

Air

Is there a flight to ...?
  ehŕ dehŕ id flü ti ...?   *Er der et fly til ...?*

When is the next flight to ...?
  vo-*nor* gor *nehs*-deh flü ti ...?   *Hvornår går næste fly til ...?*

How long does the flight take?
  vor lahng tith tah *flüu*-too-ahn?   *Hvor lang tid tager flyveturen?*

What is the flight number?
  va ehŕ *flaid*-nām-mahth?   *Hvad er flight-nummeret?*

You must check in at ... (time)
  doo sga cheh-geh in *klog*-gehn ...   *Du skal checke ind klokken ...*

airport tax	*lāfd*-haown-sgad	*lufthavnsskat*
boarding pass	*boŕ*-ding-koŕd	*boardingkort*
customs	tol	*told*

SIGNS

BAGAGE(AFHENTNING)	LUGGAGE PICKUP
BAGAGE(SKRANKE)	BAGGAGE COUNTER
CHECK IN/	CHECKING IN
INDCHEKNING	
CHECK-IN (SKRANKE)	CHECK-IN COUNTER
REGISTRERING	REGISTRATION
TOLD	CUSTOMS

DANISH

Bus

Where is the bus stop?
    vor ehŕ *boos*-stop-   *Hvor er*
    peh-stehth-ehd?   *busstoppestedet?*
Which bus goes to ...?
    vil-gehn boos gor ti ...?   *Hvilken bus går til ...?*
Does this bus go to ...?
    gor *dehn*-neh *boos* ti ...? *Går denne bus til ...?*
How often do buses pass by?
    vor *of*-deh *gor boos*-sen?   *Hvor ofte går bussen?*
Could you let me know
when we get to ...?
    koo-neh dee/doo *see*-eh ti   *Kunne De/du sige til*
    nor vee *kom*-ah ti ...?   *når vi kommer til ...? (pol/inf)*

I want to get off!   yai vi a!   *Jeg vil af!*

What time is the ...   vo-*nor* gor dehn ...   *Hvornår går den ...*
bus?   boos?   *bus?*
    next   *nehs*-deh   næste
    first   *fers*-deh   første
    last   *sees*-deh   sidste

Metro

The first phase of the Copenhagen metro is operational from 2002,
the second from 2003.
(See the Train section, page 32)

Train

Which line takes me to ...?
  *vil-*gehth tāw gor ti ...?   *Hvilket tog går til ...?*
What is the next station?
  va ehŕ *nehs-*deh sda-*shorn*?   *Hvad er næste station?*
Is this the right platform for ...?
  ehŕ *di-*deh dehn *ŕig-*dee   *Er dette den rigtige*
  pa-*ŕong* nor yai sga   *perron når jeg skal*
  meh *tā-*wehth ti ...?   *med toget til ...?*
The train leaves from platform ...
  *tā-*wehth gor ffah pa-*ŕong* ...   *Toget går fra perron ...*
Passengers must change trains/
platforms.
  pa-sa-*shi-*ah-neh sga   *Passagererne skal*
  *sgeef-*deh *tāw*/pa-*ŕong*   *skifte tog/perron.*

dining car   *sbee-*seh-vown   *spisevogn*
express   ehgs-*ŕahs*   *ekspres*
local   lor-*kal*   *lokal*
sleeping car   *sow-*eh-vown   *sovevogn*

SIGNS	
AFGANG	DEPARTURES
ANKOMST	ARRIVALS
BILLETKONTOR	TICKET OFFICE
BUSSTOPPESTED	BUS STOP
HOVEDBANEGÅRD	CENTRAL STATION
KØREPLAN	TIMETABLE
MINIMETRO	SUBWAY
PERRONNUMMER	PLATFORM NO.
STATION	STATION
TOGSTATION	TRAIN STATION
UDGANG	WAY OUT
VEKSEL	CHANGE (for coins)

Taxi

Can you take me to ...?
ka dee/doo ker
mai ti ...?
Kan De/du køre
mig til ...? (pol/inf)

How much does it cost to go to ...?
vor *mah*-eth kos-dah
di ad ker ti ...?
Hvor meget koster
det at køre til ...?

Here is fine, thank you.
sdob hehŕ tahg
Stop her, tak.

The next corner, please.
vi *nehs*-deh *yer*-neh tahg
Ved næste hjørne, tak.

The next street to the left/right.
nehs-deh *gath*-eh ti
vehns-dŕah/*hoy*-yah
Næste gade til
venstre/højre.

Please slow down.
vehŕ so *vehn*-lee ad ker
lahng-som-ah
Vær så venlig at køre
langsommere.

Continue!	*foŕd*-sehd!	*Fortsæt!*
Stop here!	sdob hehŕ!	*Stop her!*
Please wait here.	vehnd *vehn*-leesd hehŕ	*Vent venligst her.*

Some Useful Phrases

The train is delayed/cancelled.
tāw-ehth ehŕ fo-*sing*-gehth/
aw-lüsd
Toget er forsinket/
aflyst.

How long will it be delayed?
vor *mah*-ehth ehŕ *tāw*-ehth
fo-*sing*-gehth?
Hvor meget er toget
forsinket?

Can I reserve a place?
ehŕ di *moo*-lid ad
ŕeh-sehŕ-*vi*-ah plas?
Er det muligt at
reservere plads?

How long does the trip take?
vor lahng teeth tah *too*-ahn?
Hvor lang tid tager turen?

Is it a direct route?
ehŕ di in *dee*-ŕaig-deh
fo-*bin*-ehl-seh?
Er det en direkte
forbindelse?

DANISH

Is that seat taken?
 ehŕ dehn plas *ob*-ta-ehth?   *Er den plads optaget?*
I want to get off at ...
 yai vi *gehŕ*-neh a vi ...   *Jeg vil gerne af ved ...*
Where can I hire a bicycle?
 vor ka yai *lai*-eh in *sü*-gehl? *Hvor kan jeg leje en cykel?*

Car

Where can I rent a car?
 vor ka yai *lai*-eh in beel?   *Hvor kan jeg leje en bil?*
How much is it daily/weekly?
 vor *mah*-eth *kos*-dah di   *Hvor meget koster det*
 pehŕ da/pehŕ *oo*-eh?   *per dag/per uge?*
Does that include insurance/
mileage?
 ing-kloo-*di*-ah di fo-*sig*-ŕing/ *Inkluderer det forsikring/*
 oo-bi-gŕahn-seh-theh   *ubegrænsede*
 kee-lor-*mi*-dah?   *kilometer?*
Where's the next petrol station?
 vor ehŕ *nehs*-deh   *Hvor er næste*
 bin-*seen*-sda-*shorn*?   *benzinstation?*
How long can I park here?
 vor *lehng*-eh mä yai   *Hvor længe må jeg*
 pah-*ki*-ah hiŕ?   *parkere her?*
Does this road lead to ...?
 fer-ah *dehn*-neh vai ti ...? *Fører denne vej til ...?*
I need a mechanic.
 yai hah *bŕoo* for in   *Jeg har brug for en*
 mi-*ka*-ni-gah   *mekaniker.*
What make is it?
 vil-gehth *mehŕ*-geh ehŕ di? *Hvilket mærke er det?*
The battery is flat.
 ba-dah-*ŕee*-ehth ehŕ derd *Batteriet er dødt.*

The radiator is leaking.
    ker-lahn ehŕ *oo*-tehd   *Køleren er utæt.*

I have a flat tyre.
    yai ehŕ pāng-*ti*-ahth   *Jeg er punkteret.*

It's overheating. (engine)
    mor-toŕ-ahn *kā*-wah *ow*-ah   *Motoren koger over.*

It's not working.
    dehn *veeŕ*-gah ig   *Den virker ikke.*

air (for tyres)	lāfd	*luft*
battery	ba-dah-*ŕee*	*batteri*
brakes	*bŕahm*-sah	*bremser*
clutch	*kob*-ling	*kobling*
driver's licence	*ker*-kord	*kørekort*
engine	*mor*-toŕ	*motor*
lights	lüs	*lys*
oil	*orl*-yeh	*olie*
radiator	*ker*-lah	*køler*
road map	*vai*-koŕd	*vejkort*
tyres	dehg	*dæk*
windscreen	for-*ŕoo*-theh	*forrude*

DANISH

SIGNS

BLYFRI	UNLEADED
ENSRETTET	ONE WAY
GARAGE/AUTOVÆRKSTED	GARAGE
INDKØRSEL FORBUDT	NO ENTRY
MEKANIKER	MECHANIC
MOTORVEJ	FREEWAY
OKTAN	OCTANE
OMKØRSEL	DETOUR
PARKERING FORBUDT	NO PARKING
SELVBETJENING	SELF SERVICE
VEJARBEJDE	ROADWORKS
VIGEPLIGT	GIVE WAY

ACCOMMODATION

Where is a ...?	vor ehŕ dah id ...?	*Hvor er der et ...?*
cheap hotel	*bee*-leed hor-*tehl*	*billigt hotel*
good hotel	god hor-*tehl*	*godt hotel*
nearby hotel	hor-*tehl* ee *nehŕ*-hith-ehn	*hotel i nærheden*

What's the address?
va ehŕ a-*dŕah*-sehn? *Hvad er adressen?*

Could you write the address, please?
koo-neh dee *sgŕee*-w a-*dŕah*-sehn nith? *Kunne De skrive adressen ned? (pol)*

At the Hotel

Do you have any rooms available?
hah ee *lith*-ee *vehŕl*-sah? *Har I ledige værelser?*

I'd like ...	yai vi *gehŕ*-neh ha ...	*Jeg vil gerne have ...*
a single room	id *ehng*-gild-vehŕl-seh	*et enkeltværelse*
a double room	id *dob*-ehld-vehŕl-seh	*et dobbeltværelse*
to share a dorm	plas ee in *sow*-sahl	*plads i en sovesal*
a bed	in sehng	*en seng*

I want a room with a ...	yai vi *gehŕ*-neh ha id *vehŕl*-seh meh ...	*Jeg vil gerne have et værelse med ...*
bathroom	bath	*bad*
double bed	*do*-behld-sehng	*dobbeltseng*
shower	*bŕoo*-seh-bath	*brusebad*
TV	ti vi	*TV*
window	*vin*-doo	*vindue*

I'm going to stay for ...	yai bleeŕ ...	*Jeg bliver ...*
one day	in nad	*en nat*
two days	tor *nehd*-ah	*to nætter*
one week	in *oo*-eh	*en uge*

Do you have identification?
  hah dee/doo
  li-gee-tee-ma-*shorn*?
  Har De/du
  legitimation? (pol/inf)

Your (pl) membership card, please.
  yehŕs *mehth*-lehms-kord tahg
  Jeres medlemskort, tak.

Sorry, we're full.
  bi-*kla*-ah ald ehŕ *ob*-ta-ehth
  Beklager, alt er optaget.

How long will you (pl) be staying?
  vor *lehng*-eh bleeŕ ee?
  Hvor længe bliver I?

How many nights?
  vor *mahng*-eh *neh*-dah?
  Hvor mange nætter?

It's ... per day/per person.
  di *kos*-dah ... pehŕ da/
  pehŕ pehŕ-*sorn*
  Det koster ... per dag/
  per person.

DANISH

How much is it per night/
per person?
  vor *mah*-eth *kos*-dah
  di pehŕ nad/pehŕ pehŕ-*sorn*?
  Hvor meget koster
  det per nat/per person?

Can I see it?
  mā yai si *vehŕl*-sehth?
  Må jeg se værelset?

Are there any others?
  ehŕ dehŕ *ahn*-dŕah *vehŕl*-sah?
  Er der andre værelser?

Are there any cheaper rooms?
  fin-ehs dehŕ *bee*-lee-ah
  vehŕl-sah?
  Findes der billigere
  værelser?

Can I see the bathroom?
  mã yai si *ba*-theh-vehŕl-sehth?   *Må jeg se badeværelset?*
Is there a reduction for
students/children?
  ehŕ dehŕ sdoo-*dehn*-dah-ŕah-bad/   *Er der studenterrabat/*
  ber-neh-ŕah-bad?   *børnerabat?*
Does it include breakfast?
  ehŕ *morn*-math ing-kloo-*di*-ahth?   *Er morgenmad inkluderet?*

It's fine, I'll take it.
  di ehŕ feend yai tah di   *Det er fint, jeg tager det.*
I'm not sure how long I'm staying.
  yai vith ig vo *lehng*-eh   *Jeg ved ikke hvor længe*
  yai bleeŕ   *jeg bliver.*

Where is the bathroom?
  vor ehŕ toy-*lehd*-ehth?   *Hvor er toilettet?*
Is there somewhere to wash clothes?
  ehŕ dehŕ id sdehth yai   *Er der et sted jeg*
  ka vas-geh toy?   *kan vaske tøj?*
Is there a lift?
  ehŕ dehŕ i-leh-*va*-tor?   *Er der elevator?*
Can I use the kitchen?
  mã yai bŕoo *kerg*-nehth?   *Må jeg bruge køkkenet?*
Can I use the telephone?
  mã yai bi-*ner*-deh   *Må jeg benytte*
  ti-leh-*for*-nehn?   *telefonen?*

DANISH

SIGNS	
CAMPINGPLADS	CAMPING GROUND
HOTEL	HOTEL
KRO	INN
MOTEL	MOTEL
PENSIONAT/HOTELPENSION	GUEST HOUSE
VANDREHJEM	YOUTH HOSTEL

Requests & Complaints

Please wake me up at ...
koo-neh dee *veh*-geh
mai *klog*-gehn ...?

*Kunne De vække
mig klokken ...?* (pol)

The room needs to be cleaned.
vehŕl-sehth *tŕaing*-ah ti
ad blee gyooŕd fehnd

*Værelset trænger til
at blive gjort rent.*

Please change the sheets.
vi dee *vehn*-leesd *sgeef*-deh
sehng-eh-toy-yehth?

*Vil De venligst skifte
sengetøjet?* (pol)

I can't open/close the window.
yai ka ig *āb*-neh/
lā-geh *vin*-doo-ehth

*Jeg kan ikke åbne/
lukke vinduet.*

I've locked myself out of my room.
yai hah lāsd mai *oo*-theh
a *vehŕl*-sehth

*Jeg har låst mig ude
af værelset.*

The toilet won't flush.
toy-*lehd*-dehth *sger*-lah ig

Toilettet skyller ikke.

I don't like this room.
yai süns ig om *di*-deh
vehŕl-seh

*Jeg synes ikke om dette
værelse.*

It's (too) ...	di ehŕ (fo) ...	*Det er (for) ...*
small	*lee*-leh	*lille*
noisy	*sdoy*-yeh-neh	*støjende*
dark	mergd	*mørkt*
expensive	düŕd	*dyrt*

Some Useful Words & Phrases

I'm/We're leaving now/tomorrow.
yai/vee *ŕai*-sah noo/i morn

Jeg/Vi rejser nu/i morgen.

I'd like to pay the bill.
yai vi *gehŕ*-neh bi-*ta*-leh
ŕai-ning-ehn

*Jeg vil gerne betale
regningen.*

DANISH

DANISH

name	naown	*navn*
surname	*ehf*-dah-naown	*efternavn*
address	a-*dŕah*-seh	*adresse*
room number	*vehŕl*-sehs-nām-mah	*værelsesnummer*
air-conditioning	*ehŕ*-kon-dee-shon	*aircondition*
balcony	bal-*kong*/al-*tan*	*balkon/altan*
bed	sehng	*seng*
bill	*ŕai*-ning	*regning*
blanket	*teh*-beh	*tæppe*
chair	sdorl	*stol*
clean	*ŕehn*	*ren*
dirty	*snaow*-sehth	*snavset*
doona	dü-neh	*dyne*
electricity	i-lehg-tŕee-see-*tid*	*elektricitet*
excluded	*ehgs*-kloo-siw	*ekslusive*
included	ing-kloo-*di*-ahth	*inkluderet*
key	*noy*-leh	*nøgle*
lift (elevator)	i-leh-*va*-tor	*elevator*
light bulb	i-*lehg*-tŕeesg pehŕ	*elektrisk pære*
lock	lās	*lås*
mattress	ma-*dŕahs*	*madras*
mirror	sbail	*spejl*
padlock	*hehng*-eh-lās	*hængelås*
pillow	*hor*-wehth-poo-theh	*hovedpude*
quiet	*sdil*-eh	*stille*
sheet	*la*-yehn	*lagen*
soap	*seh*-beh	*sæbe*
suitcase	*käf*-ahd	*kuffert*
swimming pool	*sver*-meh-ba-sehng	*svømmebassin*
table	booŕ	*bord*
toilet	toy-*lehd*	*toilet*
toilet paper	toy-*lehd*-pah-peeŕ	*toiletpapir*
towel	*hon*-kleh-theh	*håndklæde*
water	van	*vand*
hot/cold water	vahmd/kold van	*varmt/koldt vand*

AROUND TOWN

I'm looking for ...	yai *li*-thah *ehf*-dah ...	*Jeg leder efter ...*
the art gallery	*kānsd*-moo-sehth	*kunstmuseet*
a bank	in bang-g	*en bank*
the church	*keeŕ*-gehn	*kirken*
the city centre	*sehn*-tŕām	*centrum*
the ...	dehn ...	*den ...*
embassy	ahm-ba-*sa*-theh	*ambassade*
my hotel	meed hor-*tehl*	*mit hotel*
a market	id *mah*-gehth	*et marked*
the museum	moo-*sehth*	*museet*
the police	por-lee-*tee*-eht	*politiet*
the post office	*posd*-kon-toŕ-eht	*postkontoret*
a public toilet	id *o*-fehnd-leed toy-*lehd*	*et offentligt toilet*
a telephone centre	in ti-leh-*forn*	*en telefon*
the tourist information office	too-*ŕeesd*-in-for-ma-*shor*-nehn	*turist-informationen*

What time does it open/close?
vo-*nor* āb-nah/*lā*-gah di?   *Hvornår åbner/lukker det?*
What street/suburb is this?
vil-gehn ga-theh/ *for*-sdath ehŕ *di*-deh?   *Hvilken gade/ forstad er dette?*

For directions, see the Getting Around section, page 28.

At the Post Office

I'd like to send ...	yai vi *gehŕ*-neh sehn-eh ...	*Jeg vil gerne sende ...*
a letter	id *bŕeh*-w	*et brev*
a postcard	id *posd*-kord	*et postkort*
a parcel	in *pah*-geh	*en pakke*
a telegram	id ti-leh-*gŕahm*	*et telegram*

I'd like some stamps.
  yai vi *gehŕ*-neh ha *nor*-leh   *Jeg vil gerne have nogle*
  fŕee-mehŕ-gah   *frimærker.*

How much is the postage?
  vor *mah*-eth ehŕ *poŕ*-tor-ehn? *Hvor meget er portoen?*

How much does it cost to
send this to ...?
  vor *mah*-ehth *kos*-dah di ad   *Hvor meget koster det at*
  sehn-eh *di*-deh ti ...?   *sende dette til ...?*

an aerogram	id eh-ŕor-*gŕahm*	*et aerogram*
air mail	*lāfd*-posd	*luftpost*
envelope	kon-vor-*lood*	*konvolut*
mailbox	*posd*-ka-seh	*postkasse*
parcel	*pah*-geh	*pakke*
registered mail	*ŕeh*-kom-man-di-ahth	*rekommanderet*
surface mail	*ow*-ah-fla-theh-posd	*overfladepost*

Telephone & Internet

I want to ring ...
  yai vi *gehŕ*-neh *ŕehng*-eh ti ... *Jeg vil gerne ringe til ...*

The number is ...
  nām-mahth ehŕ ...   *Nummeret er ...*

I want to speak for three minutes.
  yai vi *gehŕ*-neh *ta*-leh   *Jeg vil gerne tale*
  tŕeh mee-*noo*-dah   *tre minutter.*

How much does a
three-minute call cost?
  vo *mah*-ehth *kos*-dah di fo   *Hvor meget koster det for*
  tŕeh mee-*noo*-dah?   *tre minutter?*

DANISH

How much does each extra
minute cost?

    vo *mah*-ehth *kos*-dah vehŕd   *Hvor meget koster hvert*
    mee-*nood* ehgs-dŕah?   *minut ekstra?*

I'd like to speak to (Mr Pedersen).

    yai vi *gehŕ*-neh *ta*-leh meh   *Jeg vil gerne tale med*
    (hehŕ *pih*-dah-sehn)   *(Hr. Pedersen).*

It's engaged.

    dah ehŕ *ob*-ta-ehth   *Der er optaget.*

I want to make a reverse-charges
phone call.

    yai *erns*-gah ad *morth*-ta-ahn   *Jeg ønsker at modtageren*
    sga bi-*ta*-leh   *skal betale.*

I've been cut off.

    yai bli *aow*-bŕood   *Jeg blev afbrudt.*

Where can I get Internet access?

    vor ka yai for *in*-tuh-neht   *Hvor kan jeg få*
    ath-guhng?   *Internet adgang?*

I'd like to send an email.

    yai vil *gehŕ*-neh *sehn*-neh   *Jeg vil gerne*
    ehn *ee*-mayl   *sende en email.*

At the Bank

I want to exchange some money/
travellers cheques.

    yai vi *gehŕ*-neh *vehgs*-leh   *Jeg vil gerne veksle*
    nor-leh *pehng*-eh/   *nogle penge/*
    ŕai-seh-shehgs   *rejsechecks.*

What is the exchange rate?

    va ehŕ *kooŕ*-sehn?   *Hvad er kursen?*

How many kroner per dollar?

    vo *mahng*-eh *kŕor*-nah   *Hvor mange kroner*
    pehŕ *dol*-ah?   *per dollar?*

Can I have money transferred
here from my bank?

    ka yai få *pehng*-eh *ow*-ah-ferd   *Kan jeg få penge overført*
    hehŕ-*til* fŕah meen *bahng*-g?   *hertil fra min bank?*

DANISH

How long will it take to arrive?
vo lahng teeth vi di *ta*
fer dee *kom*-ah?

*Hvor lang tid vil det tage
før de kommer?*

Has my money arrived yet?
ehŕ *meen*-eh *pehng*-eh
kom-ehth?

*Er mine penge
kommet?*

bank draft	*bahng*-g-an-vees-ning	*bankanvisning*
bank notes	*sehth*-lah	*sedler*
cashier	ka-*si*-ah	*kasserer*
coins	*mern*-dah	*mønter*
credit card	kŕeh-*deed*-kord	*kreditkort*
to exchange	at *vehg*-sleh	*at veksle*
loose change	*smo*-pehng-eh	*småpenge*
signature	*ān*-ah-sgŕehfd	*underskrift*

INTERESTS & ENTERTAINMENT
Sightseeing

Do you (pl) have a guidebook/
local map?
hah ee in *ŕai*-seh-hon-bāw/
id lor-*kal*-kord?

*Har I en rejsehåndbog/
et lokalkort?*

What are the main attractions?
va ehŕ *hor*-wehth-
a-tŕahg-shorn-ah-neh?

*Hvad er
hovedattraktionerne?*

What is that?
va ehŕ di?

Hvad er det?

How old is it?
vo *gah*-mehl ehŕ
dehn/di?

*Hvor gammel er
den/det?*

Can I take photographs?
mā yai ta *bil*-thah?

Må jeg tage billeder?

What time does it open/close?
vo-*nor* *āb*-nah/
lāg-ah di?

*Hvornår åbner/
lukker det?*

ancient	*gah*-mehl/	*gammel*/
	hee-*stor*-reesg	*historisk*
archaeological	ah-keh-or-*lor*-isg	*arkæologisk*
beach	sdrahn	*strand*
building	*büg*-ning	*bygning*
castle	slod	*slot*
cathedral	ka-deh-*drahl*/	*katedral*/
	dom-keer-geh	*domkirke*
church	*keer*-geh	*kirke*
concert hall	kon-*sehrd*-sal	*koncertsal*
library	beeb-lee-or-*tig*	*bibliotek*
main square	*hor*-wehth-torw	*hovedtorv*
market	*mah*-gehth	*marked*
monastery	*klos*-dah	*kloster*
monument	mor-noo-*mehnd*	*monument*
mosque	mor-*sgi*	*moské*
the old city	dehn *gahm*-leh *bü*-dil	*den gamle bydel*
opera house	*or*-pi-rah-hoos	*operahus*
palace	pa-*las*	*palads*
ruins	*roo-een*-ah	*ruiner*
stadium	*sdad*-yon	*stadion*
statues	*sda*-too-ah	*statuer*
synagogue	sü-na-*gor*	*synagoge*
temple	*tehm*-behl	*tempel*
university	oo-nee-vehr-see-*tid*	*universitet*

DANISH

DANISH

Going Out

What's there to do in the evenings?
va ehŕ dah o *la*-w om
ahfd-nehn?

*Hvad er der at lave om
aftenen?*

Are there any discos?
ehŕ dah dees-gor-*ti*-gah?

Er der diskoteker?

Are there places where you can
hear local folk music?
fin-ehs dah *sdeh*-thah vor
man ka *her*-ah *lor*-kal
fol-geh-moo-seeg?

*Findes der steder hvor
man kan høre lokal
folkemusik?*

How much does it cost to get in?	vo *mah*-eth *kos*-dah di ad *kom*-eh in?	*Hvor meget koster det at komme ind?*
cinema	bi-or-*gŕahf*	*biograf*
concert	kon-*sehŕd*	*koncert*
discotheque	dees-gor-*tig*	*diskotek*
theatre	ti-*a*-dah	*teater*

Sports & Interests

What do you do in your spare time?
va *la*-wah doo ee
deen *fŕee*-teeth?

*Hvad laver du i
din fritid?* (inf)

What sport do you play?
vil-gehn spord *düŕ*-gah doo?

Hvilken sport dyrker du? (inf)

art	kānsd	*kunst*
basketball	*bah*-sgehd-borl	*basketball*
boxing	*bogs*-ning	*boksning*
cooking	math-la-w-ning	*madlavning*
fishing	fis-gah-*ree*	*fiskeri*
going out	gor ee *bü*-ehn	*gå i byen*
going to the cinema	gor ee bee-or-*grahf*-ehn	*gå i biografen*
music	moo-*seeg*	*musik*
photography	for-tor-*grah*-*fi*-ring	*fotografering*
reading	*leh*-seh	*læse*
rugby	*rog*-bee	*rugby*
shopping	*han*-leh	*handle*
soccer	*forth*-bold	*fodbold*
sport	sbord	*sport*
the theatre	ti-*a*-dahth	*teatret*
travelling	*rai*-seh	*rejse*
writing	*sgree*-weh	*skrive*

DANISH

Festivals

In Denmark the main Christmas celebration takes place on the evening of 24 December, juleaften. The Christmas tree, juletræ, is normally decorated with home-made paper hearts and tinsel. After dinner, which traditionally consists of duck, and and/or roast pork, flæskesteg, followed by ris a l'amande, the family join hands and 'dance' around the tree singing julesalmer (Christmas carols). If you want to exchange Christmas greetings with a Dane, the phrase is god/glædelig jul (merry Christmas).

Fastelavn (Shrovetide) celebrations take place seven weeks before Easter. Children get fastelavnsris, birch rods decorated with sweets and paper cats. During the day they dress up in fancy costumes and walk from door to door singing, for which they receive sweets. A traditional Shrovetide game involves a barrel (fastelavnstønde) full of sweets hanging from a rope, which children take turns to try to break with a bat. During Shrovetide people eat fastelavnsboller (Shrovetide buns).

Påske (Easter) goes from Maundy Thursday (skærtorsdag), including Good Friday (langfredag), until the Monday after Easter Sunday. Traditionally, children look for påskeæg (Easter eggs) hidden by påskeharen (the Easter bunny) on Easter Sunday (påskesøndag), or they paint their own Easter eggs. The Easter greeting in Denmark is god påske (happy Easter).

Pinse (Whitsun) is a Christian holiday on the seventh Sunday after Easter which includes pinsedag (Whit Sunday) and anden pinsedag (Whit Monday). People greet each other with god pinse (Happy Whitsun).

DANISH

Music festivals play a big role in weekend outdoor entertainment during the Danish summer.

Probably the biggest international music event in Denmark, Roskilde Festival takes place near the town of Roskilde. It attracts as many as 70,000 visitors from all over Europe and spans a huge variety of music, including rock, pop, folk and ethnic music.

Midtfynsfestival, on the island of Funen, is a smaller version of Roskilde, focusing on rock and pop.

Langelandsfestival is a family festival that takes place on the island of Langeland, with a focus on rock, folk and popular music, and lots of fun for kids.

Copenhagen Jazz Festival runs for several weeks over summer. It attracts many brilliant (primarily Danish but also international) jazz, folk and blues artists.

MAD MEAL!

After a meal you should always say Tak for mad (thanks for the meal) before getting up.

IN THE COUNTRY
Weather

What's the weather like?
vo-*dan* ehŕ *vehŕ*-ehth?   *Hvordan er vejret?*

It's ... today.	di ehŕ ... ee da	*Det er ... i dag.*
Will it be ...	bleer di ...	*Bliver det ...*
tomorrow?	ee morn?	*i morgen?*
cloudy	*ow*-ah-sgü-ehth	*overskyet*
cold	kold	*koldt*
foggy	*tā*-wehth	*tåget*
frosty	*fŕosd*-vehŕ	*frostvejr*
hot	vahmd	*varmt*
raining	*ŕain*-vehŕ	*regnvejr*
snowing	sni-vehŕ	*snevejr*
sunny	*sorl*-sgins-vehŕ	*solskinsvejr*
windy	*bleh*-seh-vehŕ	*blæsevejr*

Camping

Am I allowed to camp here?
mā yai kahm-*pi*-ah hehŕ?   *Må jeg campere her?*

Is there a campsite nearby?
fin-ehs dah in *kahm*-ping-plas   *Findes der en campingplads*
ee *nehŕ*-hith-ehn?   *i nærheden?*

backpack	*ŕerg*-sehg	*rygsæk*
can opener	*dā*-seh-*āb*-nah	*dåseåbner*
compass	kom-*pas*	*kompas*
crampons	*klad*-ŕah-yehŕn	*klatrejern*
firewood	*bŕahm*-eh	*brænde*
gas cartridge	*gas*-bi-hol-ah	*gasbeholder*
hammock	*hehng*-eh-koy-yeh	*hængekøje*
ice axe	*ees*-erg-seh	*isøkse*
mattress	ma-*dŕahs*	*madras*
penknife	*lom*-eh-knee-w	*lommekniv*
rope	tow	*tov*
sleeping bag	*sow*-eh-por-seh	*sovepose*

DANISH

stove	*kahm*-ping-vown	*campingovn*
tent	tehld	*telt*
tent pegs	*tehld*-peh-leh	*teltpæle*
torch (flashlight)	*lom*-eh-lerg-deh	*lommelygte*
water bottle	*fehld*-flas-geh	*feltflaske*

FOOD

Traditional Danish cooking is dominated by, although not to the same extent as the other Scandinavian countries, smoked, cured, pickled or otherwise preserved food, due to the short growing season and long winters. Regional variations are not strong, although proximity to the ocean flavours menus with seafood.

breakfast	*morn*-math	*morgenmad*
lunch	*frä*-kosd	*frokost*
dinner	mi-da/*ahf*-dehns-math	*middag/aftensmad*

Table for ..., please.
  id boof ti ... tahg   *Et bord til ..., tak.*
Can I see the menu please?
  mā yai si mi-*nü*-ehn?   *Må jeg se menuen?*
I'd like the set menu, please.
  yai tah *dah*-ehns fahd tahg   *Jeg tager dagens ret, tak.*
What does it include?
  va ing-kloo-*di*-ah dehn?   *Hvad inkluderer den?*
Not too spicy please.
  ig fo *krerth*-fahth tahg   *Ikke for krydret, tak.*

Vegetarian Meals

I'm a vegetarian.
  yai ehŕ veh-geh-*tah*   *Jeg er vegetar.*
I don't eat meat.
  yai *sbees*-ah ig kerth   *Jeg spiser ikke kød.*
I don't eat chicken, or fish, or pork.
  yai *sbees*-ah ig *kü*-ling eh-lah *Jeg spiser ikke kylling eller*
  fisg eh-lah *svee*-neh-kerth   *fisk eller svinekød.*

DANISH

ashtray	*as*-geh-beh-ah	*askebæger*
the bill	*rai*-ning-ehn	*regningen*
a cup	in kob	*en kop*
dessert	di-*sehrd*	*dessert*
a drink	in *dring*-g	*en drink* (always alcoholic)
a fork	in *gahf*-ehl	*en gaffel*
fresh	fehrsg/frehsg	*fersk/frisk*
a glass	id glas	*et glas*
a knife	in knee-w	*en kniv*
a plate	in ta-*lehr*-gehn	*en tallerken*
spicy	*krerth*-fahth	*krydret*
a spoon	in sgi	*en ske*
stale	*gah*-mehl/*dor*-lee	*gammel/dårlig*
sweet	serth	*sød*
a teaspoon	in *ti*-sgi	*en teske*
toothpicks	*tan*-sdi-gah	*tandstikker*

Staple Foods & Condiments

beef	*og*-seh-kerth	*oksekød*
bread	*brerth*	*brød*
butter	smer	*smør*
cucumber	a-*goorg*	*agurk*
garlic	*vith*-loy	*hvidløg*
meat	kerth	*kød*
mustard	*seh*-nob	*sennep*
mutton	lahm	*lam*
oil	*orl*-yeh	*olie*
pasta	*pas*-da	*pasta*
pepper	*pi*-wah	*peber*
pork	*svee*-neh-kerth	*svinekød*
potatoes	kah-*tof*-lah	*kartofler*
rice	*rees*	*ris*
salt	sald	*salt*
sugar	*sä*-gah	*sukker*
veal	*kal*-veh-kerth	*kalvekød*
vegetables	*grern*-sa-ah	*grønsager*
vinegar	*ith*-geh	*eddike*

DANISH

MENU DECODER

Breakfast Menu

cheese	*āsd*	ost
coffee	*kaf*-eh	kaffe
corn flakes	*koorn*-flehgs	cornflakes
fried egg	*spail*-ehg	spejlæg
(always sunny side up)		
fruit	*frāgd*	frugt
hardboiled egg	*hor*-kogd ehg	hårdkogt æg
jam	*sül*-deh-toy	syltetøj
milk	mehlg	mælk
oatmeal	*hah*-wah-grün	havregryn
porridge	*hah*-wah-grerth	havregrød
scrambled eggs	*rehr*-ehg	røræg
softboiled egg	*blerth*-kogd ehg	blødkogt æg
tea	ti	te
toast	*ris*-dehth brerth/	ristet brød/
	tāwsd	toast
yoghurt	*yoo*-goord	yoghurt

Sandwiches

bøftartar   *berf*-ta-tah
   beef tartar – raw ground beef topped with a raw egg
   yolk, onion and capers

dyrlægens natmad   *dür*-leh-ehns *nad*-math
   'the veterinarian's midnight snack' – liver paté topped
   with a thin slice of salt beef, raw onions and beef jelly

gravad laks   *grah*-wath lahgs
   cured salmon

leverpostej   *li*-wah-por-sdai
   liver paté

marineret sild   mah-ee-*ni*-ath seel
   pickled herring; served with raw onions

ostemad   *ās*-deh-math
   cheese – Denmark is famous for its cheeses, and
   produces an enormous variety

rejemad   *rai*-yeh-mahth
   small shrimp served with mayonnaise and lemon slices

røget laks   *roy*-yehth lahgs
   smoked salmon, served with scrambled eggs
røget sild   *roy*-yehth seel
   smoked herring on rye bread with chives and a raw egg yolk
røget ål   *roy*-yehth āl
   smoked eel, a delicacy

baguette	*frahns*-*brerth*	franskbrød
bread	*brerth*	brød
crusty roll	*rän*-sder-geh	rundstykke
Danish pastry	*vee*-nah-brerth	wienerbrød
rye bread	*roo*-brerth	rugbrød
soft roll	*bol*-eh	bolle

> **Danish Delights**
> Danish open rye bread sandwiches are ornate and tasty
> – a feast for the eye and a delight to the palate!

øllebrød   *er*-leh-brerth
   a smooth beer and bread dish, a bit like porridge, served
   hot with milk or whipped cream

Soup
fiskesuppe   *fis*-geh-sā-beh
   fish soup, usually creamy
grønsagssuppe   *grern*-sas-sā-beh
   vegetable soup
gule ærter   *goo*-leh *ehr*-dah
   split pea soup served with pork
hønsekødssuppe   *hern*-seh-kerth-sā-beh
   chicken soup

Meat
bankekød   *bahng*-geh-kerth
   similar to Wienerschnitzel
boller i karry   bol-ah ee kah-ee
   meat balls in a curry sauce, served with rice or potatoes
bøf med løg   berf meh loy
   hamburger served with fried onions, potatoes and
   brown gravy

DANISH

DANISH

flæskeæggekage *(flehs*-geh)-eh-geh-ka-eh
   egg dish with bacon (a bit like an omelette, but made
   with flour)
flæskesteg   *flehs*-geh-sdai
   pork roast with crispy crackling, served with potatoes,
   brown gravy and pickled cucumbers
frikadeller   fri-ga-*dehl*-ah
   meat patties made of pork, veal and onion served with
   potatoes, brown gravy, and pickled cucumbers
fyldt   füld
hvidkålshoved   *veeth*-kåls-hor-wehth
   cabbage leaves wrapped around ground beef
medisterpølse   mi-*dees*-dah-*perl*-seh
   large fried sausage served with potatoes, brown gravy
   and pickled cucumbers
spaghetti med   sba-*gehd*-dee meh
kødsovs   *kerth*-sows
   spaghetti with ground beef in a tomato sauce
stegt flæsk med   sdehgd flehsg meh
persillesovs   pehr-*sil*-eh-sows
   thick slices of fried bacon with potatoes and a white
   parsley sauce

chicken	*kül*-ing	kylling
duck	an	and
hamburger	*hag*-eh-berf	hakkebøf
meat chops	ko-deh-*leh*-dah	koteletter
roast beef	*og*-seh-sdai	oksesteg
roast lamb	*lahm*-meh-sdai	lammesteg
roast pork	*flehs*-geh-sdai	flæskesteg
sausage	*perl*-seh	pølse
sirloin	*mer*-bråh	mørbrad
steak	*ehng*-ehlsg berf	engelsk bøf
turkey	kal-*koon*	kalkun

Denmark is a major meat exporter, and is best known
for its pork, ham and bacon.

Seafood

kogt torsk kogd torsg
  poached cod in a mustard sauce served with boiled potatoes
stegt sild sdehgd seel
  fried herring served with potatoes and a white parsley sauce
stegt ål med sdehgd ål meh
stuvede kartofler sdoo-weh-theh kah-tof-lah
  fried eel with boiled potatoes in a white sauce

cod	torsk	torsk
fish	fis-g	fisk
haddock	kool-ah	kuller
halibut	hehl-eh-flün-ah	helleflynder
herring	seel	sild
plaice	rerth-sbeh-deh	rødspætte
salmon	lahgs	laks
shrimp	rai-yah	rejer
sole	ser-täng-eh	søtunge
trout	for-rahl	forel

Vegetables

asparagus	a-sbahs	asparges
beets	rerth-bi-thah	rødbeder
(usually served pickled)		
broccoli	bro-kor-lee	broccoli
cabbage	käl	kål
carrots	goo-leh-rerth-ah	gulerødder
cauliflower	blom-käl	blomkål
celery	blath-si-lah-ree	bladselleri
cucumber	a-goorg	agurk
lettuce	grern sa-lad	grøn salat
mushrooms	shahm-pin-yong-ah	champignoner
onions	loy	løg
peas	ehr-dah	ærter
pickled	soord/	surt/
cucumbers	sül-dehth a-goor-gah	syltede agurker
potato	kah-tof-ehl	kartoffel
rice	rees	ris
string beans	snee-deh-bern-ah	snittebønner
tomatoes	tor-ma-dah	tomater

DANISH

DANISH

Fruit

apple	*eh*-bleh	*æble*
banana	ba-*nayn*	*banan*
grapes	*vin*-droo-ah	*vindruver*
lemon	sit-*rorn*	*citron*
orange	ah-behl-*seen*	*appelsin*
pear	*peh*-rah	*pære*
strawberry	*yor*-behr	*jordbær*

Desserts

budding   *boo*-thing
   a kind of pudding flavoured with, for example, rum or
   almonds, served warm
chokoladeis/   shor-gor-*la*-theh-ees/
vanilleis   va-*neel*-yeh-ees
   chocolate ice cream/vanilla ice cream
fromage   *fror-ma*-sheh
   a kind of mousse served cold flavoured with, for example,
   lemon
jordbær   *yor*-behr
med fløde   meh *fler*-theh
   strawberries with cream
kage   *ka*-eh
   cake
konditorkager   kon-*dee*-dah-ka-ah
   French pastries
rødgrød   *rerth*-grerth
med fløde   meh *fler*-theh
   fruit pudding (red currant, raspberry, strawberry) served
   with cream
pandekager   *pa*-neh-ka-ah
   crepes rolled around a jam, sugar, or ice cream filling

Non-Alcoholic Drinks

apple juice	*eh-*bleh-djoos	*æblejuice*
cordial	*sahf-*deh-van	*saftevand*
coffee (with cream)	*kah-*feh (meh *fler-*theh)	*kaffe (med fløde)*
orange juice	ah-behl-*seen-*djoos	*appelsinjuice*
skim milk	*sgā-*mehtt-mehlg	*skummetmælk*
soft drink/	*sor-*da-van/	*sodavand/*
carbonated water	*dansg-*van	*danskvand*
tea	ti	*te*
water/ice water	van/*ees-*van	*vand/isvand*
full cream milk	*serth-*mehlg	*sødmælk*

Alcoholic Drinks

øl	erl	beer/lager
hvidvin	*veeth-*veen	white wine
rødvin	*rerth-*veen	red wine

bajer   *bay-*yah
  beer – specifically means a darker beer more like ale, but
  is used colloquially to mean any beer
snaps/akvavit   snahbs/ak-va-*veed*
  various kinds of clear grain alcohol flavoured with different
  herbs, often with caraway. Traditionally consumed with
  pickled herring.
bitter   *bi-*dah
  a darker variant of snaps flavoured with different herbs.
  The most popular kinds are Jägermeister and Gammel
  Dansk. Believed to help settle an uneasy stomach and consumed either at breakfast or with beer.

DANISH

SKÅL OR SKULL?

When Danes raise their glasses to you and say Skål! it
means 'Cheers!', not to be confused with the Australian
concept 'to skull', meaning emptying your drink in one go!
Also, be prepared to say Skål! a lot more than once
during a meal.

DANISH

AT THE MARKET

Basics

bread	bŕerth	brød
butter	smer	smør
cheese	åsd	ost
chocolate	sho-koh-la-theh	chokolade
eggs	ehg	æg
flour	meh-l	mel
jam	sül-deh-toy	syltetøj
margarine	mah-gah-ree-neh	margarine
marmalade	mah-meh-la-theh	marmelade
milk	mehlg	mælk
oil	orl-yeh	olie
pasta	pas-da	pasta
rice	ŕees	ris
sugar	så-gah	sukker
carbonated water	dansg-van	danskvand
water	van	vand
yoghurt	yoo-goord	yoghurt

Meat & Poultry

beef	og-seh-kerth	oksekød
chicken	kül-ing	kylling
duck	an	and
ham	skin-keh	skinke
meat	kerth	kød
mutton	lahm	lam
pork	svee-neh-kerth	svinekød
sausage	perl-seh	pølse
veal	kal-veh-kerth	kalvekød

Vegetables

beets	ŕerth-bi-thah	rødbeder
broccoli	bŕo-kor-lee	broccoli
cabbage	kål	kål

AT THE MARKET

carrots	*goo*-leh-ŕerth-ah	gulerødder
cauliflower	*blom*-kāl	blomkål
celery	*blath*-si-lah-ŕee	bladselleri
cucumber	a-*goorg*	agurk
lettuce	ǵrern sa-*lad*	grøn salat
mushrooms	*shahm*-pin-yong-ah	champignoner
onions	loy	løg
peas	*ehŕ*-dah	ærter
pickled	soorď/	surt/
cucumbers	*sül*-dehth a-*goor*-gah	syltede agurker
potato	kah-*tof*-ehl	kartoffel
string beans	*snee*-deh-bern-ah	snittebønner
tomatoes	tor-*mø*-dah	tomater
vegetables	ǵrern-sa-ah	grønsager

Seafood

cod	torsk	torsk
fish	*fis*-g	fisk
herring	seel	sild
salmon	lahgs	laks
shrimp	*ŕai*-yah	rejer
sole	*ser*-tāng-eh	søtunge
trout	for-*ŕahl*	forel

Fruit

apple	*eh*-bleh	æble
banana	ba-*nayn*	banan
fruit	*frägd*	frugt
grapes	*vin*-droo-ah	vindruver
lemon	sit-*ŕorn*	citron
orange	ah-behl-*seen*	appelsin
pear	*peh*-ŕah	pære
strawberry	*yoŕ*-behŕ	jordbær

SHOPPING

bookshop	*bāw*-han-ehl	*boghandel*
camera shop	*for*-tor-han-ehl	*fotohandel*
clothing store	*toy*-boo-teeg	*tøjbutik*
delicatessen	de-lee-ka-*teh*-seh-fo-*ŕahd*-ning	*delikatesseforretning*
general store/shop	boo-*teeg*	*butik*
laundry	vas-gah-*ŕee*	*vaskeri*
market	*mah*-gehth	*marked*
newsagency	a-*vees*-kee-yosg	*aviskiosk*
pharmacy	ah-por-*tig*	*apotek*
shoeshop	*sgor*-toys-fo-*ŕahd*-ning	*skotøjsforretning*
souvenir shop	soo-veh-*neeŕ*-boo-teeg	*souvenirbutik*
stationers	pah-*peeŕ*-han-ehl	*papirhandel*
supermarket	*soo*-bah-mah-gehth	*supermarked*
vegetable shop	*ǵernd*-han-lah	*grønthandler*

I'd like to buy ...
    yai vi *gehŕ*-neh ha ...   *Jeg vil gerne have ...*
How much is it?
    vo *mah*-ehth *kos*-dah di?   *Hvor meget koster det?*
Do you (inf) have others?
    hah doo *an*-ehth?   *Har du andet?*
I don't like it.
    dehn/di ka yai ig li   *Den/Det kan jeg ikke lide.*
Can I look at it?
    mā yai si dehn/di?   *Må jeg se den/det?*
I'm just looking.
    yai *kee*-gah bah   *Jeg kikker bare.*
Can you write down the price?
    ka doo *sgŕee*-w *pŕee*-sehn nith?   *Kan du skrive prisen ned?*
Do you accept credit cards?
    tah ee *kŕeh-deed*-kord?   *Tager I kreditkort?*

DANISH

Can I help you?
    ka yai *yehl*-beh dehm?

Kan jeg hjælpe Dem? (pol)

Will that be all?
    ehŕ di di *hi*-leh?

Er det det hele?

Would you like it wrapped?
    ern-sgah dee di
    pah-gehth in?

Ønsker De det
pakket ind? (pol)

Sorry, this is the only one.
    dis-vehŕ *di*-deh ehŕ
    dehn *i*-nehs-deh

Desværre, dette er
den eneste.

How much/many do you want?
    vo *mah*-ehht/*mahng*-eh
    ern-sgah dee?

Hvor meget/mange
ønsker De? (pol)

DANISH

Essential Groceries

bread	*bŕerth*	*brød*
butter	smer	*smør*
milk	mehlg	*mælk*
rice	ŕees	*ris*
salt	sald	*salt*
shampoo	*sham*-por	*shampoo*
sugar	*sä*-gah	*sukker*
toilet paper	toy-*lehd*-pah-peeŕ	*toiletpapir*
toothpaste	*tan*-pas-da	*tandpasta*
vegetables	*gŕern*-sa-ah	*grønsager*

Souvenirs

earrings	er-*ŕing*-eh	*øreringe*
handicraft	*känsd*-hon-vehŕg	*kunsthåndværk*
necklace	*hals*-keh-theh	*halskæde*
pottery	ki-ah-*meeg*	*keramik*
ring	ŕing	*ring*
rug	*teh*-beh	*tæppe*

DANISH

Clothing

clothing	*toy*	*tøj*
coat	*fŕah*-geh	*frakke*
dress	*kyor*-leh	*kjole*
jacket	*yah*-geh	*jakke*
jumper (sweater)	*sweh*-dah	*sweater*
shirt	*sgyoŕ*-deh	*skjorte*
shoes	sgor	*sko*
skirt	*nith*-ah-dil	*nederdel*
trousers	*bāg*-sah	*bukser*

It doesn't fit.	dehn *pas*-ah ig	*Den passer ikke.*
It's too ...	dehn ehŕ fo ...	*Den er for ...*
big	sdooŕ	*stor*
small	*lee*-leh	*lille*
short	koŕd	*kort*
long	lahng	*lang*
tight	sdŕahm	*stram*
loose	lers	*løs*

Materials

cotton	*bom*-ool	*bomuld*
handmade	*hon*-la-wehth	*håndlavet*
leather	*lehth*-ah	*læder*
brass	*mehs*-sing	*messing*
gold	gool	*guld*
silver	serl	*sølv*
silk	*sil*-geh	*silke*
wool	ool	*uld*

Colours

black	soŕd	*sort*
blue	blā	*blå*
brown	bŕoon	*brun*
green	gŕern	*grøn*

orange	or-*rang*-sheh	*orange*
pink	*ror*-sa	*rosa*
purple	*li*-la	*lilla*
red	*rerth*	*rød*
white	veeth	*hvid*
yellow	gool	*gul*

Toiletries

comb	kahm	*kam*
condoms	kon-*dorm*-ah	*kondomer*
deodorant	di-or-dor-*rahnd*	*deodorant*
hairbrush	*hor*-bers-deh	*hårbørste*
moisturising cream	*fåg*-dee-hiths-krehm	*fugtighedscreme*
razor	bah-*bir*-knee-w	*barberkniv*
sanitary napkins	bin	*bind*
shampoo	shahm-poo	*shampoo*
shaving cream	bah-*bir*-krehm	*barbercreme*
soap	*seh*-beh	*sæbe*
sunblock cream	*sorl*-krehm	*solcreme*
tampons	tahm-*pong*-ah	*tamponer*
tissues	*rahn*-seh-sehr-vee-ehd	*renseserviet*
toilet paper	toy-*lehd*-pah-peer	*toiletpapir*
toothbrush	*tan*-bers-deh	*tandbørste*
toothpaste	*tan*-pas-da	*tandpasta*

DANISH

Stationery & Publications

map	kord	*kort*
newspaper	a-*vees*	*avis*
newspaper in English	a-*vees* på *ehng*-ehlsg	*avis på engelsk*
novels in English	ro-*man*-ah på *ehng*-ehlsg	*romaner på engelsk*
paper	pa-*peer*	*papir*
pen (ballpoint)	*koo*-leh-pehn	*kuglepen*
scissors	sahgs	*saks*

DANISH

Photography

How much is it to process this film?
    vo *mah*-ehth *kos*-dah
    di ad *frahm*-ka-leh
    dehn-neh feelm?
When will it be ready?
    vo-*nor* ehŕ dehn *fehŕ*-dee?
I'd like a film for this camera.
    yai vi *gerh*-neh ha in feelm
    ti *deh*-deh ka-meh-ŕah

Hvor meget koster det
at fremkalde
denne film?

Hvornår er den færdig?

Jeg vil gerne have en film
til dette kamera.

B&W (film)	*soŕd*-veeth	*sort-hvid*
camera	*ka*-meh-ŕah	*kamera*
colour (film)	*fah*-weh	*farve*
film	feelm	*film*
flash	bleeds	*blitz*
lens	ob-yehg-*tee*-w	*objektiv*
light meter	*lüs*-mā-lah	*lysmåler*

Smoking

A packet of cigarettes, please.
    in *pah*-geh
    see-gah-*ŕah*-dah tahg
Are these cigarettes strong/mild?
    ehŕ *dees*-eh see-gah-*ŕah*-dah
    sdehŕ-geh/*meel*-eh?
Do you have a light?
    hah doo il?

En pakke
cigaretter, tak.

Er disse cigaretter
stærke/milde?

Har du ild? (inf)

cigarette papers	see-gah-*ŕahd*-pah-peeŕ	*cigaretpapir*
cigarettes	see-gah-*ŕah*-dah	*cigaretter*
filtered	meh *feel*-dah	*med filter*
lighter	*lai*-dah	*lighter*
matches	*tehm*-sdig-ah	*tændstikker*
menthol	mehn-*torl*	*mentol*
pipe	*pee*-beh	*pibe*
tobacco (pipe)	*pee*-be-tor-bahg	*pibetobak*

Sizes & Comparisons

small	*lee*-leh	*lille*
big	sdoor´	*stor*
heavy	tāng	*tung*
light	lehd	*let*
more	*mi*-ah	*mere*
less	min-dŕah	*mindre*
too much/many	fo *mah*-ehth/	*for meget/*
	mahng-eh	*mange*
many	*mahng*-eh	*mange*
enough	nog	*nok*
also	os-eh	*også*
a little bit	in *lee*-leh *smoo*-leh	*en lille smule*

DANISH

HEALTH

Where is the ...?	voŕ ehŕ ...?	*Hvor er ...?*
hospital	hors-bi-*ta*-lehth	*hospitalet*
chemist	ah-por-*tig*-ehth	*apoteket*
the casualty ward	sga-theh-sdoo-ehn	*skadestuen*
Where is a ...?	voŕ ehŕ dehŕ in ...?	*Hvor er der en ...?*
doctor	*leh*-eh	*læge*
dentist	*tan*-leh-eh	*tandlæge*

I'm sick.
  yai ehŕ sü — *Jeg er syg.*
My friend is sick.
  meen vehn ehŕ sü — *Min ven er syg.*
Could I see a female doctor?
  mā yai fā in *kvin*-lee *leh*-eh? — *Må jeg få en kvindelig læge?*
What's the matter?
  va ehŕ dah ee *vai*-yehn? — *Hvad er der i vejen?*

DANISH

Where does it hurt?
voŕ ger di ānd?   *Hvor gør det ondt?*
It hurts here.
di ger ānd heeŕ   *Det gør ondt her.*
My ... hurts.
meen/meed ... ger ānd   *Min/mit ... gør ondt.*

Parts of the Body

ankle	*ahng-gehl*	*ankel*
arm	ahm	*arm*
back	ŕerg	*ryg*
chest	bŕersd	*bryst*
ear	er-ah	*øre*
eye	oy-yeh	*øje*
finger	*fing-ah*	*finger*
foot	forth	*fod*
hand	hon	*hånd*
head	*hor*-wehth	*hoved*
heart	*yehŕ-deh*	*hjerte*
leg	bin	*ben*
mouth	mān	*mund*
ribs	*ŕee-bin*	*ribben*
skin	hooth	*hud*
stomach	*ma-weh*	*mave*
teeth	*tehn-ah*	*tænder*
throat	hals	*hals*

Ailments

I have (a/an) ...	yai hah ...	Jeg har ...
allergy	a-lah-*gee*	*allergi*
anaemia	a-neh-*mee*	*anæmi*
blister	in *va*-behl	*en vabel*
burn	id *bŕahn*-sor	*et brandsår*
cold	in fo-*kerl*-seh	*en forkølelse*
constipation	fo-*sdob*-ehl-seh	*forstoppelse*
cough	*hors*-deh	*hoste*
diarrhoea	dee-a-*ŕeh*	*diarré*
fever	*fi*-bah	*feber*
headache	*hor*-wehth-pee-neh	*hovedpine*
hepatitis	hi-pa-*tee*-tees	*hepatitis*
indigestion	*ma*-weh-bi-svehŕ	*mavebesvær*
infection	in in-fehg-*shorn*	*en infektion*
influenza	in-floo-*ehn*-sa	*influenza*
lice	loos	*lus*
low/high	*la*-wd/hoyd	*lavt/højt*
blood pressure	*blorth*-tŕerg	*blodtryk*
sore throat	ānd ee *hal*-sehn	*ondt i halsen*
sprain	in fo-*sdoo*-ning	*en forstuvning*
stomachache	ānd ee *ma*-wehn	*ondt i maven*
temperature	*fi*-bah	*feber*
venereal disease	in *kerns*-sü-dom	*en kønssygdom*
worms	ooŕm	*orm*

Some Useful Words & Phrases

I'm ...	yai hah ...	Jeg har ...
asthmatic	*asd*-ma	*astma*
diabetic	dee-a-*bi*-tehs	*diabetes*
epileptic	eh-pee-lehb-*see*	*epilepsi*

I'm allergic to antibiotics/penicillin.
yai ehŕ a-*lehŕ*-geesg *ow*-ah	*Jeg er allergisk over*
fo an-tee-bee-*or*-tee-ka/	*for antibiotika/*
pin-ee-see-*leen*	*penicillin.*

DANISH

DANISH

I'm pregnant.
    yai ehŕ gŕah-*veeth*   *Jeg er gravid.*
I'm on the pill.
    yai bŕoo-ah *pi*-pil-lah   *Jeg bruger p-piller.*
I haven't had my period for ... months.
    yai hah ig hahfd   *Jeg har ikke haft*
    mins-dŕoo-ah-*shorn* ee ...   *menstruation i ...*
    mā-neh-thah   *måneder.*
I have been vaccinated.
    yai ehŕ *bli*-wehth   *Jeg er blevet*
    vahg-see-*ni*-ahth   *vaccineret.*
I have my own syringe.
    yai hah meen *ai*-yehn ka-*nü*-leh   *Jeg har min egen kanyle.*
I feel better/worse.
    yai hah di *behth*-ah/*vehŕ*-ah   *Jeg har det bedre/værre.*

At the Chemist

I need medication for ...
    yai sga bŕoo-eh *nā*-ehth   *Jeg skal bruge noget*
    mi-dee-*seen* morth ...   *medicin mod ...*
I have a prescription.
    yai hah in ŕeh-*sehbd*   *Jeg har en recept.*

At the Dentist

I have a toothache.
    yai hah *tan*-pee-neh   *Jeg har tandpine.*
I've lost a filling.
    yai hah tahbd en *plām*-beh   *Jeg har tabt en plombe.*
I've broken a tooth.
    yai hah *kneh*-gehth in tan   *Jeg har knækket en tand.*
My gums hurt.
    meed *tan*-kerth ger ānd   *Mit tandkød gør ondt.*
I don't want it extracted.
    yai vi ig ha dehn   *Jeg vil ikke have den*
    tŕā-gehth ooth   *trukket ud.*
Please give me an anaesthetic.
    yai vi gehŕ-neh bi-*der*-wehs   *Jeg vil gerne bedøves.*

Some Useful Words

accident	*oo*-ler-geh	*ulykke*
addiction	ahw-*hehng*-ee-hith	*afhængighed*
aspirin	as-bee-*r̀een*	*aspirin*
a bandage	in ban-*da*-sheh	*en bandage*
blood test	*blorth*-p̀fer-veh	*blodprøve*
contraception	p̀feh-vehn-*shorn*	*prævention*
medicine	mi-dee-*seen*	*medicin*
menstruation	mins-d̀fo-oah-*shorn*	*menstruation*
nausea	*kval*-meh	*kvalme*
oxygen	og-sü-*gin*/eeld	*oxygen/ilt*
vitamins	vee-ta-*meen*-ah	*vitaminer*

TIME & DATES

What date is it today?
vil-gehn *da*-tor eh̀f di ee da?   *Hvilken dato er det i dag?*
What time is it?
va eh̀f *klog*-gehn?   *Hvad er klokken?*
It's ... am/pm.
klog-gehn eh̀f ...   *Klokken er ...*
om *mor̀n*-n/*ahfd*-nehn   *om morgenen/aftenen.*

in the morning	om *mor̀*-n	*om morgenen*
in the afternoon	om *ehf*-dah-mi-da-ehn	*om eftermiddagen*
in the evening	om *ahfd*-nehn	*om aftenen*

Days of the Week

Monday	*man*-da	*mandag*
Tuesday	*teer̀s*-da	*tirsdag*
Wednesday	*āns*-da	*onsdag*
Thursday	*tor̀s*-da	*̀torsdag*
Friday	*f̀feh*-da	*fredag*
Saturday	*ler*-da	*lørdag*
Sunday	*sern*-da	*søndag*

DANISH

Months

January	*yan*-oo-ah	*januar*
February	*feb*-foo-ah	*februar*
March	mahds	*marts*
April	a-*preel*	*april*
May	mai	*maj*
June	*yoo*-nee	*juni*
July	*yoo*-lee	*juli*
August	ahw-*gäsd*	*august*
September	sib-*tehm*-bah	*september*
October	org-*tor*-bah	*oktober*
November	nor-*vehm*-bah	*november*
December	di-*sehm*-bah	*december*

Seasons

summer	*som*-ah	*sommer*
autumn	*ehf*-dah-or	*efterår*
winter	*vin*-dah	*vinter*
spring	*for*-or	*forår*

Present

today	ee da	*i dag*
this morning	ee *mor*-seh	*i morges*
tonight	ee nad	*i nat*
this week	*dehn*-neh *oo*-eh	*denne uge*
this year	ee or	*i år*
now	noo	*nu*

Past

yesterday	ee gor	*i går*
day before yesterday	ee *for*-gors	*i forgårs*
yesterday morning	ee gor mor-seh	*i går morges*
last night	ee (gor) nad;	*i (går) nat;*
	ee (gor) *ahf*-dehs	*i (går) aftes*
last week	*for*-ee *oo*-eh	*forrige uge*
last year	*sees*-deh or	*sidste år*

Future

tomorrow	ee morn	*i morgen*
day after tomorrow	ee *ow*-ah-morn	*i overmorgen*
tomorrow morning	ee morn *teeth*-lee	*i morgen tidlig*
tomorrow afternoon/ evening	ee morn *ehf*-dah-mi-da/ *ahf*-dehn	*i morgen eftermiddag/ aften*
next week	*nehs*-deh *oo*-eh	*næste uge*
next year	*nehs*-deh or	*næste år*

During the Day

afternoon	*ehf*-dah-mi-da	*eftermiddag*
dawn	*daow*-grü	*daggry*
day	da	*dag*
early	*teeth*-lee	*tidlig*
midnight	*meeth*-nad	*midnat*
morning	morn	*morgen*
night	nad	*nat*
noon	*mi*-das-teeth	*middagstid*
sundown	*sorl*-nith-gahng	*solnedgang*
sunrise	*sorl*-ob-gahng	*solopgang*

DANISH

NUMBERS & AMOUNTS

0	nāl	*nul*
1	in	*en*
2	tor	*to*
3	tŕeh	*tre*
4	feeŕ	*fire*
5	feh	*fem*
6	sehgs	*seks*
7	sü-w	*syv*
8	*ā*-deh	*otte*
9	nee	*ni*
10	tee	*ti*
11	*ehl*-veh	*elve*

DANISH

12	tol	tolv
13	*trah*-dehn	tretten
14	*fyor*-dehn	fjorten
15	*fehm*-dehn	femten
16	*sais*-dehn	seksten
17	*ser*-dehn	sytten
18	*a*-dehn	atten
19	*ni*-dehn	nitten
20	*tü*-weh	tyve
21	*in*-o-tü-weh	enogtyve
30	*trahth*-veh	tredive
40	*fer*-eh	fyrre
50	hal-*trehs*	halvtreds
60	*trehs*	tres
70	hal-*fyehrs*	halvfjerds
80	*feers*	firs
90	hal-*fehms*	halvfems
100	*hoon*-ahth	hundrede
1000	*too*-sehn	tusind
one million	in mee-lee-*orn*	en million

1st	*fers*-deh	første
2nd	*an*-ehn	anden
3rd	*trehth*-yeh	tredje
1/4	in *fyi*-ah-dil	en fjerdedel
1/3	in *trehth*-yeh-dil	en tredjedel
1/2	in hal	en halv
3/4	*treh fyi*-ah-di-leh	tre fjerdedele

Some Useful Words

a little (amount)	en *lee*-leh *smoo*-leh	*en lille smule*
double	*dob*-ehld	*dobbelt*
a dozen	id doo-*seen*	*et dusin*
enough	nog	*nok*
few	fã	*fã*
less	*min*-dfah	*mindre*
many	*mahng*-eh	*mange*
more	*mi*-ah	*mere*
once	*in* gahng	*en gang*
a pair	id pah	*et par*
percent	pfor-*sehnd*	*procent*
some	*nor*-leh	*nogle*
too much	fo *mah*-ehth	*for meget*
twice	tor *gahng*-eh	*to gange*

ABBREVIATIONS

0800/2000	am/pm
a/s – aktieselskab	Ltd/Inc.
BZ – besættere	squatters
DSB – de Danske Statsbaner	the Danish National Railways
DUH – de Danske Ungdomsherberger	Danish Youth Hostel Association
DVH – de Danske Vandrehjem	Danish Youth Hostel Association
dagl. – dagligt	daily (Monday to Saturday)
EF – det Europæiske Fællesmarked	EEC, the Common Market
ekskl. – eksklusive	excluded, except
EU – den Europæiske Union	the European Union
FN – de Forenede Nationer	UN
f.kr/e.kr.	BC/AD
frk. – frøken	Miss
fr – fredag	Friday
fru	Mrs
Gd/V	St/Rd

DANISH

DANISH

hel. – hellig	holy (as in holiday)
hlp. – holdeplads	bus stop
Hr. – herr	Mr/Sir
inkl. – inklusive	including
jb – jernbane	railway
jrbst – jernbanestation	station/railway station
Kbh – København	Copenhagen
KDAK	the Royal Danish Automobile Association
kgl. – kongelig	royal
kl. – klasse	class (on trains and aeroplanes)
kl. – klokken	o'clock
km/t – kilometer i timen	kilometres per hour
kr – krone	crown (Danish monetary unit)
lø – lørdag	Saturday
m. – med	with
ma – mandag	Monday
moms	VAT, sales tax (included in the price on all goods and services)
ndf. – nedenfor	below (used in notices, timetables, etc)
Ndr. – nordre	to the north (pertaining to place names)
on – onsdag	Wednesday
SAS	Scandinavian Airline System
Sdr. – søndre	to the south (pertaining to place names)
sø – søndag	Sunday
t.h. – til højre	to the right (used in addresses)
ti – tirsdag	Tuesday
tlf. – telefon	telephone
to – torsdag	Thursday
t.v. – til venstre	to the left (used in addresses)

EMERGENCIES

Go away!	fo-*svin*!	*Forsvind!*
Help!	yehlb!	*Hjælp!*
Thief!	tüw!	*Tyv!*

It's an emergency!
  deh-deh ehf en
  nerth-si-too-a-shorn!
  Dette er en nødsituation!

There's been an accident!
  dah ehf skid in *oo*-ler-geh!
  Der er sket en ulykke!

Call a doctor!
  fing *ehf*-dah in *leh*-eh!
  Ring efter en læge!

Call an ambulance!
  fing *ehf*-dah in
  ahm-boo-*lahng*-seh!
  Ring efter en ambulance!

I've been raped.
  yai ehf *bli*-wehth *vol*-ta-ehth
  Jeg er blevet voldtaget.

I've been robbed.
  yai ehf *bli*-wehth bi-*sdyä*-lehth!
  Jeg er blevet bestjålet!

Call the police!
  fing ehf-dah por-li-*tee*-ehth!
  Ring efter politiet!

Where is the police station?
  vor ehf por-li-*tee*-sda-shor-nehn?
  Hvor er politistationen?

I'll call the police!
  yai *ring*-ah ti por-li-*tee*-ehth!
  Jeg ringer til politiet!

I'm/My friend is ill.
  yai ehr/meen vehn ehf sü
  Jeg er/Min ven er syg.

I'm lost.
  yai ehf *fah*-ehth vil
  Jeg er faret vild.

Where are the toilets?
  vor ehf toy-*lehd*-dah-neh?
  Hvor er toiletterne?

Could you help me please?
  ka dee *yehl*-beh mai?
  Kan De hjælpe mig? (pol)

Could I please use the telephone?
  mä yai *lä*-neh ti-leh-*for*-nehn?
  Må jeg låne telefonen?

DANISH

DANISH

I'm sorry. I apologise.
bi-*kla*-ah. *ān*-sgül   *Beklager. Undskyld.*

I didn't realise I was doing anything wrong.
yai *vis*-deh *ig* ad yai   *Jeg vidste ikke at jeg*
gyoŕ *nā*-ehth gald   *gjorde noget galt.*

I didn't do it.
di vah ig *mai* dah *gyoŕ* di   *Det var ikke mig der gjorde det.*

I wish to contact my embassy/ consulate.
yai vi *gehŕ*-neh kon-*tahg*-deh   *Jeg vil gerne kontakte*
meen ah-mba-*sa*-theh/   *min ambassade/*
meed kon-soo-*lad*   *mit konsulat.*

I speak English.
yai *ta*-lah *ehng*-elhsg   *Jeg taler engelsk.*

I have medical insurance.
yai hah *sü*-eh-fo-sig-*ŕing*   *Jeg har sygeforsikring.*

My possessions are insured.
mee-neh *ai*-ehn-*di*-leh ehŕ   *Mine ejendele er*
fo-*sig*-ŕahth   *forsikret.*

My ... was stolen.	meed/meen ... ehŕ	*Mit/min... er*
	bli-wehth *sdyā*-lehth	*blevet stjålet.*
I've lost my...	yai hah *mis*-dehth ...	*Jeg har mistet ...*
bags	meen ba-*ga*-sheh	*min bagage*
handbag	meen *hon*-tas-geh	*min håndtaske*
money	*mee*-neh *pehng*-eh	*mine penge*
passport	meed pas	*mit pas*
travellers cheques	*mee*-neh *ŕai*-seh-shehgs	*mine rejsechecks*

FAROESE

QUICK REFERENCE

Hello.	huh-lloh!/huhy!	*Halló!/Hey!*
Goodbye.	for-vael	*Farvæl.*
Yes./No.	yae/nai	*Ja./Nei.*
Excuse me.	or-sae-kuh!	*Orsaka!*
Sorry.	um-shil-duh/ or-saek-i-meh	*Umskylda/ Orsakið meg.*
Please.	djehr-i so vael	*Gerið so væl.*
Thank you.	tuhk	*Takk.*
That's fine./	on-chi uh	*Onki at*
You're welcome.	tuhk-kuh fi-ri	*takka fyri.*

I'd like ...	kun-di ehg fin-dji ...	*Kundi eg fingið ...*
a one-way ticket	ain-veh-yis fehr-uh-seh-yil	*einvegis ferðaseðil*
a return ticket	fehr-uh-seh-yil uht-tur o fruhm	*ferðaseðil aftur og fram*

I (don't) understand.
  eh shil-yi (ich-i)   *Eg skilji (ikki).*
Do you speak English?
  du-vir too ain-gilst?   *Dugir tú eingilskt?*
Where is ...?
  kvaer ehr ...?   *Hvar er ...?*
Go straight ahead.
  faer baint fruhm   *Far beint fram.*
Turn left/right.
  faer teel vin-stru/herg-ru.   *Fær til vinstru/høgru.*
Do you have any rooms
available?
  ehr-u nerk-ur luhys   *Eru nøkur leys*
  kerm-ur?   *kømur?*
I'm looking for a public toilet.
  eh lait-eh eht-tir   *Eg leiti eftir*
  uhl-mehn-nun vehs-eh   *almennum vesi.*

1	aitt	*eitt*	6	sehks	*seks*
2	tvuhy	*tvey*	7	shuhy	*sjey*
3	trooi	*trý*	8	ot-tuh	*átta*
4	fooir-uh	*fíra*	9	nooi-djeh	*níggju*
5	fim	*fimm*	10	tooi-djeh	*tíggju*

FAROESE

FAROESE

Faroese (often spelled Faeroese) is a twig of the North Germanic branch of the Indo-European tree, which includes Icelandic, Danish, Norwegian and Swedish.

The population of the Faroe Islands, or Faroes, is about 46,000, which means that Faroese is the mother tongue of only a very small number of people.

The Norwegian settlers (about 900 AD) brought their own language to the places they colonised, among them the Faroes, and over the centuries a distinct language developed in the Faroe Islands. The most important factor in the preservation of the language was the oral literature, particularly the kvæði, long epic ballads dealing with ancient legendary characters and events, which are a unique cultural heritage.

Historically the Faroe Islands have been under Norwegian and Danish rule. For several centuries Danish was the dominating language in all administration and in public institutions like schools and the church, and Faroese was degraded to the privacy of the home. In 1846 a Faroese scholar set out to recreate a written norm for Faroese. Today books and newspapers are in Faroese, as are church services and school lessons.

Modern Faroese is under the constant influence of the surrounding world, particularly through the mass media, and there is an ongoing struggle to promote and nourish Faroese in the face of the massive influence of Danish and American English.

PRONUNCIATION

The written norm, created in 1846 and still in use, is based on etymology and thus reflects an older stage of Faroese than does the pronunciation.

STRESS

Stress is normally on the first syllable of the word.

Pronunciation is given in the pronunciation guide at the front of this book, with the following exceptions:

Vowels

In front of two or more consonants, vowels are short and have a more open quality than their long equivalents.

Semivowels

FAROESE	GUIDE	SOUND
á long	wah	as the 'oi' in French *moi*
í, ý long	ooi	as in Spanish *muy*

Consonants

FAROESE	GUIDE	SOUND
ð		silent in a final position; otherwise taking on the value of surrounding vowels
ðr	gr	as the 'gr' in 'grab'
dj, ge, gi, gy, gey, gj, ggj	dj	as the 'j' in 'jaw'
ft	tt	as the 'tt' in 'bitter'
g		silent in a final position; otherwise taking on the value of surrounding vowels
hj	y	as the 'y' in 'yet'
ke, ki, ky, key, kj	ch	as the 'ch' 'chew'
r	r	as the 'r' in 'grab'
rn	dn	as the 'dn' in 'hadn't'
ll	dl	as the 'dl' in 'saddle'
sj, sk, ske, ski, sky, skey, skj	sh	as in 'ship'

FAROESE

GREETINGS & CIVILITIES
Top Useful Phrases

Hello.	huh-lloh!/huhy!	*Halló!/Hey!*
How do you do?	goh-uhn dae(-yin)	*Góðan dag(in).*
Goodbye.	for-vael	*Farvæl.*
See you later.	veet sooi-djuhst	*Vit síggjast.*
Yes/No.	yae/nai	*Ja./Nei.*
Excuse me.	or-sae-kuh!	*Orsaka!*
Maybe.	kuhn-skuh	*Kanska.*
Please.	djehr-i so vael	*Gerið so væl.*
Thank you.	tuhk	*Takk.*

May I? Do you mind?
    kuhn eh? slehp-pi eh?   *Kann eg? Sleppi eg?*
Sorry. (excuse me, forgive me)
    um-shil-duh/or-saek-i-meh   *Umskylda/Orsakið meg.*
Many thanks.
    too-sun tuhk   *Túsund takk.*
                   (lit. thousand thanks)

You too!
    sholv/-ur tuhk!   *Sjálv/-ur takk!* (f/m)
                   (lit. self thanks)

That's fine. You're welcome.
    on-chi uh tuhk-kuh fi-ri   *Onki at takka fyri.*
That's all right.
    tae ehr ooi lae-yee   *Tað er í lagi.*

FAROESE

THANKS FOR THE MEMORIES

Takk fyri seinast.   tuhk fi-ri sain-uhst
    Thanks for the last time I saw you – used when you
    meet someone again after a party or a social event
Manga takk!   muhn-guh tuhk!
    Many thanks – used to your hostess after a meal
Væl gagnist!   vael guhg-nist
    May the food do you good – answer to the above

Greetings

Good morning.	goh-uhn mor-gun	*Góðan morgun.*
Good afternoon.	goh-uhn dae(-yin)	*Góðan dag(in).*
Good evening.	gott kverld	*Gott kvøld.*
Good night.	goh-uh nott	*Góa nátt.*
How are you?	kvus-seh heh-vur too tae?	*Hvussu hevur tú tað?*
Well, thanks.	gott tuhk	*Gott takk.*

Forms of Address

Madam/Mrs	froo	*frú*
Sir/Mr	huhr-ruh	*harra*
Miss	frer-kun	*frøkun*
companion/friend	vin-kon-uh/vee-nur	*vinkona/vinur* (f/m)

FAROESE

PRONOUNS		
SG		
I	eh	*eg*
you	too	*tú*
she/he/it	hon/huhn/tae	*hon/hann/tað*
PL		
we	veed	*vit*
you (pl)	teed	*tit*
they	taer/tair/tuhy	*tær/teir/tey* (f/m/n)

SMALL TALK
Meeting People

What is your name?	kvus-seh ai-tuh ti-yun?	*Hvussu eita tygum?*
My name is ...	eh ai-ti ...	*Eg eiti ...*

I'd like to introduce you to ...
	chehn-nir too ...?	*Kennir tú ...?*
		(lit. know you ...?)

I'm pleased to meet you.
	stutt-litt aet hitt-uh teh	*Stuttligt at hitta teg.*

Nationalities

Where are you from?
kvae-uhn-i ehr-u tiy-un?	*Hvaðani eru tygum?*

I'm from ...	eh ehr-i oor ...	*Eg eri úr ...*
Australia	uhu-strah-li-uh	*Avstralia*
Canada	kah-nuh-duh	*Kanada*
Denmark	duhm-muhrsk	*Danmark*
England	ong-luhn-di	*Onglandi*
Iceland	ooish-luhn-di	*Íslandi*
Ireland	ur-luhn-di	*Írlandi*
New Zealand	nooi-sae-luhn-di	*Ný Sælandi*
Norway	nor-ruh	*Noregi*
Scotland	sgot-luhn-di	*Skotlandi*
Sweden	sverr-ooi-chi	*Svøríki*
the USA	uh-mehr-i-kuh/	*Amerika/*
	u-ehs-ah	*USA*

Age

How old are you?
kvus-seh go-mul/	*Hvussu gomul/*
gae-muhl ehrs-too?	*gamal ert tú?* (f/m)

I'm ... years old.
eh ehr-i ... wah-ruh go-mul/	*Eg eri ... ára gomul/*
gae-muhl	*gamal.* (f/m)

FAROESE

Occupations

What do you do?
kvaet djeh-ruh ti-yun?   *Hvat gera tygum?* (pol)

I work as ...	eh uhr-buh-yi sum ...	*Eg arbeiði sum ...*
artist	lis-tuh-ferlk	*listafólk*
business person	huhn-dils-kvin-nuh/	*handilskvinna/*
	huhn-dil-mae-vur	*handilsmaður* (f/m)
doctor	luhk-ni/dok-tuhr-i	*lækni/doktari*
engineer	muh-sheen-mai-stuhr-i	*maskinmeistari*
farmer	bern-di	*bóndi*
journalist	tooin-duh-ferlk	*tíðindafólk*
lawyer	saek-ferr-uhr-i	*sakførari*
manual worker	uhr-bais-kvin-nuh/	*arbeiðskvinna/*
	uhr-bais-mae-vur	*arbeiðsmaður* (f/m)
mechanic	meh-kahn-i-kuhr-i	*mekanikari*
nurse	shook-ruh-sis-tir	*sjúkrasystir*
office worker	skriv-sto-vu-ferlk	*skrivstovufólk*
sailor/seaman	shoh-mae-vur	*sjómaður*
scientist	voois-in-duh-ferlk	*vísindafólk*
student	stu-dehn-tur	*studentur*
teacher	lae-ruhr-i	*lærari*
waiter	tae-nuhr-i	*tænari*
writer	rit-her-vun-dur	*rithøvundur*

Religion

What is your religion?
kverr-yuh trigv heh-vur too?   *Hvørja trúgv hevur tú?*
I'm not religious.
eh ehr-i ich-i reh-li-gi-ers/-ur   *Eg eri ikki religøs/-ur.* (f/m)

I'm (a) ...	eh ehr-i ...	*Eg eri ...*
Buddhist	budd-is-tur	*buddistur*
Catholic	kuh-to-lik-kur	*katolikkur*
Christian	kris-tin	*kristin*
Hindu	hin-du	*hindu*
Jewish	yer-di	*jødi*
Muslim	mus-lee-mur	*muslimur*

FAROESE

Family

Are you married?	ehrs-too djift/-ur	*Ert tú gift/-ur?* (f/m)
I'm ...	eh ehr-i ...	*Eg eri ...*
single	oh-djift/-ur	*ógift/-ur* (f/m)
married	djift/-ur	*gift/-ur* (f/m)
divorced	shild/-ur	*skild/-ur* (f/m)
a widow/er	ain-chuh/	*einkja/*
	ain-chu-mae-vur	*einkjumaður* (f/m)
available	luhys/-ur	*leys/-ur* (f/m)

How many children do you have?
kvus-su nehgv
berdn heh-vur too? — *Hvussu nógv børn hevur tú?*

I don't have any children.
eh hae-vi on-dji berdn — *Eg havi ongi børn.*

I have a daughter/a son.
eh hae-vi ain-uh der-ttur/ ain son — *Eg havi eina dóttur/ ein son.*

How many brothers/ sisters do you have?
kvus-su nehgv sish-in heh-vur too? — *Hvussu nógv systkin hevur túu?*

Do you have a boyfriend/girlfriend?
Heh-vur too shaik/dah-mu? — *Hevur tú sjeik/damu?*

FAROESE

brother	brohir/bai-dji	*bróðir/beiggi*
children	berdn	*børn*
daughter	der-ttir	*dóttir*
family	fuhm-il-yuh/shil-ferlk	*familja/skyldfólk*
father	fae-yir/pwah-pi	*faðir/pápi*
grandfather	uhb-i	*abbi*
grandmother	om-uh	*omma*
husband	mae-vur	*maður*
mother	moh-ir/muhm-uh	*móðir/mamma*
sister	sis-tir	*systir*
son	son-ur	*sonur*
wife	ko-nuh	*kona*

Kids' Talk

How old are you?
  kvu-su nehgv wahr ehrs-too?   *Hvussu nógv ár ert tú?*

When's your birthday?
  naer fidl-ir too?   *Nær fyllir tú?*

What do you do after school?
  kvaet gehrs-too ehtt-ir   *Hvat gert tú eftir*
  skoo-luh-tooi?   *skúlatíð?*

Do you have a pet at home?
  Heh-vur too nae-kuh   *Hevur tú nakað*
  chehl-i-dooir?   *kelidýr?*

I have/own a ...	eh hae-vi/ai-yi ...	*eg havi/eigi ...*
bird	ain fugl	*ein fugl*
budgerigar	un-du-laht	*undulat*
canary	kuhn-ahr-i-u-fugl	*kanariufugl*
cat	cheht-u	*kettu*
dog	hund	*hund*

Feelings

I (don't) like ...
  maer dwah-muhr (ich-i) ...   *Mær dámar (ikki)...*

I love/hate ...
  eh ehl-shi/hae-ti ...   *Eg elski/hati ...*

I'm in a hurry.
  eh mwah skund-uh maer   *Eg má skunda mær.*
      (lit. I must hurry me)

I'm well.
  eh hae-vi tae got   *Eg havi tað gott.*

I'm sorry. (condolence)
  tae vaer sind ooi taer/   *Tað var synd í tær/*
  tik-un   *tykkum.* (sg/pl)

I'm grateful.
  eh si-yi stohr-uh tuhk   *Eg sigi stóra takk.*
      (lit. I say great thank-you)

FAROESE

You're right.	too heh-vur ruhtt	*Tú hevur rætt.*
I'm ...	eh ehr-i ...	*Eg eri ...*
angry	idl/-ur	*ill/-ur* (f/m)
cold	kerld/kuhld-ur	*køld/kaldur* (f/m)
full/satisfied	mehtt/-ur	*mett/-ur* (f/m)
happy	glae/-vur	*glað/-vur* (f/m)
hot	hait/-ur	*heit/-ur* (f/m)
hungry	svong/svehng-ur	*svong/svangur* (f/m)
sad	chehdd/-ur	*kedd/-ur* (f/m)
thirsty	tist/-ur	*tyst/-ur* (f/m)
tired (fatigued)	moh/-ur	*móð/-ur* (f/m)
worried	stoor-in	*stúrin*

FAROESE

Some Useful Phrases

Just a minute.
  booi-yuh aitt sin-dur   *Bíða eitt sindur.*
It's (not) important.
  tae ehr (ich-i) um-rwahn-di   *Tað er (ikki) umráðandi.*
It's (not) possible.
  tae ehr (ich-i) mer-vi-litt   *Tað er (ikki) møguligt.*
Wait!
  booi-yuh!/booi-yi!   *Bíða!/Bíðið!* (sg/pol & pl)
Good luck!
  goh-uh ehd-nu!   *Góða eydnu!*

BODY LANGUAGE

The Faroese are rather shy or wary when it comes to expressing their feelings, be it in words or in physical manifestation.

Shaking hands is the usual form of greeting when you meet someone for the first time. Friends and family who meet after having been apart for some time may hug each other, and good friends also kiss each other. Women tend to hug and kiss more than men, who mostly prefer to slap each other's back. When you meet people who you see often, you don't shake hands every time, nor do you shake hands every time you leave.

Gesticulation is not a characteristic of the Faroese, more typically they keep their hands and arms still, and some – particularly men – keep one or both hands in their pockets.

BREAKING THE LANGUAGE BARRIER

Do you speak English?
  du-vir too ain-gilst?   *Dugir tú eingilskt?*

Does anyone speak English?
  du-vir nae-gar ain-gilst?   *Dugir nakar eingilskt?*

I speak a little ...
  eh du-vi aitt sin-dur ...   *Eg dugi eitt sindur ...*

I don't speak ...
  eh du-vi ich-i ...   *Eg dugi ikki ...*

I (don't) understand.
  eh shil-yi (ich-i)   *Eg skilji (ikki).*

Could you repeat that?
  kuhnst too tae-kuh
  huhtt-uh up-uhtt-ur?   *Kanst tú taka
                                            hatta uppaftur?*

Could you speak more
slowly please?
  kuhns-too djehr-uh so
  vael uht tos-uh saint?   *Kanst tú gera so
                                            væl at tosa seint?*

How do you say ...?
  kvus-u si-yuh teet ...?   *Hvussu siga tit ...?*

I speak ...	eh du-vi ...	*Eg dugi ...*
English	ain-gilst	*eingilskt*
French	fruhnkst	*franskt*
German	tooikst	*týskt*
Italian	i-tuhlst	*italskt*
Spanish	spuhnkst	*spanskt*

PAPERWORK

address	boos-tae-vur	*bústaður*
age	uhld-ur	*aldur*
birth certificate	fer-yi-braev	*føðibrøv*
car owner's title	beel-skrwah-seht-ing-uhr-vott-uhn	*bilskrásetingarváttan*
car registration	vot-tuhn	*váttan*
customs	to-dlur	*tollur*
date of birth	fer-ying-uhr-dae-vur	*føðingardagur*
driver's licence	koy-ri-korst	*koyrikort*
identification	suhm-lai-kuh-prehgv	*samleikaprógv*
immigration	in-fleet-ing	*innflyting*
marital status	choon-uh-ster-vuh	*hjúnastøða*
name	nuhun	*navn*
nationality	choh-skae-pur	*tjóðskapur*
passport (number)	puhs(-num-uhr)	*pass(nummar)*
place of birth	fer-ying-uhr-stae-vur	*føðingarstaður*
profession	uhr-bai-yi	*arbeiði*
reason for travel	ehn-duh-mwahl vee fehr-in-i	*endamál við ferðini*
religion	trigv	*trúgv*
sex	cheen	*kyn*
visa	vee-suh	*visa*

FAROESE

PREPOSITIONS

English 'at' corresponds to a number of Faroese prepositions (*í ooi*, *á wah*, *við vee*).

GETTING AROUND

What time does the ... leave/arrive?	naer fehr/ chehm-ur ...?	*Nær fer/ kemur ...?*
(air)plane	flog-faer-i	*flogfarið*
boat	bwaht-ur-in	*báturin*
bus (city)	(booi)bus-ur-in	*(bý)bussurin*
bus (intercity)	bus-ur-in	*bussurin*
car ferry	beel-fehr-yuhn	*bilferjan*

Directions

Where is ...?
    kvaer ehr ...?   *Hvar er ...?*
How do I get to ...?
    kvus-seh slehp-i eh teel ...?   *Hvussu sleppi eg til ...?*
Is it far from here?
    ehr tae lehnkt hee-yuhn-i?   *Er tað langt hiðani?*
Can I walk there?
    kuhn eh faer-uh til   *Kann eg fara til*
    gong-u hae-uhr?   *gongu hagar?*
Can you show me (on the map)?
    kun-nu tiy-um vooi-suh maer   *Kunnu tygum vísa mær*
    (wah korst-in-um)?   *(á kortinum)?*
Are there other means of
getting there?
    kvus-seh kuhn ain uhn-uhrs   *Hvussu kann ein*
    faer-uh hae-uhr?   *annars fara hagar?*
I want to go to ...
    ehg uht-li maer uht   *Eg ætli mær at*
    faer-uh teel ...   *fara til ...*
Go straight ahead.
    faer baint fruhm   *Far beint fram.*
It's two streets down.
    tae ehr tvaer gert-ur   *Tað er tvær gøtur*
    o-muhn-ehtt-ir   *omaneftir.*

Turn left/ right at the ...	faer teel vin-stru/ herg-ru ...	*Fær til vinstru/ høgru ...*
next corner	wah nuhst-uh hod-ni	*á næsta horni*
traffic lights	vee fehrs-leh-lyohs-in-i	*við ferðsluljósini*

behind	uht-tuhn-feer-i	*aftanfyri*
far	lehnkt	*langt*
in front of	fruhm-muhn-feer-i	*frammanfyri*
near	naer	*nær*
opposite	ee-vir-aev	*yvirav*

SIGNS

ATGONGD BANNAÐ/ EINGIN ATGONGD	ENTRANCE PROHIBITED
BUSSUR	BUS
EINVEGIS	ONE WAY
FARSTØÐIN	TERMINAL
FERÐASEÐLAR	TICKETS
FLOGVØLLUR	AIRPORT
FRÁFERÐ	DEPARTURE
HÝRUVOGNUR	TAXI
KOMA	ARRIVAL
NEYÐÚTGONGD	EMERGENCY EXIT
ROYKING BANNAÐ	NO SMOKING
TOLLUR	CUSTOMS
UPPLÝSINGAR	INFORMATION

FAROESE

Booking Tickets

Where can I buy a ticket?
kvaer fwah-yi ehg chuhypt   *Hvar fái eg keypt*
fehr-uh-seh-yil?   *ferðaseðil?*

I want to go to ...
eh veel feh-yin faer-uh teel ...   *Eg vil fegin fara til ...*

Do I need to book?
mwah eh booi-leh-djuh?   *Má eg bíleggja?*

I'd like to book a seat to ...
eh sgael bi-yuh um   *Eg skal biðja um*
aitt plos teel ...   *eitt pláss til ...*

Is it completely full?
ehr tae hailt ootsehlt?   *Er tað heilt útselt?*

Can I get a stand-by ticket?
kuhn eh fwah ain fehr-uh-seh-yil   *Kann eg fái ein ferðaseðil*
ooi sooist-u lert-u?/kuhn eh   *í síðstu løtu?/Kann eg*
slehp-uh wah booi-yeh-list-uh?   *sleppa á bíðilista?*

I'd like ...	kun-di ehg fin-dji ...	*Kundi eg fingið ...*
a one-way ticket	ain-veh-yis	*einvegis*
	fehr-uh-seh-yil	*ferðaseðil*
a return ticket	fehr-uh-seh-yil	*ferðaseðil*
	uht-tur o fruhm	*aftur og fram*
		(lit. ticket back
		and forth)
two tickets	tvair fehr-uh-	*tveir ferðaseðlar*
	sehl-uhr	
a student's fare	ain fehr-uh-seh-yil	*ein ferðaseðil*
	teel leh-suhn-di	*til lesandi*
a child's fare	ain buhd-nuh-	*ein barnaferðaseðil*
	fehr-uh-seh-yil	
a pensioner's fare	fehr-uh-seh-yil	*ein ferðaseðil*
	teel pehn-sion-ist	*til pensionist*
1st class	fis-ti kluhs-si	*fyrsti klassi*
2nd class	uhn-nuhr kluhs-si	*annar klassi*

FAROESE

Air

Is there a flight to ...?
    ehr naek-uh flo-faer teel ...?   *Er nakað flogfar til ...?*
How long does the flight take?
    kvus-seh long ehr   *Hvussu long er*
    flig-vi-tooi-yin?   *flúgvitíðin?*

airport tax	flo-vuhdl-uhr-skuht-tur	*flogvallarskattur*
boarding pass	bor-ding puhs	*boarding pass*

Bus

Where is the bus stop?
    kvaer ehr bus-steh-dji-plos-si?   *Hvar er bussteðgiplássið?*
Which bus goes to ...?
    kverr bus-sur fehr teel ...?   *Hvør bussur fer til ...?*
Could you let me know
when we get to ...?
    kun-nuh ti-yun si-yuh maer   *Kunna tygum siga mær*
    frwah twah ooi veet   *frá tá ið vit*
    ko-muh teel ...?   *koma til ...?*
I want to get off!
    eh veel slehp-puh aev!   *Eg vil sleppa av!*
Must I change buses?
    sgael eh shif-tuh bus?   *Skal eg skifta buss?*

What time is the ... bus?	naer fehr ... bus-sur-in?	*Nær fer ... bussurin?*
next	nuhs-ti	*næsti*
first	fis-ti	*fyrsti*
last	sain-uhs-ti	*seinasti*

FAROESE

DID YOU KNOW ...	There are no trains in the Faroe Islands.

Boat

Which harbour is next?
    kverr ehr nuhs-tuh huhvn?   *Hvør er næsta havn?*

Is this the ferry for ...?
    ehr heht-tuh fehr-yuhn teel ...?   *Er hetta ferjan til ...?*

cafeteria	kuhff-eh-teh-ri-uh	*kafeteria*
car deck	beel-dehk	*bildekk*
smoking saloon	roy-chi-suh-long	*roykisalon*
sun deck	sohl-dehk	*sóldekk*
ticket including a bunk	koy-dju-plos	*koyggjupláss*

Taxi

Can you take me to ...?
    kun-nuh ty-djun koy-ruh
    meh teel ...?   *Kunna tygum koyra meg til ...?*

How much does it cost to go to ...?
    kvus-seh nehgv kos-tuhr
    tae teel ...?   *Hvussu nógv kostar tað til ...?*

Here is fine, thank you.
    hehr ehr fooint tuhk   *Her er fint, takk.*

Continue!
    koyr long-ur!   *Koyr longur!*

The next street to the left/right.
    nuhs-tuh ger-tuh teel
    vin-stru/herg-ru   *Næsta gøta til vinstru/høgru.*

Stop here!
    stehg-guh hehr!   *Steðga her!*

Please slow down.
    djehr-i so vael uht min-kuh
    fehr-in-uh   *Gerið so væl at minka ferðina.*

Please wait here.
    djehr-i so vael uht
    booi-yuh hehr!   *Gerið so væl at bíða her!*

FAROESE

Some Useful Phrases

The ... is delayed/cancelled.
    ... ehr sain-kuh-vur/
    aev-loois-tur
    ... er seinkaður/
    avlýstur.

How long will it be delayed?
    kvus-seh nehgv ehr huhn
    sain-kuh-vur?
    Hvussu nógv er hann
    seinkaður?

There is a delay of ... hours.
    sain-chin-djin ehr ...
    tooi-muhr
    Seinkingin er ...
    tímar.

Can I reserve a place?
    kuhn eh booi-leh-djuh
    plos?
    Kann eg bíleggja
    pláss?

How long does the trip take?
    kvus-su lehng-uh tooi
    tehk-ur toor-ur-in?
    Hvussu langa tíð
    tekur túrurin?

Is it a direct route?
    ehr tae ain bain-lai-yis
    rut-uh?
    Er tað ein beinleiðis
    ruta?

Is that seat taken?
    ehr huht-tuh plos-si
    up-teech-i?
    Er hatta plássið
    upptikið?

I want to get off at ...
    eh sgael aev ooi ...
    Eg skal av í ...

Where can I hire a bicycle?
    kvaer fwah-yi eh lai-yuh
    ain-uh sük-klu?
    Hvar fái eg leigað
    eina súkklu?

FAROESE

Car

Where can I rent a car?
kvaer fwah-yi eh
lai-yuh ain beel?

*Hvar fái eg
leigað ein bil?*

How much is it daily/weekly?
kvus-seh nehgv kos-tuhr
huhn um dae-yin/vee-ku-nuh?

*Hvussu nógv kostar
hann um dagin/vikuna?*

Does that include insurance/
mileage?
ehr tri-djing/keel-o-meh-truh-
tael rok-nuh up-ooi?

*Er trygging/
kilometratal roknað uppí?*

Where's the next petrol station?
kvaer ehr nuhst-uh
behns-een-ster?

*Hvar er næsta
bensinstøð?*

How long can I park here?
kvus-su lain-dji ehr lov aet
puhr-kehr-uh hehr?

*Hvussu leingi er lov at
parkera her?*

Does this road lead to ...?
ehr heht-tuh veh-vur-in
teel ...?

*Er hetta vegurin
til ...?*

English	Pronunciation	Faroese
air (for tyres)	luft (teel dehk)	*luft (til dekk)*
battery	uhk-ku-mo-lah-tor-ur	*akkumolatorur*
brakes	brehm-sir	*bremsur*
clutch	kob-ling	*kobling*
driver's licence	koy-ri-korst	*koyrikort*
engine	mo-tor-ur	*motorur*
lights	lyohs	*ljós*
oil	ol-yuh	*olja*
puncture	punk-tehr-ing	*punktering*
radiator	ker-luhr-i	*kølari*
road map	veh-korst	*vegkort*
tyres	dehk	*dekk*
windscreen	fruhm-roo-tur	*framrútur*

FAROESE

I need a mechanic.
eh haev-i brook fir-i ain-un
meh-kahn-i-kuhr-uh

*Eg havi brúk fyri einum
mekanikara.*

The battery is flat.
buht-tuhr-ooi-yi er fluhtt

Battaríið er flatt.

The radiator is leaking.
kerl-uhr-in lehk-ur

Kølarin lekur.

I have a flat tyre.
ehg ehr-i punk-tehr-uh-vur

Eg eri punkteraður.

It's overheating. (engine)
huhn gong-ur hait-ur

Hann gongur heitur.

It's not working.
huhn rig-guhr i-chi

Hann riggar ikki.

ACCOMMODATION

Where is a ...?	kvaer ehr aitt ...?	*Hvar er eitt ...?*
cheap hotel	booil-itt ho-tehll	*bíligt hotell*
good hotel	gott ho-tehll	*gott hotell*
nearby hotel	ho-tehll ooi nond	*hotell í nánd*

What is the address?
kvus-seh ait-ur gert-uhn?

Hvussu eitur gøtan?

Could you write the address,
please?
kun-nu ti-yun djehr-uh so vael
aet sgree-vuh ger-tu-nuhv-ni?

*Kunnu tygum gera so væl
at skriva gøtunavnið?* (pol)

FAROESE

SIGNS

GISTINGARHÚS	GUESTHOUSE
HOTELL	HOTEL
VALLARAHEIM	YOUTH HOSTEL

FAROESE

At the Hotel

Do you have any rooms available?
ehr-u nerk-ur luhys kerm-ur? *Eru nøkur leys kømur?*

Sorry, we're full.
tooi-vehr-ri hehr ehr fult *Tíverri, her er fult.*

How many nights?
kvus-seh nehg-vuhr naet-ur? *Hvussu nógvar nætur?*

It's ... per day/per person.
tae kos-tuhr ... *Tað kostar ...*
um dae-yin fyr-i kvern *um dagin fyri hvønn.*

How much is it per night/per person?
kvus-seh nehgv kos-tuhr *Hvussu nógv kostar tað*
tae fir-i kvern ain-uh nott? *fyri hvønn eina nátt?*

I'd like ...	ehg veel feh-yin	*Eg vil fegin*
	haev-uh ...	*hava ...*
a single room	aitt	*eitt*
	ain-kult-kaem-uhr	*einkultkamar*
a double room	aitt	*eitt*
	du-bult-kaem-uhr	*dupultkamar*
to share a dorm	aitt	*eitt*
	feh-luhks-kaem-uhr	*felagskamar*
a bed	ain-uh song	*eina song*

I want a room	eh veel haev-uh aitt	*Eg vil hava eitt*
with a ...	kaem-uhr vee ...	*kamar við ...*
bathroom	bae	*bað*
shower	broos-u	*brúsu*
TV	shohn-vuhrs-pi	*sjónvarpi*
window	vin-dae	*vindeyga*

I'm going to	eh steh-dji ooi ...	*Eg steðgi í ...*
stay for ...		
one day	ain dae	*ein dag*
two days	tvair dehahr	*tveir dagar*
one week	ain-uh veek-u	*eina viku*

Requests & Complaints

Can I see it?
    kuhn eh slehp-puh aet
    sooi-djuh tae?
                    Kann eg sleppa at
                    síggja tað?

Are there any other/cheaper rooms?
    ehr-u nerk-ur on-nur/
    booi-li-yuhr-i kerm-ur?
                    Eru nøkur onnur/
                    bíligari kømur?

Is there a reduction for students/
children?
    ehr aev-slot-tur fir-i
    stu-dehnt-uhr/berdn?
                    Er avsláttur fyri
                    studentar/børn?

Does it include breakfast?
    ehr mor-gun-maet-ur
    up-pi ooi?
                    Er morgunmatur
                    uppi í?

It's fine, I'll take it.
    tae ehr fooint eh tae-chi tae
                    Tað er fínt, eg taki tað.

I'm not sure how long I'm staying.
    eh vait i-chi kvus-seh
    lain-dji eh steh-dji
                    Eg veit ikki hvussu
                    leingi eg steðgi.

Where is the bathroom?
    kvaer ehr bae-yi-room-i?
                    Hvar er baðirúmið?

Is there somewhere to wash clothes?
    behr teel aet vuhs-kuh klae-yi?
                    Ber til at vaska klæði?

Can I use the kitchen?
    kuhn eh broo-kuh ker-chin?
                    Kann eg brúka køkin?

Can I use the telephone?
    kuhn eh broo-kuh
    tehl-eh-fon-in-uh?
                    Kann eg brúka
                    telefonina?

Some Useful Words & Phrases

I'm/We're leaving now/tomorrow.
    eh faer-i/veet faer-uh noo/
    ooi mor-djin
                    Eg fari/Vit fara nú/
                    í morgin.

I'd like to pay the bill.
    kuhn eh fwah rok-nin-djin-uh?
                    Kann eg fáa rokningina?

FAROESE

name	nuhun	*navn*
surname	eht-tir-nuhun	*eftirnavn*
address	boo-stae-vur	*bústaður*
room number	kaem-uhr-num-muhr	*kamarnummar*
bathroom	bae-yi-room	*baðirúm*
bed	song	*song*
blanket	tehp-peh	*teppi*
chair	sdohl-ur	*stólur*
clean	raint	*reint*
dirty	shee-ti	*skitið*
double bed	dub-ilt-song	*dupultsong*
electricity	ruhu-muhgn	*ravmagn*
excluded	i-chi ooi-rok-nuh	*ikki írokna*
included	ooi-rok-nuh	*íroknað*
key	lee-chil	*lykil*
lift (elevator)	lif-tuh	*lyfta*
light bulb	lyohs-pehr-uh	*ljóspera*
a lock	lwahs	*lás*
mattress	muh-druhs-suh	*madrassa*
mirror	spehgl	*spegl*
padlock	hon-dji-lwahs	*heingilás*
pillow	kod-di	*koddi*
room (in hotel)	kaem-uhr	*kamar*
quiet	free-yuhr-litt	*friðarligt*
sheet	laek	*lak*
shower	broos-uh	*brúsa*
soap	swahb-uh	*sápa*
suitcase	kuf-fehrst	*kuffert*
swimming pool	svim-yeh-heel-ur	*svimjihylur*
table	bor	*borð*
toilet (paper)	veh-seh(-puhp-pooir)	*vesi(pappír)*
towel	huhn-klae	*handklæði*
(hot/cold) water	(haitt/kuhlt) vuhtn	*(heitt/kalt) vatn*
window	vin-dae	*vindeyga*

FAROESE

AROUND TOWN

I'm looking	eh lait-eh	*Eg leiti*
for the/a ...	eht-tir ...	*eftir ...*
art gallery	list-uh-suhun-in-un	*listasavninum*
bank	ain-un buhn-kuh	*einum banka*
church	ain-uhr-eh chir-cheh	*einari kirkju*
city centre	mib-booi-nun	*miðbýnum*
... embassy	... uhm-buhs-sah-dun-eh	*... ambassaduni*
hotel	ain-eh ho-tehll-i	*einum hotelli*
market street	huhn-dils-gert-ehn-eh	*handilsgøtuni*
museum	fon-min-ni-	*fornminnis-*
	su-hun-in-un	*savninum*
police	lerg-rehg-lun-eh	*løgregluni*
post office	post-hoos-in-un	*posthúsinum*
public toilet	uhl-mehn-nun vehs-eh	*almennum vesi*
telephone	teh-leh-fon-ster-yin-eh	*telefonstøðini*
centre		
tourist	fehr-uh-	*ferða-*
information	skreev-sto-vun-eh/	*skrivstovuni/*
office	tu-rist-kon-tohr-in-un	*turistkontórinum*

What time does it open/close?
naer klok-kuhn leht-ur   *Nær klokkan letur*
tae up/uht-tur?   *tað upp/aftur?*

What ... is this? kvus-seh ait-ur ...?   *hvussu eitur ...?*
  street   hehn-duh gert-uhn   *henda gøtan*
  suburb   hehs-in   *hesin*
                    booi-uhr-puhrs-tur-in *býarparturin*

For directions, see the Getting Around section, page 90.

At the Post Office

I'd like to send ...   eh sgael sehn-duh ...   *Eg skal senda ...*

a letter	aitt braev	*eitt bræv*
a postcard	aitt post-korst	*eitt postkort*
a parcel	ain puhk-kuh	*ein pakka*
a telegram	aitt teh-leh-gruhm	*eitt telegramm*

I'd like some stamps.
   kuhn eh fwah nerg-ur   *Kann eg fáa nøkur*
   frooi-mehr-cheh?   *frímerki?*

How much does it cost
to send this to ...?
   kvus-seh nehgv kos-tuhr tae   *Hvussu nógv kostar tað*
   aet sehn-duh heht-tuh teel ...?   *at senda hetta til ...?*

an aerogram	aitt luft-braev	*eitt luftbræv*
air mail	luft-post-ur	*luftpostur*
e-mail	tehl-deh-post-ur	*teldupostur*
envelope	braev-bdjolv-eh/	*brævbjálvi/*
	kon-vo-lut-tur	*konvoluttur*
mailbox	post-kuhs-seh	*postkassi*
registered mail	in-sgree-vuh braev	*innskrivað bræv*
surface mail	ships-post-ur	*skipspostur*
		(lit. ship post)

FAROESE

Telephone & Internet

I want to ring ...
    eh sgael rin-djuh teel ...   *Eg skal ringja til ...*
The number is ...
    num-muhr-eh ehr ...   *Nummarið er ...*
How much does a three-minute
call cost?
    kvus-seh nehgv kos-tuhr aet   *Hvussu nógv kostar at*
    tos-uh ooi trooi-djuhr min-ut-tir?   *tosa í tríggjar minuttir?*
How much does each extra minute cost?
    kvus-seh nehgv kos-tuhr   *Hvussu nógv kostar*
    kverr uhy-kuh min-ut-tur?   *hvør eyka minuttur?*
I'd like to speak to (Mr Pedersen).
    kuhn eh slehp-puh aet tos-uh   *Kann eg sleppa at tosa*
    vee (huhr-ruh peh-dehr-sehn)?   *við (harra Pedersen)?*

It's engaged.
    tae ehr bun-deh   *Tað er bundið.*
I want to make a reverse-charges
phone call.
    eh sgael rin-djuh   *Eg skal ringja*
    moh-tae-kuhr-in beh-tae-lir   *móttakarin betalir.*
I've been cut off.
    eh bluhyv aev-brot-in   *Eg bleiv avbrotin.*

Where can I get Internet access?
    kvaer fwah-yeh eh brookt   *Hvar fái eg brúkt*
    in-tehr-neh-ti?   *internetið?*
I'd like to send an email.
    eh veel feh-yin sehn-duh   *Eg vil fegin senda*
    ain ee-mayl   *ein e-mail.*

FAROESE

At the Bank

I want to exchange some money/
travellers cheques.

eh sgael vehk-sluh aitt sin-dur		*Eg skal veksla eitt sindur*
aev pehng-um/fehr-uh-chehk-kum		*av pengum/ferðakekkum.*

What is the exchange rate?

kvaet ehr kurs-ur-in? *Hvat er kursurin?*

How many kroner per dollar?

kvus-seh nehg-vuhr krohn-ur   *Hvussu nógvar krónur*
fir-i doll-uhr-uhn?   *fyri dollaran?*

bank draft	pehng-uh-wah-vooi-sing	*pengaávísing*
bank notes	pehng-uh-sehl-uhr	*pengaseðlar*
cashier	kuhs-suh-dahm-uhn	*kassadaman*
coins	min-tir	*myntir*
credit card	kreh-ditt-korst	*kredittkort*
exchange	vehk-sling	*veksling*
loose change	smwah-pehng-uhr	*smápengar*
signature	un-dir-skrift	*undirskrift*

INTERESTS & ENTERTAINMENT
Sightseeing

Do you have a guidebook/local map?

haev-uh tee-yun naek-ruh	*Hava tygum nakra*
fehr-uh-huhnd-bohk/	*ferðahandbók/*
naek-uh korst?	*nakað kort?* (pol)

What are the main attractions?

kvaet ehr vehrst aet sooi-djuh?   *Hvat er vert at síggja?*
  (lit. what is worth to see?)

What is that?

kvaet ehr huht-tuh?   *Hvat er hatta?*

How old is it?

kvus-seh gaem-uhlt ehr tae?   *Hvussu gamalt er tað?*

Can I take photographs?

kuhn eh taek-uh min-dir   *Kann eg taka myndir?*

What time does it open/close?

naer leht-ur tae up/uhtt-ur? *Nær letur tað upp/aftur?*

ancient	fod-nur	*fornur*
archaeological	fon-frer-yi-lee-yur	*fornfrøðiligur*
beach	suhn-dur/strond	*sandur/strond*
building	big-ning-ur	*bygningur*
castle	slott	*slott*
cathedral	dohm-chir-chuh	*dómkirkja*
church	chir-chuh	*kirkja*
concert hall	kon-sehrt-herdl	*konserthøll*
library	boh-kuhs-uhun	*bókasavn*
main square	mib-booi-yur	*miðbýur*
market	huhn-dils-chuhd-neh	*handilskjarni*
monastery	klos-tur	*klostur*
monument	min-nis-vaer-eh	*minnisvarði*
old city	gaem-uhl	*gamal*
	booi-uhr-puhrst-ur	*býarpartur*
opera house	op-ehr-uh-hoos	*opera hús*
palace	kongs-borg	*kongsborg*
ruins	hoos-uh-laiv-dir	*húsaleivdir*
stadium	ooi-trot-uhr-verdl-ur	*ítróttarvøllur*
statues	stuhnd-min-dir	*standmyndir*
temple	tehm-pil	*tempul*
university	froh-sgae-buhr-seh-dur	*fróðskaparsetur*

FAROESE

Going Out

What's there to do in the evenings?

kvaet kuhn muhn djehr-uh *Hvat kann mann gera*
um kverl-deh? *um kvøldið?*

Are there places where you can
hear local folk music?

behr teel uh hoy-ruh *Ber til at hoyra*
ferr-is-guhn tohn-laig? *føroyskan tónleik?*

Can one see Faroese dancing anywhere?

behr teel uh sooi-djuh ferr-is-guhn *Ber til at síggja føroyskan*
duhns nae-gruh-staen-i? *dans nakra staðni?*

How much does it cost to get in?
kvus-seh nehgv kos-tuhr
tae uh slehp-puh in?

*Hvussu nógv kostar
tað at sleppa inn?*

cinema	bi-o-gruhf-ur	*biografur*
concert	kon-sehrst	*konsert*
discotheque	dis-ko-tehk	*diskotek*
theatre	shohn-laig-uhr-hoos	*sjónleikarhús*

UNDER AGE?

aldursmark	uhl-durs-muhrsk	age limit

Sports & Interests

What do you do in your spare time?
kvaet djehr-stoo ooi
frooi-tooi-yin-eh?

*Hvat gert tú í
frítíðini?*

What sport do you play?
kvern ooi-trott ooik-kuhr too?

Hvønn ítrótt iðkar tüu?

art	list	*list*
basketball	kurv-uh-berlt	*kurvabólt*
boxing	bok-sing	*boksing*
cooking	muh-djehr	*matgerð*
fishing trout	uh fis-kuh sooil	*at fiska síl*
football/soccer	foht-berlt	*fótbólt*
going/out	uh faer-uh/ooi booi-yin	*at fara í býin*
to the cinema	ooi bi-o-gruhf	*í biograf*
music	tohn-laig	*tónleik*
photography	fo-to-gruh-fehr-ing	*fotografering*
reading	leh-sing	*lesing*
shopping	uh faer-uh teel huhn-dils	*at fara til handils*
sport	ooi-trott	*ítrótt*
the theatre	shohn-laig	*sjónleik*
travelling	uh fehr-uhst	*at ferðast*
writing	uh sgreev-uh	*at skriva*

FAROESE

Festivals

During the summer months, June and July, almost every weekend offers a village festival. The first one is Norðoyastehvna in Klaksvík, and the last one is Ólavsøka in Tórshavn. There are sports events, music and dancing, and many people wear their national costume. The traditional rowing competition features the ancient Faroese rowing boat – a descendant from the Viking ship. Participants are boys and girls from the competing villages.

Grækarismessa 12 March – celebrated as the arrival day of the national bird **tjaldur**. Boy- and girlscouts march in procession and speeches are delivered.

Flag Day 25 April – celebrated in memory of the sanctioning of the Faroese flag by the British during WWII.

Ólavsøka 29 July – celebration in the capital Tórshavn lasting at least two days. In ancient times the celebration was for the Holy King Olav of Norway who died in 1030 AD.

A relatively new custom is having a bonfire on the small beach in Tórshavn on the shortest night of the year, 21 June.

IN THE COUNTRY
Weather

What's the weather like?
    kvus-seh ehr vehg-reh?   *Hvussu er veðrið?*
It's ... today.
    vehg-reh ehr ... ooi dae   *Veðrið er ... í dag.*

Will it be ...	Vehr-ur tae ...	Verður tað ...
tomorrow?	ooi mor-djin?	í morgin?
cloudy	sgooi-djuh	skýggjað
cold	kuhlt	kalt
foggy	myerr-cheh	mjørki
frosty	frost	frost
hot	haitt	heitt
raining	rehgn	regn
snowing	kaev-eh	kavi
sunny	serl-shin	sólskin
windy	vin-dur	vindur

FAROESE

Camping

Am I allowed to camp here?
  ehr loyft uh chuhl-duh hehr?   *Er loyvt at tjalda her?*
Is there a campsite nearby?
  ehr naeg-uh chuhld-plos   *Er nakað tjaldpláss*
  ooi nond?   *í nánd?*

FAROESE

backpack	rigg-sehk-kur	*ryggsekkur*
can opener	dohs-uh-op-nuhr-eh	*dósaopnari*
compass	kum-puhs	*kumpass*
firewood	brehn-neh	*brenni*
gas cartridge	guhs-puh-trohn	*gass patrón*
mattress	muh-druhs-suh	*madrassa*
penknife	fehd-leh-knooi-vur	*felliknívur*
rope	buhnd	*band*
sleeping bag	so-veh-pos-eh	*soviposi*
stove	ohn-ur	*ovnur*
tent (pegs)	chuhld (hael-ir)	*tjald (hælir)*
torch/flashlight	ligt	*lykt*
water bottle	vuhn-flers-guh	*vatnfløska*

SIGNS
TJÁLDPLASS   CAMPING GROUND

FOOD

Traditional Faroese food includes fish, mutton, whalemeat and birds from the steep cliffs. Not many vegetables are cultivated in the Faroes, but potatoes and rhubarb are popular.

A Faroese specialty is skerpikjøt, mutton which has been wind dried, eaten mostly with bread. Another dish is ræst kjøt, the same meat only half dried and then cooked or roasted. The same drying methods are used with fish and whalemeat.

Some Useful Words & Phrases

breakfast	mor-gun-drehk-kuh	*morgundrekka*
lunch	mor-gun-maet-ur	*morgunmatur*
dinner	derv-reh	*døgurði*

Table for ..., please.   bor teel ... tuhk   *Borð til ... takk.*

Can I see the menu please?
  kuhn eh fwah maet-seh-yil-in?   *Kann eg fáa matseðilin?*
What does it include?
  kvaet hoy-rir teel?   *Hvat hoyrir til?*

ashtray	ers-keh-beek-uhr	*øskubikar*
the bill	rok-nin-djin	*rokningin*
a cup	ain kop-pur	*ein koppur*
dessert	deh-sehrst/	*dessert/*
	o-muhn-wah	*omaná*
a drink	ok-kurst uh drehk-kuh	*okkurt at drekka*
a fork	ain guhf-fil	*ein gaffil*
fresh	nooi-djur/fehs-kur	*nýggjur/feskur*
a glass	aitt glaes	*eitt glas*
a knife	ain knooi-vur	*ein knívur*
a plate	ain bor-isk-ur	*ein borðiskur*
spicy	krid-duh	*kryddað*
a spoon	ain sgai	*ein skeið*
stale	sbil-tur	*spiltur*
sweet	sert-ur	*søtur*
a teaspoon	ain teh-sgai	*ein teskeið*
toothpicks	tuhn-nuhs-tuhy-tuhr-uhr	*tannasteytarar*

FAROESE

Vegetarian Meals

I'm a vegetarian.
eh eht-i baer-uh grern-meht-eh;   *Eg eti bara grønmeti;*
eh ehr-eh veh-geh-tuhr-ur   *Eg eri vegetarur.*
I don't eat meat.
eh eht-i i-chi chert   *Eg eti ikki kjøt.*
I don't eat chicken, or fish, or pork.
eh eht-i ich-i hers-nuhr-ung-uh   *Eg eti ikki høsnarunga*
edl-uh fisk edl-uh grwees-uh-chert *ella fisk ella grísakjøt.*

Staple Foods & Condiments

bread	bruhy	*breyð*
butter	smerr	*smør*
garlic	kvooit-luhy-gur	*hvítleykur*
meat	chert	*kjøt*
mustard	sin-nop-pur	*sinoppur*
oil	ol-yuh	*olja*
pepper	pee-puhr	*pipar*
pickled cucumbers	sült-uh-yuhr	*súltaðar*
	uh-gursk-ir	*agurkir*
rice	roois	*rís*
salt	suhlt	*salt*
string beans	bern-ir	*bønir*
sugar	suk-ur	*sukur*
vinegar	eh-dik-kur	*edikur*

FAROESE

Vegetables

beets	ruhy-rert-ur	*reyðrøtur*
(usually served pickled)		
cabbage	kwahl	*kál*
carrots	gu-luh-rert-ur	*gularøtur*
cauliflower	blom-kwahl	*blomkál*
celery	sehl-luh-rooi	*sellarí*
cucumber	uh-gursk	*agurk*
mashed potatoes	eh-pluh-morl	*eplamorl*
mushrooms	hun-duh-luhnd	*hundaland*
onions	luhy-kur	*leykur*
peas	ehrs-truhr	*ertrar*
pickled cucumbers	sült-uh-yuhr	*súltaðar*
	uh-gursk-ir	*agurkir*
potato	eh-pli	*epli*
(boiled/baked)	(kohg-uh/baeg-uh)	*(kókað/bakað)*
rice	roois	*rís*
string beans	bern-ir	*bønir*

Fruit

apple	süur-eh-pleh	*súrepli*
banana	buh-nahn	*banan*
grapes	vooin-drüu-vir	*víndrúvur*
lemon	si-trohn	*sitrón*
orange	uh-pil-seen	*appilsin*
pear	peh-ruh	*pera*
strawberry	jar-ber	*jarðber*

FAROESE

FAROESE

MENU DECODER

Breakfast Menu

toast	rist-uh bruhy	ristað breyð
bacon	buhy-kon	bacon
cheese	ost-ur	ostur
eggs	ehgg	egg
jam	sül-teh-toy	súltutoy
milk	myerlk	mjólk
rye bread	rub-bruhy	rugbreyð
white bread	fruhns-bruhy	fransbreyð

Main Meals

chicken	hers-nuhr-un-djeh	høsnarungi
lamb chops	luhms-chert	lambskjøt
roast beef	nuhy-tuh-staik	neytasteik
roast lamb	luhms-staik	lambssteik
roast pork	groois-uh-staik	grísasteik
sausage	pil-suh	pylsa
steak	büf-fur	búffur
whale meat with blubber	grind o speek	grind og spik
wind-dried meat (boiled or roasted)	ruhst chert	ræst kjøt
wind-dried meat	turt chert/ shehr-peh-chert	turt kjøt/ skerpikjøt
wind-dried fish (boiled)	ruhst-ur fis-kur	ræstur fiskur
wind-dried fish	tur-rur fis-kur	turrur fiskur

Seafood

fish	fis-kur	fiskur
haddock	hoois-uh	hýsa
halibut	kuhlv-i	kalvi
herring	sild	sild
plaice	rehs-prerk-uh	reyðsprøka
salmon	luhk-sur	laksur
shrimp	raech-ur	rækjur
sole	tung-uh	tunga
trout	sooil	síl

Soups

fesk súpan   fehsk soop-uhn
  broth from boiled meat with vegetables
røst súpan   rerst soop-uhn
  broth from boiled *ræst kjøt* with vegetables and rice
breyðsúpan   bruhy-soop-uhn
  soup made from bread, sugar and non-alcoholic beer

fiskasúpan   fis-kuh-soop-uhn   fish soup
asparssúpan   uhs-puhrs-soop-uhn   asparagus soup
blábersúpan   blwah-behr-soop-uhn   blueberry soup

Desserts

ice cream	oois-ur	*ísur*
cake	kaek-uh	*kaka*
rhubarb cake	ruh-buhr-beh-kaek-uh	*rabarbukaka*
rhubarb jelly	ruh-buhr-beh-gruhyt-ur	*rabarbugreytur*
pancakes	puhn-neh-kaek-ur	*pannukakur*

Drinks

coffee(with cream)	kuhf-fi (vee roh-muh)	*kaffi (við róma)*
orange juice	uhp-pil-seen-djoos	*appelsindjús*
skim/	skoo-muh/	*skúmað/*
full cream milk	vuhn-li myerlk	*vanlig mjólk*
soft drink,	suhft, so-duh-vuhtn	*saft,sodavatn*
carbonated water		
tea	teh	*te*
(ice) water	(oois-)vuhtn	*(ís)vatn*

snapsur   snuhp-sur
  small glass 2-4 cl of (particularly) akvavit
flúgvari   flig-vuhr-i
  mixture of coke and akvavit (lit. flyer)
svartideyð   svuhr-steh-duhy-yeh
  Icelandic brand of alcohol (lit. the black death)
durasnapsur   dur-uh-snuhp-sur
  snaps offered at the door as you enter (lit. door *snaps*)
bjóða ein lítlan   byoh-uh ain looitl-uhn
  also *snaps* (lit. offer a 'small one')

FAROESE

SHOPPING

How much is it?

kvus-seh nehgv kos-tuhr tae?   *Hvussu nógv kostar tað?*

bookshop	bohk-huhnd-il	*bókhandil*
camera shop	foto huhnd-il	*foto handil*
clothing store	kluhd-nuh-huhnd-il	*klædnahandil*
general store/shop	huhnd-il	*handil*
laundry	vuhs-kuhr-ooi	*vaskarí*
market	muhrk-nuh-vur	*marknaður*
newsagency	ki-osk	*kiosk*
pharmacy	uh-po-tehk	*apotek*
shoeshop	skoh-huhnd-il	*skóhandil*
souvenir shop	su-vehn-eer huhnd-il	*souvenir handil*
stationers	puhp-pooirs-huhnd-il	*pappírshandil*
supermarket	sholvt-erk-eh-huhnd-il	*sjálvtøkuhandil*
vegetable shop	grern-meht-is-huhnd-il	*grønmetishandil*

I'd like to buy ...

eh sgael chuhy-puh ...   *Eg skal keypa ...*

Do you have others?

haev-uh teet aer-uhr?   *Hava tit aðrar?* (inf)

I don't like it.

maer dwahm-uhr haen-uh/   *Mær dámar hana/*
huhn/tae i-chi   *hann/tað ikki.* (f/m/n)

Can I look at it?

kuhn eh sooi-djuh haen-uh/   *Kann eg síggja hana/*
huhn/tae?   *hann/tað?* (f/m/n)

I'm just looking.

eh baer-uh hi-djeh   *Eg bara hyggi.*

Can you write down the price?

kuhns-too sgreev-uh   *Kannst tú skriva*
proois-in nee-yur?   *prísin niður?*

Do you accept credit cards?

    taek-uh teet kreh-ditt-korst?   *Taka tit kredittkort?*

Can I help you?

    fwah-yeh eh yolt tee-yuhn?   *Fái eg hjálpt tygum?* (pol)

Will that be all?

    naeg-uh uhn-nuh?   *Nakað annað?*

Essential Groceries

bread	bruhy	*breyð*
butter	smerr	*smør*
milk	myerlk	*mjólk*
rice	roois	*rís*
salt	suhlt	*salt*
shampoo	shuhm-po	*shampo*
sugar	suk-ur	*sukur*
toilet paper	veh-seh-puhp-pooir	*vesipappír*
toothbrush	tuhn-bust	*tannbust*
vegetables	grern-meht-i	*grønmeti*

Souvenirs

earrings	oyr-nuhr-ing-uhr	*oyrnaringar*
handicraft	hond-uhr-bai-yeh	*handarbeiði*
necklace	hols-buhnd	*hálsband*
pottery	stain-toy	*steintoy*
ring	ring-ur	*ringur*
rug	tehp-pi	*teppi*

Clothing

coat	fruh-chi	*frakki*
dress	chohl-eh	*kjóli*
jacket	yuh-cheh	*jakki*
jumper (sweater)	troy-djuh	*troyggja*
shirt	shür-tuh	*skjúrta*
shoes	skehg-vuhr	*skógvar*
skirt	shürt	*skjúrt*
trousers	buk-sir	*buksur*

FAROESE

It doesn't fit.

    tae puhs-suhr i-chi   *Tað passar ikki.*

It's too ...	tae ehr o ...	*Tað er ov ...*
big	sterrst	*stórt*
small	looit-i	*lítið*
short	stutt	*stutt*
long	lehnkt	*langt*
tight	tronkt	*trongt*
loose	vooit	*vítt*

Materials

cotton	bum-udl	*bumull*
handmade	hond-djerrt	*hondgjørt*
leather	leh-vur	*leður*
brass	mehs-sing	*messing*
gold	gudl	*gull*
silver	sil-vur	*silvur*
silk	sil-chi	*silki*
wool	udl	*ull*
of wool	ud-lint	*ullint*

Colours

black	svuhrt	*svart*
blue	blott	*blátt*
brown	brünt	*brúnt*
green	grernt	*grønt*
orange	uhp-pil-seen-gult	*appelsingult*
pink	lyohs-uh-rehtt	*ljósareytt*
purple	lil-luh	*lilla*
red	rehtt	*reytt*
white	kvooitt	*hvítt*
yellow	gult	*gult*

Toiletries

comb	kuhm-bur	*kambur*
condoms	hooit-ir	*hítir*
deodorant	deh-o-do-ruhnt	*deodorant*
hairbrush	ho-uhr-bust	*hárbust*
moisturising cream	vae-teh-krehm	*vætukrem*
razor	rae-cheh-muh-sheen-uh	*rakimaskina*
sanitary napkins	(duh-meh)bind	*(damu)bind*
shampoo	shuhm-po	*shampo*
shaving cream	rae-cheh-swah-puh	*rakisápa*
soap	swah-puh	*sápa*
sunblock cream	sohl-krehm	*sólkrem*
tampons	tuhm-pon-djir	*tampongir*
tissues	sehr-vi-eht-tuhr	*serviettar*
toilet paper	veh-seh-puhp-pooir	*vesipappír*
toothpaste	tuhn-krehm	*tannkrem*

Stationery & Publications

map	korst	*kort*
newspaper	(ain-gilst)	*(eingilskt)*
(in English)	duhg-blae	*dagblað*
novels in English	ain-gils-guhr	*eingilskar*
	skuhld-ser-vur	*skaldsøgur*
paper	puhp-pooir	*pappír*
pen (ballpoint)	koo-lu-pehn-nur	*kúlupennur*
scissors	suhk-sur	*saksur*

FAROESE

FAROESE

Photography

How much is it to process this film?
kvus-seh nehgv kos-tuhr duh uh   *Hvussu nógv kostar tað at*
fruhm-kuhd-luh hehn-duh film-in?   *framkalla henda filmin?*

When will it be ready?
naer vehr-ur huhn li-yu-vur?   *Nær verður hann liðugur?*

I'd like a film for this camera.
eh sgael haev-uh ain film   *Eg skal hava ein film*
teel heht-tuh fo-to-toh-leh   *til hetta fototólið.*

B&W (film)	svuhrt kvooit-ur film-ur	*svart hvítur filmur*
camera	fo-to-tohl	*fototól*
colour (film)	leet-film-ur	*litfilmur*
film	fil-mur	*filmur*
flash	blits	*blits*
lens	lin-suh	*linsa*
light meter	lyohs-mwah-tuhr-eh	*ljósmátari*

Smoking

A packet of cigarettes, please.
ain si-guh-rehtt-puhk-kuh tuhk   *Ein sigarettpakka, takk.*

Are these cigarettes strong/mild?
ehr-u hehs-uhr si-guh-rehtt-ir-nuhr *Eru hesar sigarettirnar*
stehr-kuhr/mil-duhr?   *sterkar/mildar?*

Do you have a light?
heh-vur too ehld?   *Hevur tú eld?*

cigarette papers	si-guh-rehtt-puhp-pooir	*sigarettpappír*
cigarettes	si-guh-reht-tir	*sigarettir*
filtered	vee fil-tri	*við filtri*
lighter	tehn-druh-ri	*tendrari*
matches	svvah-vul-pin-nuhr	*svávulpinnar*
menthol	mehn-tol	*mentol*
pipe	pooi-puh	*pípa*
tobacco (pipe)	tub-buhk	*tubbakk*

Sizes & Comparisons

big	sterrt	*stórt*
small	looiti	*lítið*
heavy	tunkt	*tungt*
light	luhtt	*lætt*
more	mai-ri/flai-ri	*meiri/fleiri*
less	min-ni	*minni*
too much/many	o mic-hi/o nehgv	*ov mikið/ov nógv*
many	nehgv	*nógv*
enough	noh mi-chi/noh nehgv	*nóg mikið/nónógv*
also	ai-sin-i	*eisini*
a little bit	aitt sin-dur	*eitt sindur*

HEALTH

Where is ...?	kvaer ehr ...?	*Hvar er ...?*
the chemist	uh-po-teh-cheh	*apotekið*
a doctor	ain luhk-neh	*ein lækni*
a dentist	ain tuhn-luhk-neh	*ein tannlækni*
the hospital	shook-ruh-hoos-eh	*sjúkrahúsið*

I'm sick.
 eh ehr-i shook/-ur   *Eg eri sjúk/-ur.* (f/m)
My friend is sick.
 veen-ur mooin ehr shook-ur   *Vinur mín er sjúkur.*
Could I see a female doctor?
 kuhn eh slehp-puh uh tos-uh   *Kann eg sleppa at tosa*
 vee ain kvin-neh-li-yuhn   *við ein kvinnuligan*
 luhk-nuh?   *lækna?*
What's the matter?
 kvaet bae-yir?   *Hvat bagir?*
Where does it hurt?
 kvaer heh-vur too ilt?   *Hvar hevur tú ilt?*
It hurts here.
 eh haev-i ilt hehr   *Eg havi ilt her.*

FAROESE

FAROESE

Ailments

I have (a/an) ...	eh haev-i ...	Eg havi ...
allergy	o-vee-kvae-meh	*ovviðkvæmi*
anaemia	bloh-muhng-ul	*blóðmangul*
blister	bler-ru	*bløðru*
burn	bruhnd-swahr	*brandsár*
cold	krooim	*krím*
constipation	haer-uhn book	*harðan búk*
cough	hos-tuh	*hosta*
diarrhoea	lehst looiv	*leyst lív*
fever	fehb-ur	*fepur*
headache	her-vu-pooin-eh	*høvuðpínu*
hepatitis	liv-ruh-brun-uh	*livrabruna*
indigestion	ilt ooi boo-chin-un	*ilt í búkinum*
infection	brun-uh	*bruna*
influenza	in-flu-ehn-suh	*influensa*
lice	loois	*lýs*
low/high	logt/herkt	*lágt/høgt*
blood pressure	bloh-trooist	*blóðtrýst*
sore throat	ilt ooi hol-sin-un	*ilt í hálsinum*
a sprained foot	kok-tuhn foht	*keiktan fót*
stomachache	boo-kil-sku	*búkilsku*
temperature	fehb-ur	*fepur*
venereal disease	cheen-shoo-ku	*kynssjúku*
worms	orm	*orm*

Parts of the Body

ankle	er-kul	*økul*
arm	uhrm-ur	*armur*
back	baek	*bak*
chest	bring-uh/brerst	*bringa/bróst*
ear	oy-ruh	*oyra*
eye	uhy-yuh	*eyga*
finger	fing-ur	*fingur*
foot	foht-ur	*fótur*
hand	hond	*hond*
head	herdd	*høvd*

heart	yuhrt-uh	*hjarta*
leg	bain	*bein*
mouth	mun-nur	*munnur*
ribs	riv-yuh-bain	*rivjabein*
skin	hoo	*húð*
stomach	book-ur	*búkur*
teeth	tehn	*tenn*
throat	hols-ur	*hálsur*

Some Useful Words & Phrases

I'm ...	eh ehr-i ...	*Eg eri ...*
diabetic	su-kur-shook/-ur	*sukursjúk/-ur* (f/m)
epileptic	eh-pi-lehp-ti-kuhr-eh	*epileptikari*
asthmatic	uhs-muh-shook/-ur	*astmasjúk/-ur* (f/m)

I'm allergic to antibiotics/penicillin.
eh tol-i i-cheh uhn-ti-bi-o-tik-uh/   *Eg toli ikki antibiotika/*
pehn-i-sill-een   *penisillin.*

I'm pregnant.
eh ehr-i up wah veh-yin   *Eg eri upp á vegin.*

I haven't had my period for ... months.
eh haevi- i-cheh huhft   *Eg havi ikki havt*
mwah-nuh-shook-un-uh ooi ...   *mánasjúkuna í ...*
mwahn-uhr   *mánaðar.*

I have been vaccinated.
eh ehr-i vuhk-si-nehr-uh/-vur   *Eg eri vaksineraði/-ur.* (f/m)

accident	oh-luk-kuh	*ólukka*
addiction	trongd	*trongd*
aspirin	pooin-eh-tuhb-leht-tir	*pínutablettir*
a bandage	for-bind-ing	*forbinding*
blood test	bloh-roynd	*blóðroynd*
contraceptive	fi-ri-bir-djing	*fyribyrging*
medicine	hai-li-vwah-vur	*heilivágur*
nausea	vuhml	*vaml*
oxygen	soo-rehv-ni	*súrevni*
vitamins	vi-tuh-meen-ir	*vitaminir*

FAROESE

At the Chemist

I need medication for ...
    kuhn eh fwah hail-i-vwah   *Kann eg fáa heilivág*
    fi-ri ...?   *fyri ...?*
I have a prescription.
    eh haev-i reh-sehpt   *Eg havi resept.*

At the Dentist

I have a toothache.
    eh haev-i tuhn-nuh-pooin-eh   *Eg havi tannapínu.*
I've lost a filling.
    eh haev-i mist ain-uh plom-beh   *Eg havi mist eina plombu.*
I've broken a tooth.
    eh haev-i brot-i ain-uh ton   *Eg havi brotið eina tonn.*
My gums hurt.
    tae pooin-ir ooi   *Tað pínir í*
    tuhn-huhl-din-un   *tannhaldinum.*
Please give me an anaesthetic.
    kuhn eh fwah doy-ving?   *Kann eg fáa doyving?*

TIME & DATES

What date is it today?
    kverr dae-vur ehr ooi dae?   *Hvør dagur er í dag?*
What time is it?
    kvaet ehr klok-kuhn?   *Hvat er klokkan?*
It's ... am/pm.
    hon ehr ...   *Hon er ...*

in the morning	um mor-gun-in	*um morgunin*
in the afternoon	said-nuh-puhrst-in	*seinnapartin*
in the evening	um kverl-deh	*um kvøldið*

FAROESE

Days of the Week

Monday	mwah-nuh-dae-vur	*Mánadagur*
Tuesday	toois-dae-vur	*Týsdagur*
Wednesday	mee-ku-dae-vur	*Mikudagur*
Thursday	hers-dae-vur	*Hósdagur*
Friday	frooi-djuh-dae-vur	*Fríggjadagur*
Saturday	luhy-yuhr-dae-vur	*Leygardagur*
Sunday	sun-nu-dae-vur	*Sunnudagur*

Months

January	djuhn-vwahr	*Januar*
February	feh-bruv-uhr	*Februar*
March	muhrs	*Mars*
April	uhp-rooil	*Apríl*
May	mai	*Mai*
June	dju-ni	*Juni*
July	dju-li	*Juli*
August	uhu-gust	*August*
September	sehp-tehm-bir	*September*
October	ok-to-bir	*Oktober*
November	no-vehm-bir	*November*
December	dehs-ehm-bir	*Desember*

Seasons

summer	sumuhr	*summar*
autumn	hehst	*heyst*
winter	veh-tur	*vetur*
spring	vwahr	*vár*

Present

today	ooi dae	*í dag*
this morning	ooi mor-gun	*í morgun*
tonight	ooi kverld/ooi nott	*í kvøld/í nátt*
this week/	heh-suh vee-ku-nuh/	*hesa vikuna/*
this year	ooi wahr	*í ár*
now	noo	*nú*

Past

yesterday	ooi djwahr	*í gjár*
day before yesterday	ooi fir-ruh-dae-yin	*í fyrradagin*
yesterday morning	ooi djwahr-uh-mor-gun-in	*í gjáramorgunin*
last night	djwahr-kverl-di	*í gjárkvøldið*
last week/last year	ooi soois-tu vee-ku/soois-tuh wahr	*í síðstu viku/síðsta ár*

Future

tomorrow	ooi mor-djin	*í morgin*
day after tomorrow	o-vur-mor-djin	*ovurmorgin*
tomorrow morning	ooi mor-djin-wahr-i	*í morginári*
tomorrow afternoon	said-nuh-puhrs-tin	*seinnapartin*
	ooi mor-djin	*í morgin*
tomorrow evening	ooi uhn-nuh-kverld	*í annaðkvøld*
next week	nuhs-tu vee-ku	*næstu viku*
next year	nuhs-uh wahr	*næsta ár*

During the Day

afternoon	said-nuh-puhrs-tur	*seinnapartur*
dawn	ooi loois-in-djin-i	*í lýsingini*
day	dae-vur	*dagur*
early	tooil-yuh	*tíðliga*
midnight	mid-nott	*midnátt*
morning	mor-gun	*morgun*
night	nottt	*nátt*
noon	wah mid-deh-yi	*á miðdegi*

NUMBERS & AMOUNTS

0	null	*null*
1	aitt	*eitt*
2	tvuhy	*tvey*
3	trooi	*trý*
4	fooir-uh	*fíra*
5	fim	*fimm*
6	sehks	*seks*
7	shuhy	*sjey*
8	ot-tuh	*átta*
9	nooi-djeh	*níggju*
10	tooi-djeh	*tíggju*
11	ehd-lehv-eh	*ellivu*
12	terlv	*tólv*
13	treht-tuhn	*trettan*
14	fdjürs-tuhn	*fjúrtan*
15	fim-tuhn	*fimtan*
16	sehks-tuhn	*sekstan*
17	suhy-chuhn	*seytjan*
18	wah-chuhn	*átjan*
19	nooi-chuhn	*nítjan*
20	choo-vu	*tjúgu*
21	ain-o-choo-vu	*einogtjúgu*
30	treh-di-veh	*tretivu*
40	fyerr-it-eh	*fjøruti*
50	fim-ti	*fimti*
60	sehks-ti	*seksti*
70	shoo-ti	*sjúti*
80	waht-tuh-ti	*áttati*
90	nooi-ti	*níti*
100	hun-druh	*hundrað*
1000	too-sin	*túsund*
one million	ain mil-liohn	*ein millión*

FAROESE

1st	fis-teh	*fyrsti*
2nd	uhn-nuhr	*annar*
3rd	tree-yi	*triðji*
1/4	ain fyoh-ring-ur	*ein fjórðingur*
1/3	ain tree-ying-ur	*ein triðjingur*
1/2	aitt holt	*eitt hálvt*
3/4	trooi-djir fyoh-ring-uhr	*tríggir fjórðingar*

Some Useful Words

a little (amount)	aitt sin-dur	*eitt sindur*
double	du-bult	*dupult*
enough	noh mi-chi/noh nehgv	*nóg mikið/nógv*
few	fwahr/fwah-yir/fwah	*fáar/fáir/fá* (f/m/n)
less	min-ni	*minni*
many	nehg-vuhr/nehg-vir/nehgv	*nógvar/nógvir/nógv* (f/m/n)
more	mai-ri/flai-ri	*meiri/fleiri*
once	ain-uh-fehr	*einaferð*
a pair	aitt paer/tvuhy	*eitt par/tvey*
percent	pro-sehnt	*procent*
some	naek-ruhr/naek-rir/nerk-ur	*nakrar/nakrir/nøku* (f/m/n)
too much	o nehgv	*ov nógv*
twice	tvaer fehr-ir	*tvær ferðir*

ABBREVIATIONS

SLS	*trandfaraskip Landsins*	Faroese national ferry company
ES	*Evropasamveldið*	European Community
ST	*Sameindu tjóðir*	United Nations
AA	*Atlantic Airways*	Faroese national airlines
km		kilometres
FO		Faroe Islands (letters used on cars/com puter adresses, etc.)

EMERGENCIES

I'm lost.	eh ehr-i vilst/-ur	*Eg eri vilst/-ur.* (f/m)
I've been raped.	eh ehr-i nuhy-ti-chin	*Eg eri neyðtikin.*
Go away!	faer burs-tur!	*Far burtur!*
Help!	djolp!	*Hjálp!*
Thief!	choh-vur!	*Tjóvur!*

SIGNS

LØGREGLA	POLICE

It's an emergency!
  heht-tuh ehr ain nuhy-ster-vuh!   *Hetta er ein neyðstøða!*
There's been an accident!
  ain oh-luk-kuh ehr hehnd!   *Ein ólukka er hend!*
Call a doctor/an ambulance!
  rin-ji eht-tir luhk-uht/   *Ringið eftir lækna/*
  shook-ruh-bee-li!   *sjúkrabili!*
Call the police!
  rin-dji eht-tir lerg-rehg-lu-neh!   *Ringið eftir løgregluni!*
Where is the police station?
  kvaer ehr lerg-rehg-lus-ter-yin?   *Hvar er løgreglustøðin?*
I'll call the police!
  eh rin-dji eht-tir lerg-rehg-lu-neh!   *Eg ringi eftir løgregluni!*
I'm/My friend is ill.
  eh ehr-i/veen-ur mooin   *Eg eri/vinur mín*
  ehr shook-ur   *er sjúkur.*
Where are the toilets?
  kvaer ehr-u veh-seh-ni?   *Hvar eru vesini?*
Could you (pol) help me please?
  kun-nu ti-yun djeh-ruh so   *Kunnu tygum gera so*
  vael uh djol-puh maer?   *væl at hjálpa mær?*
Could I please use the telephone?
  kuhn eh lae-nuh   *Kann eg læna*
  teh-leh-fon-in-uh?   *telefonina?*
I didn't do it.
  eh hae-vi i-chi djerrt duh   *Eg havi ikki gjørt tað.*

FAROESE

FAROESE

I'm sorry. I apologise.
um-shil-duh. eh bi-yeh um
fi-ri-djehv-ing

*Umskylda. Eg biði um
fyrigeving.*

I didn't realise I was doing anything wrong.
eh vis-ti i-chi aet eh djerr-di
nae-guh sgaift

*Eg visti ikki, at eg gjørdi
nakað skeivt.*

I wish to contact my embassy/
consulate.
eh veel to-suh vee mooi-nuh
uhm-buhs-suh-du/mooitt
kon-su-lwaht

*Eg vil tosa við mína
ambassadu/mítt
konsulát.*

I speak English.
eh to-si ain-djilst

Eg tosi eingilskt.

I have medical insurance.
eh hae-vi shook-ruh-tri-djing

Eg havi sjúkratrygging.

My possessions are insured.
Mooi-nuhr og-nir ehr-u
tri-djuh-yuhr

*Mínar ognir eru
tryggjaðar.*

My ...	mooin/mooitt ...	*Mín/Mítt ...*
was stolen.	ehr sto-lin/sto-li	*er stolin/stolið.*
I've lost my ...	eh hae-vi mist ...	*Eg havi mist ...*
bags	mooi-nuhr tuhs-kur	*mínar taskur*
handbag	mooi-nuh hond-tuhs-ku	*mína hondtasku*
money	mooi-nuhr pehng-uhr	*mínar pengar*
passport	mooitt puhs	*mítt pass*
travellers	mooi-nuhr	*mínar*
cheques	feh-ruh-chehk-kuhr	*ferðakekkar*

FINNISH

QUICK REFERENCE

Hello.	*hay*/ *tehrr*-veh	Hei/Terve.
Goodbye.	*na*-keh-meen	Näkemiin.
Yes.	*kül*-lah/yoo	Kyllä/Joo.
No.	ay	Ei.
Excuse me.	*uhn*-teehk-si	Anteeksi.
Sorry.	*o*-lehn	Olen
	puh-hoyl-luh-ni;	pahoillani;
	so-rri	Sori.
Thank you.	*kee*-toss	Kiitos.
You're welcome.	*o*-leh *hü*-va	Ole hyvä.
I understand.	*üm*-marr-rran	Ymmärrän.
I don't understand.	ehn *üm*-marr-rra	En ymmärrä.
Where is ...?	*mis*-sa on ...?	Missä on ...?
Go straight ahead.	*kul*-yeh *su*-o-rrahn	Kulje suoraan.

Turn left/right.
kaan-nü *vuh*-sehm-pahn/   Käänny vasempaan/
oy-keh-ahn.   oikeaan.

Do you speak English?
pu-hut-ko   Puhutko
ehng-luhn-ti-uh?   englantia?

Do you have any rooms available?
on-ko *tayl*-la *vuh*-pah-tuh   Onko teillä vapaata
hu-*o*-neht-tuh?   huonetta?

Where is a public toilet?
mis-sa on *ü*-lays-ta *vehs*-sah/   Missä on yleistä vessaa/
ü-lay-nehn *vehs*-suh?   yleinen vessa?

I'd like ...   *sahn*-ko ...   Saanko ...
  a one-way ticket   meh-no-*li*-pun   menolipun
  a return ticket   meh-no-*pa*-   meno-pa-
  loo-*li*-pun   luulipun

1	*ük*-si	yksi	6	*koo*-si	kuusi
2	*kuhk*-si	kaksi	7	*sayt*-seh-man	seitsemän
3	*kol*-meh	kolme	8	*kuhkh*-dehk-suhn	kahdeksan
4	*nehl*-ya	neljä	9	*ükh*-dehk-san	yhdeksän
5	*vee*-si	viisi	10	*küm*-meh-nehn	kymmenen

FINNISH

FINNISH

Finnish, or suomi as it's called in Finland, is almost unique. It's not closely related to any language other than Estonian and Karelian and a handful of other rare languages. Linguistically, Finnish belongs to the Finnic (or more widely, Finno-Ugric) group of languages. Hungarian is the most widely spoken of the Finno-Ugric languages, but similarities with Finnish are extremely few.

Finnish is spoken by some five million people. It isn't related to any Indo-European languages. There are, however, many loan words from Baltic, Slavonic and Germanic languages, and many words deriving from French and, especially, English.

The main difficulties with Finnish are the suffixes (endings) added to noun and verb roots, which often alter in this process, and the habit of constructing long words by putting several small words together.

Outside the large towns, few people speak fluent English, so it's advisable to learn some phrases in Finnish to make your visit more rewarding. Finns appreciate any effort made by a non-native speaker and are eager to help further. Finnish is by no means an easy language to master, but it's easy to read out loud and the phonetics are not difficult – and mistakes made by foreigners are usually disregarded. There is also a notable Swedish-speaking minority in Finland, and all Finns learn Swedish in school, so you may need your Swedish vocabulary in Finland from time to time.

PRONUNCIATION

Pronunciation is given in the pronunciation guide at the front of this book, with the following exceptions:

Vowels

Finnish has eight vowels and the alphabet also includes Swedish å (see page 308).

FINNISH	GUIDE	SOUNDS
u	u	as in 'pull'

WHAT COMES AFTER Z?

The last three letters of the alphabet are å, ä and ö. So, while Aatami would be one of the first entries in a telephone book, Äänekoski would be one of the last.

Vowel Harmony

Finnish divides vowels into two groups: those formed 'in the front of the mouth' (e, i, y, ä, ö) and those formed 'in the back of the mouth' (a, o, u). This distinction is very important when forming words with suffixes, because the vowels in the suffixes must be of the same type as the vowels in the root word. For example, koulussa, 'in school', is formed by adding -ssa, not -ssä, to the root.

Double Vowels

Double vowels are tricky to pronounce, so follow the pronunciation guide carefully. You will find that some double vowels are pronounced as one sound within one syllable, others as diphthongs, and some as separate syllables.

FINNISH	GUIDE	SOUNDS
ää	aa	as the 'a' in American 'fast', but even longer

FINNISH

Consonants

There are only 13 consonants in Finnish, although the alphabet includes English consonants. The letter x can be written as ks, and z can be written, and is pronounced, as *ts*. Finns consider v and w more or less as the same letter, and in phone books you will find both under 'V'. In literature of a certain type, w makes a word look 'older.' Vanha is 'old', but wanha is 'definitely old'.

FINNISH	GUIDE	SOUNDS
p	p	soft, as in 'spirit'
b	b	explosive, as the 'b' in 'bug'
t	t	soft, as in 'steak'
k	k	soft, as in 'skate'
g	g	explosive, as the 'g' in 'gutter'
s	s	as in 'sun', but weaker
h	h	as in 'horse'
	kh	almost as strong as the 'ch' in Scottish 'loch'

PRONOUNS

SG		
I	*mi-na*	minä
you	*si-na*	sinä
he/she/it	*han/han/seh*	hän/hän/se
PL		
we	*meh*	me
you (pl & pol)	*teh*	te
they	*heh/neh*	he/ne (inf)

Double Consonants

Double consonants like kk in viikko, 'week', or mm in summa, 'sum', are held longer and they always split the word into two syllables. Note that ng and nk both make two syllables, and are pronounced as -*ng*-ng- and -*ng*-k-. For example, vangit, 'prisons', is *vuhng*-ngit. Note also that np is pronounced as mp, as in olenpa, *o*-lehm-puh, 'I am'.

FINNISH

SIGNS

AUKI/SULJETTU	OPEN/CLOSED
KIELLETTY	PROHIBITED
KUUMA/KYLMÄ	HOT/COLD
LÄHTÖSELVITYS	CHECK-IN COUNTER
MATKATAVARAT	BAGGAGE COUNTER
OPASTUS/NEUVONTA	INFORMATION
PUHELIN	TELEPHONE
PÄÄSY KIELLETTY	NO ENTRY
SISÄÄN	ENTRANCE
TULLI	CUSTOMS
TUPAKOINTI KIELLETTY	NO SMOKING
ULOS	EXIT
VAPAA PÄÄSY	FREE ADMISSION
VARATTU	RESERVED
VARAULOSKÄYNTI	EMERGENCY EXIT
WC	TOILETS

GREETINGS & CIVILITIES
Top Useful Phrases

Hello.	*hay*/*tehrr*-veh/*moy*	*Hei/Terve/Moi.* (pol/inf)
Goodbye.	*na*-keh-meen/*moy*	*Näkemiin/Moi.* (pol/inf)
Yes.	*kül*-lah/*yoo*	*Kyllä/Joo.* (pol/inf)
No.	ay	*Ei.*
Excuse me.	*uhn*-teehk-si	*Anteeksi.*
Thank you.	*kee*-toss/*keet*-ti	*Kiitos/Kiitti.* (inf)
Many thanks.	*puhl*-yon *kee*-tok-si-uh	*Paljon kiitoksia.*

May I? Do you mind?
  sai-sin-ko? *Saisinko?*

Sorry.
  o-lehn *puh*-hoyl-luh-ni; *so*-rri   *Olen pahoillani; Sori.* (inf)

That's fine. You're welcome.
  o-leh *hü*-va; *ay*-pa *kehs*-ta   *Ole hyvä; Eipä kestä.* (inf)

FINNISH

There's no frequently used word for 'please' in Finnish. Often kiitos (thank you) is used. Another useful expression is 'could you', voisitteko, plus a verb. If you assume equality, or generally deal with informal situations, you are free to use less formal expressions. Speaking to a young clerk at a ticket booth or in a bank, you can say voitko, or even voitsä, 'are you able to', whereas an elderly lady would like to hear voisitteko, 'could you'.

Greetings

Good morning.

    (hü-vaa*) hu*-o-mehn-tuh   *(Hyvää) huomenta.*

Good afternoon.

    hü-vaa *pa*-i-vaa/*pa*-i-vaa   *Hyvää päivää./Päivää.* (inf)

Good evening/night.	*hü*-vaa *il*-tah/*ü-er*-ta	*Hyvää iltaa/yötä.*
How are you?	*mi-ta koo*-loo?	*Mitä kuuluu?*
Well, thanks.	*kee*-toss *hü*-vaa	*Kiitos hyvää.*

Forms of Address

Madam/Mrs	*rrohv*-vuh	*Rouva*
Sir/Mr	*hehrr*-rruh	*Herra*
Miss	*nay*-ti	*Neiti*
companion/friend	*üs*-ta-va/*kuh*-veh-rri	*ystävä/kaveri* (inf)

SMALL TALK

When you ask for a favour, use the most polite word: Te ('you' in the plural).

Minä means 'I', sinä is 'you'. Not everyone uses these words, however. In southern Finland, especially in Helsinki, most people say mä and sä. In Turku, Tampere and Oulu it's mää, for 'I', and sää for 'you' (nää in Oulu). In southern Savo they say mie and sie. In Helsinki it would be better to use mä instead of minä, to express that you don't place yourself above the other person. In northern Savo and places in Karelia, people still use minä – elsewhere you may sound rather egoistic if you use it. An asterisk (*) indicates where you could consider using some other form as you tour Finland.

Meeting People

What's your name?

mi-ka *tay*-dan *ni*-mehn-neh *on*?;   *Mikä teidän nimenne on?*;
mi-ka *sun ni*-mi *on*?   *Mikä sun nimi on?* (inf)

My name is ...

mi-nun *ni*-mehn-ni *on* ...;   *Minun nimeni on ...*;
mun ni-mi *on* ...   *Mun nimi on ...* (inf)

I'd like to introduce you to ...

huh-lu-ai-sin   *Haluaisin*
eh-si-tehl-la *si*-nut ...   *esitellä sinut ...-lle.*

I'm pleased to meet you.

hows-kuh *tuh*-vuh-tuh   *Hauska tavata.*

Nationalities

Where are you from?

mis-ta *si*-na *o*-let *ko*-toy-sin?   *Mistä sinä* olet kotoisin?*

I'm from ...	*o*-lehn ...	*Olen ...*
Australia	*owst*-rruh-li-uhs-tuh	*Australiasta*
Canada	*kuh*-nuh-duhs-tuh	*Kanadasta*
England	*ehng*-luhn-nis-tuh	*Englannista*
Finland	*su*-o-mehs-tuh	*Suomesta*
Ireland	*irr*-luhn-nis-tuh	*Irlannista*
New Zealand	*oo*-dehs-tuh	*Uudesta-*
	seeh-luhn-nis-tuh	*Seelannista*
Scotland	*scot*-luhn-nis-tuh	*Skotlannista*
the USA	*ükh*-düs-vuhl-loys-tuh/	*Yhdysvalloista/*
	uh-meh-rri-kuhs-tuh	*Amerikasta*
Wales	*wayl*-sis-ta	*Walesistä*

DID YOU KNOW ...	In Finnish, the word for Finland is Suomi and the word for Finnish (the language) is suomi

Age

How old are you?

    ku-in-kuh vuhm-huh si-na o-leht?   *Kuinka vanha sinä* olet?*

I'm ... years old.

    o-lehn ... vu-o-ti-uhs   *Olen ...-vuotias.*

Occupations

What work do you do?

    mi-ta si-na teeht tüh-erk-seh-si?   *Mitä sinä* teet työksesi?*

I'm (a/an) ...	*o-lehn ...*	*Olen ...*
artist	*tai-tay-li-yuh*	*taiteilija*
businessperson	*lee-keh-mi-ehs*	*liikemies*
engineer	*in-si-ner-rri*	*insinööri*
farmer	*mahn-vil-yeh-li-ya*	*maanviljelijä*
journalist	*yohrr-nuh-lis-ti/*	*journalisti/*
	lekh-ti-mi-ehs	*lehtimies*
lawyer	*yu-rris-ti/*	*juristi/*
	luh-ki-mi-ehs	*lakimies*
mechanic	*meh-kaa-nik-ko*	*mekaanikko*
doctor	*laa-ka-rri*	*lääkäri*
nurse	*sai-rrahn-hoy-tuh-yuh*	*sairaanhoitaja*
office worker	*toy-mis-to-tü-*	*toimistotyöntekijä*
	ern-teh-ki-ya	
scientist	*tut-ki-yuh/*	*tutkija/*
	ti-eh-deh-mi-ehs	*tiedemies*
student	*o-pis-keh-li-yuh*	*opiskelija*
teacher	*o-peht-tuh-yuh*	*opettaja*
waiter	*tuhrr-yoy-li-yuh*	*tarjoilija*
writer	*kihrr-yai-li-yuh*	*kirjailija*

FINNISH

Religion

What is your religion?
mi-ka *on* si-*nun* us-kon-to-si?   *Mikä on sinun uskontosi?*

I'm not religious.
ehn o-leh us-kon-nol-li-nehn/   *En ole uskonnollinen/*
us-ko-vai-nehn   *uskovainen.*

I'm (a) ...	o-lehn ...	Olen ...
Buddhist	*bud*-huh-lai-nehn	*buddhalainen*
Catholic	*kuh*-to-li-nehn	*katolinen*
Christian	*krris*-tit-tü	*kristitty*
Hindu	*hin*-du-lai-nehn	*hindulainen*
Jewish	*yoo*-tuh-lai-nehn	*juutalainen*
Lutheran	*lu*-teh-rri-lai-nehn	*luterilainen*
Muslim	*mus*-li-mi	*muslimi*

Family

Are you married?   o-*leht*-ko *nai*-mi-sis-suh?   *Oletko naimisissa?*

I'm ...	o-lehn ...	Olen ...
single	*nai*-muh-ton	*naimaton*
married	*nai*-mi-sis-suh	*naimisissa*
in a relationship	uhvo-lee-tos-suh	*avoliitossa*

How many children do you have?
ku-*in*-kuh mon-tuh   *Kuinka monta*
luhs-tuh sul-luh on?   *lasta sinulla on?*

I don't have any children.
mul-luh ay o-leh *luhp*-si-uh   *Minulla ei ole lapsia.*

I have a daughter/a son.
mul-luh on tü-tarr/*poy*-kuh   *Minulla on tytär/poika.*

How many brothers/sisters
do you have?
ku-*in*-kuh mon-tuh *vehl*-yeh-a/   *Kuinka monta veljeä/*
sis-uhrr-tuh si-nul-luh on?   *sisarta sinulla on?*

Do you have a boyfriend/girlfriend?
on-ko *sul*-luh *poy*-kuh-üs-ta-vaa/   *Onko sinulla poikaystävää/*
tüt-ter-üs-ta-vaa?   *tyttöystävää?*

brother	*veh*-li	*veli*
children	*luhp*-set	*lapset*
daughter	*tü*-tarr	*tytär*
family	*pehrr*-heh	*perhe*
father	*i*-sa	*isä*
grandfather	*i*-so-*i*-sa/*vah*-rri/*uk*-ki	*isoisä/vaari/ukki*
grandmother	*i*-so-*a*-*i*-ti/*mum*-mi	*isoäiti/mummi*
husband	*uh*-vi-o *mi*-ehs	*aviomies*
mother	*a*-*i*-ti	*äiti*
partner	*e*-lam-an-*kump*-puh-ni	*elämänkumppani*
sister	*sis*-ko	*sisko*
son	*poy*-kuh	*poika*
wife	*vai*-mo	*vaimo*

Kids' Talk

How old are you?
ku-in-kuh *vuh*-huh
si-na *o*-let?
*Kuinka vanha
sinä olet?*

When's your birthday?
kos-kuh *sun* sünt-ta-rrit on?
Koska sun synttärit on?

What do you do after school?
mi-ta *si*-na *te*-eht *koh*-lun
jal-keehn?
*Mitä sinä teet koulun
jälkeen?*

Do you have a pet at home?
on-ko *si*-nul-luh *lehm*-mik-ki-
eh-la-in-ta *ko*-to-nuh?
*Onko sinulla lemmikki-
eläintä kotona?*

I have a ...	*mi*-nul-luh on ...	*Minulla on ...*
bird	*lin*-tu	*lintu*
budgerigar	*un*-du-laht-ti	*undulaatti*
canary	*kuh*-nuhrr-i-uhn-*lin*-tu	*kanarianlintu*
cat	*kis*-suh	*kissa*
dog	*koy*-rruh	*koira*
goldfish	*kul*-tuh-*kuh*-luh	*kultakala*

Feelings

I like ...	*pi*-dan ...-sta/stuh	Pidän ...-sta/stä.
I don't like ...	*ehn pi*-da ...-sta/stuh	En pidä ...-sta/stä.
I'm well.	*voyn hü*-vin	Voin hyvin.

I'm ...	*mi*-nul-luh on ...	Minulla on ...
cold	*kül*-ma	kylmä
hot	*koo*-muh	kuuma
in a hurry	*kee*-rreh	kiire

I'm ...	*o*-lehn ...	Olen ...
angry	*vi*-hai-nehn	vihainen
grateful	*kee*-tol-li-nehn	kiitollinen
happy	*i*-loy-nehn	iloinen
right	*oy*-keh-uhs-suh	oikeassa
sad	*su*-rrul-li-nehn	surullinen
sleepy	*u*-ni-nehn	uninen
tired	*va*-sü-nüt	väsynyt
worried	*hu*-o-lis-suh-ni	huolissani

I'm sorry. (condolence)
  o-tuhn *o*-sah *o*-lehn   Otan osaa, olen
  puh-hoyl-luh-ni   pahoillani.

BREAKING THE LANGUAGE BARRIER

Do you speak English?
  pu-hut-ko *ehng*-luhn-ti-uh?   Puhutko englantia?
Does anyone speak English?
  pu-hoo-ko ku-kahn   Puhuuko kukaan
  ehng-luhn-ti-uh?   englantia?

I speak a little ...	*pu*-hun va-han ...	Puhun vähän ...
I don't speak ...	*ehn pu*-hu ...	En puhu ...
I understand.	*üm*-marr-rran	Ymmärrän.
I don't understand.	*ehn üm*-marr-rra	En ymmärrä.

FINNISH

Could you speak more slowly please?
    voy-sit-ko *pu*-hu-uh   *Voisitko puhua*
    hi-tahm-min?   *hitaammin?*
Could you repeat that?
    voyt-ko *toys*-tah?   *Voitko toistaa?*
How do you say ...?
    mi-tehn *suh*-no-tahn ...?   *Miten sanotaan ...?*
What does ... mean?
    mi-ta ... *tuhrr*-koyt-tah?   *Mitä ... tarkoittaa?*

I speak ...	*pu*-hun ...	*Puhun ...*
English	*ehng*-luhn-ti-uh	*englantia*
French	*rruhns*-kah	*ranskaa*
German	*suhk*-sah	*saksaa*
Swedish	*rru*-ot-si-uh	*ruotsia*

Some Useful Phrases

Just a minute.	*heht*-ki-nehn	*Hetkinen.*
Wait!	*o*-do-tuh!	*Odota!*

Good luck!
    on-neh-uh! (*lükh*-kü-a *tüh*-ker!)   *Onnea! (Lykkyä tykö!)*
It's (not) important.
    seh on (*ay* o-leh) *tarr*-keh-aa   *Se on (ei ole) tärkeää.*
It's (not) possible.
    seh on (*ay* o-leh)   *Se on (ei ole)*
    muhkh-dol-lis-tuh   *mahdollista.*

BODY LANGUAGE

You are in the country of the 'silent Finn': it's not felt necessary to make small talk all the time, and lack of eye contact doesn't indicate shiftiness or rudeness. If there are empty seats on a bus or in the cinema (and there always are), it's not usual to sit down right next to a stranger – leave a 'buffer zone.'

Shake hands when you meet someone for the first time.

FINNISH

PAPERWORK

address	*o*-soy-teh	osoite
age	*i*-ka	ikä
birth certificate	*sün*-tü-ma-*to*-dis-tus	syntymätodistus
border	*rruh*-yuh	raja
car registration	*rreh*-kis-teh-rri *nu*-meh-rro	rekisterinumero
customs	*tul*-li	tulli
date of birth	*sün*-tü-ma *ai*-kuh/	syntymäaika/
	hen-ki-ler-*tun*-nus	henkilötunnus
driver's licence	*uh*-yo-korrt-ti	ajokortti
identification	*hehm*-ki-ler-*puh*-peh-rrit	henkilöpaperit
make of car	*ow*-ton *mehrrk*-ki	auton merkki
marital status	*si*-vee-li-*saa*-tü	sivilisääty
name	*ni*-mi	nimi
nationality	*kuhn*-suh-lai-soos	kansalaisuus
passport	*puhs*-si	passi
passport number	*puhs*-sin *nu*-meh-rro	passin numero
place of birth	*sün*-tü-ma-*paik*-kuh	syntymäpaikka
profession	*uhm*-muht-ti	ammatti
reason for travel	*muht*-kuhn *tuhrr*-koy-tus	matkan tarkoitus
religion	*us*-kon-to	uskonto
sex	*su*-ku-*pu*-o-li	sukupuoli
visa	*vee*-su-mi	viisumi

SIGNS

AIKATAULU	TIMETABLE
ALIKULKUKÄYTÄVÄ	SUBWAY (pedestrian)
ASEMA	STATION
BUSSI/RATSIKKA PYSÄKKI	BUS/TRAM STOP
LIPPUTOIMISTO	TICKET OFFICE
LÄHTEVÄT	DEPARTURES
METRO	SUBWAY (train)
RAUTATIEASEMA	TRAIN STATION
SAAPUVAT	ARRIVALS

FINNISH

GETTING AROUND

As you look for places, visit them and leave them, you'll use different words in each case, and a little grammar is needed to gain an understanding of how words are constructed. Finnish grammar is extremely complicated. With all the possible suffixes and meanings, you can construct over 450 different words from any noun root.

-ssa or -ssä, 'in something': koulu-ssa, 'in school'
-sta or -stä, 'from something': koulu-sta, 'from school'
-double vowel plus n, 'to something': koulu-un, 'to school'
-lla or -llä, 'on', 'at' or 'in something' or 'somebody': koulu-lla, 'at school'
-lta or -ltä, 'from something' or 'somebody': koulu-lta, 'from school'
-lle, 'to something' or 'somebody': koulu-lle, 'to school'

Consider the following examples of expressing 'in ...', and 'to ...' (a town):

Helsinki:	Helsingi-ssä	Helsinki-in
Turku:	Turku-ssa	Turku-un
Varkaus:	Varkaude-ssa	Varkaute-en
Tampere:	Tamperee-lla	Tamperee-lle
Rovaniemi: (and others ending -niemi)	Rovaniemé-llä	Rovaniemé-lle
Seinäjoki: (and others ending -joki)	Seinäjoe-lla	Seinäjoe-lle
Kemijärvi: (and others ending -järvi)	Kemijärve-llä	Kemijärve-lle

To express being inside a vehicle, hotel etc, the -ssa suffix is used for 'in', and a double vowel plus -n for 'to': juna-ssa/juna-an, hotelli-ssa/hotelli-in. When you use a vehicle, you use the -lla suffix, as matkustaa juna-lla, 'to travel by train'.

What time does ...	*mi*-hin *ai*-kahn ...	*Mihin aikaan ...*
leave/arrive?	*lakh*-teeh/*sah*-poo?	*lähtee/saapuu?*
the (aero)plane	*lehn*-to-*ko*-neh	*lentokone*
the boat	*lai*-vuh	*laiva*
the bus (city)	*bus*-si	*bussi*
the bus (intercity)	*bus*-si/*lin*-yuh-*ow*-to	*bussi/linja-auto*
the train	*yu*-nuh	*juna*
the tram	*rrai*-ti-o-*vow*-nu/	*raitiovaunu/*
	rruh-tik-kuh	*ratikka* (inf)

Directions

Where is ...?   *mis*-sa *on* ...?   *Missä on ...?*

How do I get to ...?
mi-ten *mi*-na *paa*-sen ...?   *Miten minä* pääsen ...?*

Is it far from/near here?
on-ko *seh kow*-kuh-nuh/   *Onko se kaukana/*
la-hehl-la?   *lähellä?*

Can I walk there?
voy-ko *sin*-neh *ka*-vehl-la?   *Voiko sinne kävellä?*

Can you show me (on the map)?
voyt-ko *na*-üt-taa *mul*-leh   *Voitko näyttää minulle*
(*kuhrr*-tuhs-tuh)?   *(kartasta)?*

Are there other means of getting there?
paa-seeh-ker *sin*-neh *yol*-luh-kin   *Pääseekö sinne jollakin*
mool-luh *tuh*-vuhl-luh?   *muulla tavalla?*

I want to go to ...
huh-lu-uhn *men*-na ...   *Haluan mennä ...*

Go straight ahead.
kul-yeh *su*-o-rrahn   *Kulje suoraan.*

It's two blocks down.
seh on kuhkh-den   *Se on kahden*
korrt-teh-lin *paas*-sa   *korttelin päässä.*

Turn left/right ...	*kaan*-nü *vuh*-sehm-pahn/ *oy*-keh-ahn ...	*Käänny vasempaan/ oikeaan ...*
at the next corner	*seh-u*-rrah-vuhs-tuh *kuh-dun-kul*-muhs-tuh	*seuraavasta kadunkulmasta*
at the traffic lights	*lee*-kehn-neh- *vuh*-loys-suh	*liikenne valoissa*
behind	...-n *tuh*-kuh-nuh	*...-n takana*
far	*kow*-kuh-nuh	*kaukana*
near	*la*-hehl-la	*lähellä*
in front of	*eh*-dehs-sa	*edessä*
opposite	*vuhs*-tuh *paa*-ta ... -ta/-tuh	*vastapäätä ... -ta/-tä*

Booking Tickets

Where can I buy a ticket?
mis-ta *voy os*-tah *li*-pun? *Mistä voi ostaa lipun?*

I want to go to ...
ha-lu-uhn *men*-na ... *Haluan mennä ...-lle/ ...vowel + n*

Do I need to book?
ta-ü-tüü-ker *vuh*-rruh-tuh? *Täytyykö varata?*

I'd like to book a seat to ...
ha-lu-ai-sin *vuh*-rruh-tuh *is*-tu-muh-*pai*-kuhn ... *Haluaisin varata istumapaikan ...lle/...vowel + n*

I'd like ...	*sahn*-ko ...	*Saanko ...*
a one-way ticket	*meh*-no-*li*-pun	*menolipun*
a return ticket	*meh*-no-*pa*-loo-*li*-pun	*menopaluulipun*
two tickets	*kuhk*-si *lip*-pu-uh	*kaksi lippua*
a student's fare	*o*-pis-keh-li-ya-*li*-pun	*opiskelijalipun*
a child's fare	*luhs*-tehn-*li*-pun	*lastenlipun*
a pensioner's fare	*eh*-la-keh-*la*-is-tehn *li*-pun	*eläkeläisten lipun*
1st class	*en*-sim-ma-i-nehn *lu-ok*-kuh	*ensimmäinen luokka*
2nd class	*toy*-nehn *lu-ok*-kuh	*toinen luokka*

Is it completely full?
on-ko *se ai*-vuhn *ta-ün*-na?   *Onko se aivan täynnä?*
Can I get a stand-by ticket?
voyn-ko *sah*-duh   *Voinko saada*
li-pun *il*-muhn   *lipun ilman*
paik-kuh-*vuh*-rrows-tuh?   *paikkavarausta?*

Air

Is there a flight to ...?
on-ko ... *len*-to-uh?   *Onko ...-lle/ (vowel + n) lentoa?*
How long does the flight take?
kow-uhn-ko *len*-to *kehs*-taa?   *Kauanko lento kestää?*
What is the flight number?
mi-ka *on len*-non   *Mikä on lennon*
nu-meh-rro?   *numero?*
You must check in at ...
tay-dan (*sun*) *taü*-tüü   *Teidän (sun) täytyy*
kheh-kuh-tuh ... -la   *tsekata ...-lla*

airport tax	*lehn*-to-*kehnt*-ta *veh*-rro	*lentokenttävero*
boarding pass	*tuhrr*-kuhs-tus-*korrt*-ti	*tarkastuskortti*
customs	*tul*-li/*tul*-li-*tuhrr*-kuhs-tus	*tulli/tullitarkastus*

Bus

Does this bus go to ...?
meh-neeh-ker *ta*-ma   *Meneekö tämä*
bus-si ...?   *bussi ... vowel + n/...lle?*
Could you let me know
when we get to ...?
voyt-ko *suh*-no-uh, *mil*-loyn   *Voitko sanoa, milloin*
tul-ehm-meh ...-n *lu*-o-nuh? *tulemme ...-n luona?*
I want to get off!
mi-na *huh*-lu-uhn   *Minä* haluan*
jaa-da *poys*!   *jäädä pois!*

What time is the ... bus?	mi-hin ai-kahn on ... bus-si?	*Mihin aikaan on ... bussi?*
next	seh-u-rrah-vuh	*seuraava*
first	ehn-sim-ma-i-nehn	*ensimmäinen*
last	vee-may-nehn	*viimeinen*

Train

Is this the right platform for ...?
on-ko ta-ma oy-keh-uh
rrai-deh ...?

Onko tämä oikea raide ... vowel + n/...lle?

Passengers must change trains.
muht-kus-tuh-yi-ehn on
vaikh-deht-tuh-vuh yu-nah

Matkustajien on vaihdettava junaa

The train leaves from platform ...
yu-nuh lakh-teeh rrai-teehl-tuh ...

Juna lähtee raiteelta ...

dining car	rruh-vin-to-luh-vow-nu	*ravintolavaunu*
express	pi-kuh-yu-nuh	*pikajuna*
local	pai-kuhl-lis-yu-nuh	*paikallisjuna*
sleeping car	muh-koo-vow-nu	*makuuvaunu*

Metro

Which direction takes me to ...?
kum-pahn soon-tahn
paa-seeh ...?

Kumpaan suuntaan pääsee ...lle/...vowel + n?

What is the next station?
mi-ka on seh-u-rrah-vuh
uh-seh-muh?

Mikä on seuraava asema?

SIGNS

KAUKOLIIKENNE	LONG-DISTANCE TRAFFIC
KOLIKOT	CHANGE (for coins)
LAITURIALUE	PLATFORM AREA (for ticket check)
LÄHILIIKENNELIPPUJA	LOCAL TRAIN TICKETS
LÖYTÖTAVARAT	LOST AND FOUND
RAIDE	PLATFORM NO
VR MATKAPALVELU	TRAVEL SERVICE

FINNISH

Taxi

How much does it
cost to go to ...?
puhl-yon-ko *muhk*-sah
muht-kuh ...?
*Paljonko maksaa
matka ...vowel + n/...lle?*

Here is fine, thank you!
tas-sa on *hü*-va *kee*-toss!   *Tässä on hyvä, kiitos!*
Continue!
yuht-kuh *vi*-eh-la!   *Jatka vielä!*
Stop here!
pü-sa-ü-ta *tas*-sa!   *Pysäytä tässä!*
The next street to the left/right.
seh-*u*-rrah-vah *kuh*-tu-uh   *Seuraavaa katua*
vuh-sehm-muhl-leh/   *vasemmalle/oikealle.*
oy-keh-uhl-leh
Please slow down.
hi-das-tuh *va*-han   *Hidasta vähän.*
Please wait here.
voyt-ko *o*-dot-tah *tas*-sa *va*-han   *Voitko odottaa tässä vähän.*

Some Useful Phrases

The train is delayed/cancelled.
yu-nuh on *mü*-er-has-sa/   *Juna on myöhässä/*
peh-rroo-teht-tu   *peruutettu.*
How long will it be delayed?
kow-uhn-ko *seh* onmu-er-has-sa?   *Kauanko se on myöhässä?*
There is a delay of ... hours.
seh on ... *tun*-ti-uh *mu*-er-has-sa   *Se on ... tuntia myöhässä.*
How long does the trip take?
kow-uhn-ko *muht*-kuh *kehs*-taa?   *Kauanko matka kestää?*
Is it a direct route?
on-ko *se* su-*o*-rruh *rrayt*-ti?   *Onko se suora reitti?*
Is that seat taken?
on-ko *toy* paik-kuh *vuh*-rruht-tu?   *Onko tuo paikka varattu?*

FINNISH

I want to get off at ...
    mi-na *jaan poys* ...-ssa/lla   *Minä* jään pois ...-ssa/-lla.*
Where can I hire a bicycle?
    mis-ta *mi*-na *voyn vu-ok*-rruh-tuh   *Mistä minä* voin vuokrata*
    pol-ku-*pü-er*-rran?   *polkupyörän?*
Is there room for the bicycle?
    makh-too-ko *tan*-neh   *Mahtuuko tänne*
    pol-ku-*pü-er*-rra?   *polkupyörä?*

Car

Where can I rent a car?
    mis-ta *mi*-na *voy*-sin   *Mistä minä* voisin*
    vu-ok-rruh-tuh *ow*-ton?   *vuokrata auton?*
daily/weekly
    pehrr pa-i-va/pehrr veek-ko   *per päivä/per viikko*
Does that include insurance/
unlimited mileage?
    koo-loo-ko *see*-hen *vuh*-koo-tus/   *Kuuluuko siihen vakuutus/*
    rruh-yoyt-tuh-muh-ton   *rajoittamaton*
    ki-lo-meht-rri *maa*-rra?   *kilometrimäärä?*
Where's the next petrol station?
    mis-sa on *la*-hin *ben*-suh   *Missä on lähin bensa*
    uh-seh-muh?   *-asema?*
How long can I park here?
    kow-uhn-ko *tas*-sa *sah*   *Kauanko tässä saa*
    parrk-keeh-rruh-tuh?   *parkkeerata?*
Does this road lead to ...?
    meh-neeh-ker *ta*-ma *ti-eh* ...?   *Meneekö tämä tie*
          ...vowel + n/...lle?

I need a mechanic.
    mi-na *tarr*-vit-sehn *korr*-yah-yah   *Minä* tarvitsen korjaajaa.*
The battery is flat.
    uhk-ku on *tükh*-ya   *Akku on tyhjä.*
The radiator is leaking.
    yaakh-dü-tin *vu-o*-tah   *Jäähdytin vuotaa.*
I have a flat tyre.
    rrehng-nguhs on *tükh*-ja   *Rengas on tyhjä.*

FINNISH

It's overheating.
  seh koo-meh-neeh lee-kah   *Se kuumenee liikaa.*
It's not working.
  seh ay toy-mi   *Se ei toimi.*

air (for tyres)	*il-*muh	*ilma*
battery	*uhk-*ku	*akku*
brakes	*yuhrr-*rrut	*jarrut*
clutch	*küt-*kin	*kytkin*
driver's licence	*uh-yo-korrt-*tih	*ajokortti*
engine	*morrt-*to-rri/*ko-*neh	*moottori/kone*
lights	*vuh-*lot	*valot*
oil	*erl-*yü	*öljy*
puncture	*rrehng-*nguhs-*rrik-*ko	*rengasrikko*
radiator	*yaakh-*dü-tin	*jäähdytin*
road map	*ti-eh-*kuhrrt-*tuh	*tiekartta*
tyres	*rrehn-*kaht	*renkaat*
windscreen	*too-*li-*luh-*si	*tuulilasi*

SIGNS

BENSA-ASEMA	FILLING STATION
HUOLTOASEMA	GARAGE
ITSEPALVELU	SELF SERVICE
JÄINEN TIE	ICE ON ROAD
KELIRIKKO	BAD ROAD
KIELLETTY AJOSUUNTA	NO ENTRY
KIERTOTIE	DETOUR
KORJAAMO	MECHANIC
LYIJYTÖN 95E	UNLEADED
MOOTTORITIE	FREEWAY
PYSÄKÖINTI KIELLETTY	NO PARKING
STOP	STOP
TIETYÖ	ROADWORKS
YKSISUUNTAINEN AJOTIE	ONE WAY
97 OKTAANIA	NORMAL LEADED
99 OKTAANIA	SUPER LEADED

FINNISH

ACCOMMODATION

Where is ...?	mis-sa o-li-si ...?	Missä olisi ...?
a cheap hotel	huhl-puh ho-tehl-li	halpa hotelli
a good hotel	hü-va ho-tehl-li	hyvä hotelli
a nearby hotel	la-hin ho-tehl-li	lähin hotelli

What is the address?
mi-ka on o-soy-teh?   *Mikä on osoite?*

Could you write the address, please?
voy-sit-teh-ko *kirr*-yoyt-tah   *Voisitteko kirjoittaa*
o-soyt-teen   *osoitteen.*

At the Hotel

Do you have any rooms available?
on-ko *tayl*-la *vuh*-pah-tuh   *Onko teillä vapaata*
hu-o-neht-tuh?   *huonetta?*

I'd like ...	ha-lu-ai-sin ...	Haluaisin ...
a single room	ükh-dehn hehng-ngehn	yhden hengen
	hu-o-neehn	huoneen
a double room	kuhkh-dehn hehng-ngehn	kahden hengen
	hu-o-neehn	huoneen
to share a dorm	muh-koo-suh-lin	makuusalin
	san-kü-pai-kuhn	sänkypaikan
a bed	sang-ngün	sängyn

I want a room	mi-na huh-lu-uhn	Minä* haluan
with a ...	hu-o-neehn ...	huoneen ...
bathroom	kül-pü-hu-o-neehl-luh	kylpyhuoneella
shower	su-ih-kul-luh	suihkulla
television	yos-suh on	jossa on
	teh-leh-vi-si-o	televisio
window	yos-suh on ik-ku-nuh	jossa on ikkuna

I'm going to	mi-na ai-on	Minä* aion
stay for ...	vee-pü-a ...	viipyä ...
one day	ükh-dehn pai-van	yhden päivän
two days	kuhk-si pai-vaa	kaksi päivää
one week	vee-kon	viikon

Do you have identification?
on-ko tayl-la/sul-luh
hehn-ki-ler-puh-peh-rray-tuh?

Onko teillä/sulla
henkilöpapereita? (pol/inf)

Your membership card, please.
sahn-ko ya-sehn-korrt-tin

Saanko jäsenkortin.

Sorry, we're full.
vuh-li-teht-tuh-vuhs-ti mayl-la
on ta-üt-ta

Valitettavasti meillä
on täyttä.

How many nights?
ku-in-kuh mon-tuh u-er-ta?

Kuinka monta yötä?

How much is it per night/per person?
puhl-yon-ko seh on ü-erl-ta/
hehng-ngehl-ta?

Paljonko se on yöltä/
hengeltä?

Can I see it?
voyn-ko mi-na nakh-da sehn?

Voinko minä* nähdä sen?

Are there any others?
on-ko mi-taan mu-i-tuh?

Onko mitään muita?

Are there any cheaper rooms?
on-ko huhl-vehm-pah
hu-o-neht-tuh?

Onko halvempaa
huonetta?

Can I see the bathroom?
voyn-ko mi-na nakh-da
kül-pü-hu-o-neehn?

Voinko minä*
nähdä kylpyhuoneen?

Is there a reduction for
students/children?
sah-ko o-pis-keh-li-yuh/luhp-si
uh-lehn-nus-tuh?

Saako opiskelija/lapsi
alennusta?

Does it include breakfast?
koo-loo-ko ah-mi-ai-nehn
hin-tahn?

Kuuluuko aamiainen
hintaan?

FINNISH

It's fine, I'll take it.
   se on hü-va mi-na o-tuhn sen.   *Se on hyvä, minä* otan sen.*
I'm not sure how long I'm staying.
   mi-na ehn ti-eh-da ku-in-kuh   *Minä* en tiedä kuinka*
   kow-uhn mi-na vii-vün taal-la   *kauan minä* viivyn täällä.*

Is there a lift?
   on-ko taal-la his-si-a?   *Onko täällä hissiä?*
Where is the bathroom?
   mis-sa on kül-pü   *Missä on kylpyhuone*
   hu-o-neh (vehs-suh)?   *(vessa)?*
Is there hot water all day?
   on-ko koo-mah veht-ta   *Onko kuumaa vettä*
   ko-ko pai-van?   *koko päivän?*
Do you have a safe where
I can leave my valuables?
   on-ko tayl-la sa-ilü-tüs-lo-kehrr-   *Onko teillä säilytyslokeroa*
   oy-tuh arr-vo-tuh-vuhrr-uhl-le?   *arvotavaralle?*
Is there somewhere to wash clothes?
   voy-ko taal-la yos-sain   *Voiko täällä jossain*
   pehs-ta vaht-tay-tuh?   *pestä vaatteita?*
Can I use the kitchen?
   voyn-ko ka-üt-taa kayt-ti-er-ta?   *Voinko käyttää keittiötä?*
Can I use the telephone?
   voyn-ko ka-üt-taa pu-heh-lin-tuh?   *Voinko käyttää puhelinta?*
Is your sauna warm?
   on-ko sow-nuh lam-min?   *Onko sauna lämmin?*
Do you have a smoke sauna?
   on-ko tayl-la suh-vu-sow-nah?   *Onko teillä savusaunaa?*

SIGNS

HOTELLI	**HOTEL**
MATKUSTAJAKOTI	**GUESTHOUSE**
MOTELLI	**MOTEL**
RETKEILYMAJA	**YOUTH HOSTEL**

FINNISH

Requests & Complaints

Please wake me up at ...
voyt-teh-ko *heh*-rrat-taa
mi-nut kehl-lo ...

*Voitteko herättää
minut kello ...*

The room needs to be cleaned.
hu-o-neh ta-ü-tü-i-si *see*-vo-tuh

Huone täytyisi siivota.

Please change the sheets.
voyt-teh-ko *vaikh*-tah
luh-kuh-nuht

*Voitteko vaihtaa
lakanat.*

I can't open/turn on ...	*ehn sah ... ow*-ki	*En saa ... auki.*
I can't close/turn off ...	*ehn sah ... keen*-ni	*En saa ... kiinni.*
the window	*ik*-ku-nah	*ikkunaa*
the door	*o*-veh-uh	*ovea*
the heating	*puht*-teh-rri-uh	*patteria*
the TV	*tee*-veeh-ta	*TV:ta*

I left my key in the room.
uh-vai-meh-ni *ya-i*
hu-o-neeh-seehn

*Avaimeni jäi
huoneeseen.*

The toilet won't flush.
vehs-suh *ay veh*-da

Vessa ei vedä.

I don't like this room.
mi-na *ehn* oy-kayn *pi*-da
tas-ta *hu-o*-neehs-tuh

Minä en oikein
pidä tästä huoneesta.*

It's too small.	*se on lee*-uhn *pi-eh*-ni	*Se on liian pieni.*
It's noisy.	*si-ehl*-la on *meh*-lu-uh	*Siellä on melua.*
It's too dark.	*se on lee*-uhn *pi*-meh-a	*Se on liian pimeä.*
It's expensive.	*se on kuhl*-lis	*Se on kallis.*

Some Useful Words & Phrases

I'm/We're leaving now/tomorrow.

mi-na *luh*-dehn/*meh*
lakh-deh-taan *nüt/hu-o*-mehn-nuh

Minä lähden/Me
läh-detään nyt/huomenna.*

I'd like to pay the bill.

mi-na *muhk*-sai-sin *luhs*-kun

Minä* maksaisin laskun.

name	*ni*-mi	*nimi*
given names	*eh*-tu *ni*-meht	*etunimet*
surname	*su*-ku-*ni*-mi	*sukunimi*
address	*o*-soy-teh	*osoite*
room number	*hu-o*-neen	*huoneen*
	nu-meh-rro	*numero*
air-conditioned	*il*-muhs-toy-tu	*ilmastoitu*
balcony	*puhrr*-veh-keh	*parveke*
bathroom	*kül*-pü-*hu-o*-neh	*kylpyhuone*
bed	*san*-kü	*sänky*
bill	*luhs*-ku	*lasku*
blanket	*payt*-to	*peitto*
candle	*künt*-ti-la	*kynttilä*
chair	*tu-o*-li	*tuoli*
clean	*puh*-duhs	*puhdas*
cupboard	*kahp*-pi	*kaappi*
dirty	*li*-kai-nehn	*likainen*
double bed	*puh*-rri-*san*-kü	*parisänky*
electricity	*sakh*-ker	*sähkö*
excluded	*ay koo*-lu *hin*-tahn	*ei kuulu hintaan*
included	*koo*-loo *hin*-tahn	*kuuluu hintaan*
key	*uh*-vain	*avain*
lift (elevator)	*his*-si	*hissi*
light bulb	*heh*-ku-*luhmp*-pu/	*hehkulamppu/*
	luhmp-pu	*lamppu*
a lock	*luk*-ko	*lukko*
mattress	*puht*-yuh	*patja*
mirror	*pay*-li	*peili*
padlock	*mu*-nuh-*luk*-ko	*munalukko*

FINNISH

pillow	*tüü*-nü	*tyyny*
quiet	*hil*-jai-nehn	*hiljainen*
room (in hotel)	*hu-o*-neh/*ho*-tehl-li-*hu-o*-neh	*huone/hotelli huone*
sauna	*sow*-nuh	*sauna*
sheet	*luh*-kuh-nuh	*lakana*
shower	*su-ih*-ku	*suihku*
soap	*saip*-pu-uh	*saippua*
suitcase	*muht*-kuh-*lowk*-ku	*matkalaukku*
swimming pool	*u-i*-muh-*uhl*-luhs	*uima-allas*
table	*per-ü*-ta	*pöytä*
toilet	*veeh*-seeh/*vehs*-suh	*WC/vessa*
toilet paper	*vehs*-suh-*puh*-peh-rri	*vessapaperi*
towel	*püü*-heh	*pyyhe*
(some) water	*veht*-ta	*vettä*
cold water	*kül*-muh vesi	*kylmä vesi*
hot water	*koo*-mah vet-ta	*kuumaa vettä*
window	*ik*-ku-nuh	*ikkuna*

FINNISH

STRAIGHT TO THE POINT

When buying a pack of cigarettes or a beer, you just state the merchandise. Pitkä! means 'Could you give me a large glass of beer, please!'.

AROUND TOWN

Where is ...?	*mis-sa on ...?*	*Missä on ...?*
the art gallery	*tai-deh-guhl-leh-rri-ah/*	*taidegalleriaa/*
	tai-deh-guhl-leh-rri-uh	*taidegalleria*
a bank	*puhnk-ki-uh/puhnk-ki*	*pankkia/pankki*
the church	*kirrk-ko-uh/kirrk-ko*	*kirkkoa/kirkko*
the city centre	*kehs-kus-tah/*	*keskustaa/*
	kehs-kus-tuh	*keskusta*
the ...embassy	*...-n soorr*	*...-n suur*
	la-heh-tüs-ter-a/	*lähetystöä/*
	...-n soorr la-heh-tüs-ter	*suurlähetystö*
my hotel	*ho-tehl-li-ni*	*hotellini*
a mail box	*pos-ti-lah-tik-ko-uh/*	*postilaatikkoa/*
	pos-ti-lah-tik-ko	*postilaatikko*
the market	*to-rri-uh/to-rri*	*oria/tori*
the museum	*mu-seh-o-tuh/mu-seh-o*	*museota/museo*
the police	*po-lee-si-uh/po-lee-si*	*poliisia/poliisi*
the post office	*pos-ti-uh/pos-ti*	*postia/posti*
a public toilet	*ü-lays-ta vehs-sah/*	*yleistä vessaa/*
	ü-lay-nehn vehs-suh	*yleinen vessa*
a telephone	*pu-heh-lin-tuh/*	*puhelinta/*
	pu-heh-lin	*puhelin*
the tourist	*muht-kay-lu*	*matkailu*
information	*toy-mis-to-uh/*	*toimistoa/*
office	*toy-mis-to*	*toimisto*

What time does it open/close?
mil-loyn *seh uh*-vuh-tahn/   *Milloin se avataan/*
sul-jeh-tahn?   *suljetaan?*

What ... is this?	*mi-ka ... ta-ma on?*	*Mikä ... tämä on?*
street	*kuh-tu*	*katu*
suburb	*kow-pung-ngin-o-suh/*	*kaupunginosa/*
	eh-si-kow-pung-ki	*esikaupunki*

For directions, see the Getting Around section, page 144.

FINNISH

At the Post Office

I'd like to send ...	*huh*-lu-ai-sin	*Haluaisin*
	la-heht-taa ...	*lähettää ...*
a fax	*fuhk*-sin	*faksin*
a letter	*kirr*-yeehn	*kirjeen*
a postcard	*pos*-ti-*korr*-tin	*postikortin*
a parcel	*puh*-keh-tin	*paketin*
a telegram	*sakh*-keehn	*sähkeen*

I'd like some stamps.

huh-lu-ai-sin	*Haluaisin*
pos-ti-*mehrrk*-keh-ja	*postimerkkejä.*

How much does it cost
to send this to ...?

puhl-yon-ko *muhk*-sah	*Paljonko maksaa*
la-heht-taa ta-ma ...?	*lähettää tämä*
	...vowel + *n?*

an aerogram	*uh-eh*-rro-grruhm-mi	*aerogrammi*
air mail	*lehn*-to-*pos*-ti-nuh	*lentopostina*
envelope	*kirr*-jeh	*kirje*
registered mail	*kirr*-juht-tu *kirr*-jeh	*kirjattu kirje*
surface mail	*mah*-*pos*-ti-nuh	*maapostina*

FINNISH

CHEAP ACCESS!

You can find cybercafés in most large towns, but the best and cheapest way to access the Internet is at a public library.

Telephone & Internet

I want to ring ...
huh-lu-ai-sin *soyt*-tah ...   *Haluaisin soittaa ...*

The number is ...
pu-heh-lin-*nu*-meh-rro *on* ...   *Puhelinnumero on ...*

How much does a
three-minute call cost?
puhl-yon-ko *muhk*-sah   *Paljonko maksaa*
kol-mehn *mi*-noo-tin *pu*-heh-lu?   *kolmen minuutin puhelu?*

How much does each
extra minute cost?
puhl-yon-ko *muhk*-sah   *Paljonko maksaa*
jo-*kai*-nehn *li*-sa-*mi*-noot-ti?   *jokainen lisäminuutti?*

I'd like to speak to (Mr Nieminen).
huh-lu-ai-sin *pu*-hu-uh   *Haluaisin puhua*
(*hehrr*-rruh *ni*-*eh*-mi-sehn)   *(herra Niemisen)*
kuhns-suh   *kanssa.*

I want to make a
reverse-charges phone call.
huh-lu-uhn *soyt*-tah   *Haluan soittaa*
vuhs-tuh-*pu*-heh-lun   *vastapuhelun.*

It's engaged.
seh on vuh-rruht-tu   *Se on varattu.*

I've been cut off.
pu-heh-lu *kuht*-keh-si   *Puhelu katkesi.*

cellular phone
kan-nük-ka   *kännykkä*

Where can I access the Internet?
mis-sa *paa*-sehn   *Missä pääsen*
in-tehrr-neht-tiin?   *Internettiin?*

I'd like to send an e-mail.
huh-lu-ai-sin *la*-heht-taa   *Haluaisin lähettää*
suh-ker-*pos*-ti-uh   *sähköpostia.*

At the Bank

I want to change some money/
travellers cheques.

huh-lu-ai-sin *vaikh*-tah *rruh*-hah/   Haluaisin vaihtaa rahaa/
muht-kuh *shehk*-keh-ja   matkashekkejä.

What is the exchange rate?

mi-ka on *kurrs*-si?   Mikä on kurssi?

How many marks per dollar?

puhl-yon-ko *dol*-luh-rril-luh   Paljonko dollarilla
sah muhrrk-ko-yuh?   saa markkoja?

Can I have money transferred
here from my bank?

voyn-ko *mi*-na *sah*-duh   Voinko minä* saada
rruh-hah *seö*-rreht-tü-a   rahaa siirrettyä
o-*muhs*-tuh *puhn*-kis-tuh-ni?   omasta pankistani?

How long will it take to arrive?

kow-uhn-ko *sehn tu*-lo *kehs*-taa?   Kauanko sen tulo kestää?

Has my money arrived yet?

on-ko *mi*-nun *rruh*-huh-ni   Onko minun rahani
sah-pu-nut *vi*-eh-la?   saapunut vielä?

(some) banknotes	*seh*-teh-leh-i-ta	seteleitä
cashier	*kuhs*-suh	kassa
some coins	*ko*-li-koy-tuh	kolikoita
credit card	lu-*ot*-to-korrt-ti	luottokortti
exchange	*rruh*-huhn-*vaikh*-to	rahanvaihto
loose change	*pik*-ku-*rruh*-hah/	pikkurahaa/
	vaikh-to-*rruh*-hah	vaihtorahaa
money transfer	*ti*-li-*seer*-to	tilisiirto
signature	*uhl*-leh-*kirr*-yoy-tus	allekirjoitus

INTERESTS & ENTERTAINMENT
Sightseeing

Do you have a guidebook/
local map?
    on-ko *si*-nul-luh *muht*-kuh-*o*-
    puhs-tuh/*kuhrrt*-tah?

*Onko sinulla matkao
pasta/karttaa?*

What are the main attractions?
    mit-ka *o*-vuht *tarr*-kaym-mat
    nakh-ta-vüü- deht?

*Mitkä ovat tärkeimmät
nähtävyydet?*

What is that?
    mi-ka *tu*-o on?

Mikä tuo on?

How old is it?
    ku-*in*-kuh *vuhn*-huh *seh* on?

Kuinka vanha se on?

Can I take photographs?
    voyn-ko *mi*-na *ot*-tah
    vuh-lo-*ku*-vi-uh?

Voinko minä ottaa
valokuvia?*

What time does it open/close?
    mil-loyn *seh* *ow*-keh-ah/
    sul-yeh-tahn?

*Milloin se aukeaa/
suljetaan?*

ancient	*vuhn*-huh	*vanha*
archaeological	*uhrr*-keh-o-lo-gi-nehn	*arkeologinen*
beach	*u*-*i*-muh *rruhn*-tuh	*uimaranta*
building	*rruh*-kehn-nus	*rakennus*
castle	*lin*-nuh	*linna*
cathedral	*tu*-o-mi-o-*kirrk*-ko/	*tuomiokirkko/*
	kuh-tehd-rrah-li	*katedraali*
church	*kirrk*-ko	*kirkko*
concert hall	*kon*-sehrrt-ti-*huhl*-li	*konserttihalli*
library	*kirr*-juhs-to	*kirjasto*
main square	*kehs*-kus *to*-rri	*keskustori*
market	*to*-rri/*kowp*-puh-*to*-rri/	*tori/kauppatori/*
	muhrrk-ki-nuht	*markkinat*
monastery	*lu*-*os*-tuh-rri	*luostari*
monument	*mu*-*is*-to-*mehrrk*-ki/	*muistomerkki/*
	mo-nu-mehnt-ti	*monumentti*

FINNISH

mosque	*mos*-kay-yuh	*moskeija*
old city	*vuhn*-huh-*kow*-pun-ki	*vanhakaupunki*
palace	*puh*-luht-si	*palatsi*
opera house	*orrp*-peh-rruh-*tuh*-lo	*oopperatalo*
ruins	*rrow*-ni-ot	*rauniot*
stadium	*stuh*-di-on	*stadion*
some statues	*puht*-sai-tuh	*patsaita*
synagogue	*sü*-nuh-gorr-guh	*synagooga*
temple	*tehmp*-peh-li	*temppeli*
university	*ü*-li-*o*-pis-to/	*yliopisto/*
	korr-keh-uh *koh*-lu	*korkeakoulu*

Going Out

What's there to do in the evening?
    mi-ta *taal*-la *voy* teh-da *il*-tai-sin?   *Mitä täällä voi tehdä iltaisin?*

Are there any discos?
    on-ko *taal*-la *üch*-taan *dis*-ko-uh?   *Onko täällä yhtään diskoa?*

Are there places where you
can hear local folk music?
    voy-ko *taal*-la *mis*-saan *kool*-luh   *Voiko täällä missään kuulla*
    pai-kal-lis-tuh *mu*-seek-ki-uh?   *paikallista musiikkia?*

How much does it cost to get in?
    puhl-yon-ko *on* paa-sü *muhk*-su?   *Paljonko on pääsymaksu?*

cinema	*eh*-lo-ku-vuh-*teh*-*uht*-teh-rri	*elokuvateatteri*
concert	*kon*-sehrrt-ti	*konsertti*
discotheque	*dis*-ko	*disko*
theatre	*teh*-uht-teh-rri	*teatteri*

FRIENDS FOREVER

Traditionally Finns had to make a deal, sinunkaupat, to call each other sinä instead of Te. The deal involved an exchange of names and a formal handshake, after which you were friends forever.

Sports & Interests

What do you do in your spare time?

mi-ta *si*-na *teeht*   *mitä sinä teet*
va-pah-*ai*-kuh-nuh-si?   *vapaa-aikanasi?*

What sport do you play?

mi-ta *urr*-hay-lu-*luh*-yi-uh   *mitä urheilulajia*
huhrr-rruhs-tat?   *harrastat?*

art	*tai*-deh	*taide*
basketball	*ko*-rri-puhl-lo	*koripallo*
boxing	*nürrk*-kay-lü	*nyrkkeily*
cooking	*rru*-uuhn-*lait*-to	*ruuanlaitto*
fishing	*kuh*-luhs-tus	*kalastus*
football	*yuhl*-kuh-puhl-lo	*jalkapallo*
going out	*ul*-ko-nuh-*ka*-ün-ti	*ulkonakäynti*
going to	*eh*-lo-ku-vis-	*elokuvissakäynti*
the cinema	suh-*ka*-ün-ti	
music	*mu*-seek-ki	*musiikki*
photography	*vuh*-lo-kuv-ows	*valokuvaus*
reading	*luk*-ehm-in-ehn	*lukeminen*
shopping	*shop*-pai-luu	*shoppailu*
soccer	*yuhl*-kuh-puhl-lo	*jalkapallo*
sport	*orr*-hay-loo	*urheilu*
the theatre	*the*-uht-teh-rri	*teatteri*
travelling	*muht*-kust-uh-min-ehn	*matkustaminen*
writing	*kirr*-yoy-tuh-min-ehn	*kirjoittaminen*

FINNISH

Festivals

The best film festival is held in Sodankylä (above the Arctic Circle) in June. The longest-established summer events are both held in July: Pori Jazz and the huge festival of world and traditional music at Kaustinen in Ostrobothnia. The biggest rock festivals are held near Turku (Ruisrock, July) and Seinäjoki (Provinssirock, June). One of Europe's leading and most remarkable Chamber Music events is held in Kuhmo on the Eastern border (July). To hear some of the best choirs for which the Nordic countries are famous, go to the Choirs Festival in Vaasa in May.

IN THE COUNTRY
Weather

What's the weather like?	*mi*-ka *on saa ti*-luh?/ *mil*-lai-nehn *saa on?*	*Mikä on säätila?/ Millainen sää on?*
It's ... today.	*ta*-naan *on* ...	*Tänään on* ...
Will it be ...	*on*-ko	*Onko*
tomorrow?	*hu-o*-mehn-nuh?	*huomenna...* ?
cloudy	*pil*-vis-ta	*pilvistä*
cold	*kül*-maa	*kylmää*
foggy	*su*-mu-is-tuh	*sumuista*
forest fire alert	*meht*-sa-*puh*-lo-vuh-rroy-tus	*metsäpalo varoitus*
frosty	*puhk*-kuhs-tuh	*pakkasta*
hot	*koo*-muh	*kuuma*
raining	*suh*-deht-tuh	*sadetta*
snowing	*lun*-tuh/ *lu*-mih-*suh*-deht-tuh	*lunta/ lumisadetta*
summer night frost	*huhl*-lah	*hallaa*
sunny	*ow*-rrin-koys-tuh	*aurinkoista*
thunderstorm	*uk*-kos-tuh	*ukkosta*
sleet	*rran*-taa	*räntää*
windy	*too*-lihs-tuh	*tuulista*

Camping

Am I allowed to camp here?
  sah-ko *taal*-la *lay*-rri-ü-tü-a?   *Saako täällä leiriytyä?*
Is there a campsite nearby?
  on-ko *taal*-la *yos*-sain *la*-hehl-la   *Onko täällä jossain lähellä*
  lay-rrint-tuh-*uh*-luh-eh?   *leirintäaluetta?*

backpack	*rrehp*-pu	*reppu*
can opener	*purr*-kin-*uh*-vah-yuh	*purkinavaaja*
compass	*kom*-puhs-si	*kompassi*
some firewood	*polt*-to-*poo*-tuh	*polttopuuta*
foam mattress	*muh*-koo-*uh*-lou-tuh	*makuualusta*
gas cartridge	*kah*-su-*sa-i*-li-ö	*kaasusäiliö*
mattress	*puht*-yuh	*patja*
penknife	*link*-ku-*vayt*-si	*linkkuveitsi*
rope	*ker*-ü-si	*köysi*
tent	*tehlt*-tuh	*teltta*
torch (flashlight)	*tuhs*-ku-*luhmp*-pu	*taskulamppu*
sleeping bag	*muh*-koo-*pus*-si	*makuupussi*
stove	*rreht*-ki-*kay*-tin	*retkikeitin*
water bottle	*veh*-si-*pul*-lo	*vesipullo*

SIGNS

LEIRINTÄALUE   CAMPING GROUND

FINNISH

FOOD
Some Useful Words & Phrases

breakfast	*ah*-mi-ai-nehn	*aamiainen*
lunch	*loh*-nuhs	*lounas*
early/late dinner	*pa-i*-val-li-nehn/	*päivällinen/*
	il-luhl-li-nehn	*illallinen*

Table for ..., please.
    sah-dahn-ko *meh per-ü*-ta ...?   *Saadaanko me pöytä ... lle?*
Can I see the menu please?
    voyn-ko *mi*-na   *Voinko minä**
    nakh-da *meh*-nun?   *nähdä menun?*
I'd like the set lunch, please.
    sahn-ko *pa-i*-van *loh*-nahn   *Saanko päivän lounaan.*
What does it include?
    mi-ta *see*-hehn *koo*-loo?   *Mitä siihen kuuluu?*
Service is included in the bill.
    tuhrr-yoy-lu *koo*-loo *hin*-tahn *Tarjoilu kuuluu hintaan.*

ashtray	*tuh*-kuh-*kup*-pi	*tuhkakuppi*
the bill	*luhs*-ku	*lasku*
a cup	*kup*-pi	*kuppi*
dessert	*yal*-ki-*rru-o*-kuh	*jälkiruoka*
a drink	*yu-o*-muh	*juoma*
a fork	*hah*-rruk-kuh	*haarukka*
fresh	*tu-o*-rreh	*tuore*
a glass	*luh*-si	*lasi*
a knife	*vayt*-si	*veitsi*
a plate	*low*-tuh-nehn	*lautanen*
spicy	*tu*-li-nehn	*tulinen*
spoiled	*pi*-lahn-tu-nut	*pilaantunut*
a spoon	*lu*-sik-kuh	*lusikka*
sweet	*muh*-keh-uh	*makea*
teaspoon	*teeh*-lu-sik-kuh	*teelusikka*
toothpick	*huhm*-muhs-*tik*-ku	*hammastikku*

Vegetarian Meals

I'm a vegetarian.
   o-lehn *kuhs*-vis-*sü*-er-ya   *Olen kasvissyöjä.*
I don't eat meat.
   ehn sü-er *li*-hah   *En syö lihaa.*
I don't eat chicken, fish, or ham.
   ehn sü-er *kuh*-nah *kuh*-lah   *En syö kanaa, kalaa*
   ehn-ka *kink*-ku-uh   *enkä kinkkua.*

Staple Foods

bread	*lay*-paa	*leipää*
macaroni	*muh*-kuh-rro-ni	*makaroni*
oats	*kow*-rruh	*kaura*
rice	*rree*-si	*riisi*
rye	*rru*-is	*ruis*

Breakfast Menu

butter	*voi*	*voi*
boiled egg	*kay*-teht-tu *mu*-nuh	*keitet munah*
cereal	*hiu*-tuh-lay-ta	*hiualeitä*
cheese	*yuus*-to	*juusto*
coffee	*kuh*-vi	*kahvi*
fresh juice	*tuo*-rreh-*meh*-hu	*tuoremehu*
fried egg	*pais*-teht-tu *mun*-uh	*paisettu munah*
marmalade	*ap*-pehl-see-ni-*hil*-lo	*appelsiinihillo*
milk	*mai*-to	*maito*
oatmeal/porridge	*poo*-rro	*puuro*
orange juice	*ap*-pehl-see-ni-*meh*-hu	*appelsiinimehu*
sugar	*so*-kehrr-i	*sokeri*
tea	*teeh*	*tee*
toast	*pah*-to-*lay*-pa	*paahtoleipä*
yoghurt	*yog*-urrt-ti	*jogurtti*

Meat

beef	*now*-tuh/*harr*-ka	nauta/härkä
chicken	*kuh*-nuh/*brroy*-leh-rri	kana/broileri
ham	*kink*-ku	kinkku
liver	*muhk*-suh	maksa
minced meat	*yow*-heh-*li*-huh	jauheliha
pork	*porr*-sahs/*pos*-su	porsas/possu
reindeer	*po-rron*	poron
sausage	*muhk*-kuh-rruh	makkara
steak	*pih*-vi	pihvi

Seafood

Baltic herring	*si*-luhk-kuh	silakka
fish	*kuh*-lah	kala
herring	*sil*-li	silli
salmon	*loh*-hi	lohi
seafood (not fish)	*a*-ü-rri-ai-nehn	äyriäinen
shrimp	*kuht*-kuh-rruh-pu	katkarapu

Vegetables

cabbage	*kah*-li	*kaali*
carrot	*porrk*-kuh-nuh	*porkkana*
cucumber	*kurrk*-ku	*kurkku*
garlic	*val*-ko-*si*-pu-li	*valkosipuli*
mushroom	*si*-ehn-i	*sieni*
onion	*si*-pu-li	*sipuli*
pea	*hehrr*-ne	*herne*
potato	*peh*-rru-nuh	*peruna*
swede	*luhnt*-tu	*lanttu*
tomato	*to*-maht-ti	*tomaatti*
vegetable	*vi*-huhn-nehs	*vihannes*

Fruit

apple	*om*-ehn-a	*omena*
banana	bah-*nah*-ni	*banaani*
blueberry	*mus*-tik-kuh	*mustikka*
grapes	*vee*-ni-*rü*-pa-leh	*viinirypäle*
lemon	*si*-troo-nah	*sitruuna*
lingonberry	*puo*-kuk-kuh	*puolukka*
orange	*ap*-pehl-see-ni	*appelsiini*
pear	*paa*-rü-na	*päärynä*
pineapple	*uhn*-uhn-uhs	*ananas*
strawberry	*muhm*-sik-kuh	*mansikka*

FINNISH

MENU DECODER

Prepared Food

kiisseli laatikko   kees-seh-li lah-tik-ko
  berry or fruit soup minced vegetables and/or meat,
  baked in an oven
rieska   rrieh-ska
  thin barley bread, like chappati

herkku	hehrrk-ku	tidbits
kastike	kuhs-ti-keh	sauce
keitto/soppa	kayt-toh/sop-puh	soup
munakas	mu-nuh-kuhs	omelette
paistos	pais-tos	scalloped food or pie
pannu	puhn-nu	pan-fried food
piiras	pee-rruhs	pie
salaatti	suh-laht-ti	salad
sämpylä	sam-pü-la	roll
voileipä	voy-lay-pa	open sandwich

'Grilli' Food

The grilli can also be called katukeittiö, snägäri or nakkikioski.
Enormously popular, they prepare fast food by order until the early
hours when everything else is closed. You can also find local specialities, such as mikkeliläinen in Mikkeli.

atomi   uh-to-mi
  meat pie with ham or fried egg
kebakko   keh-buhk-ko
  finger-shaped meat ball
lihapiirakka   li-huh-pee-rruhk-kuh
  pie with meat & rice filling
makkaraperunat   muhk-kuh-rruh-peh-rrun-uht
  sausage with French fries
munakukkaro   mu-nuh-kuk-kuh-rro
  hamburger with fried egg
nakkipiiras   nuhk-ki-pee-rruhs
  small sausage inside a pie
porilainen   po-rri-lai-nehn
  thick slice of sausage in a burger roll

reissumies   *rrays*-su-*miehs*
   two slices of rye bread with filling
vety   *veh*-tü
   meat pie with ham and eggs

camping	*kuhm*-ping	sausage
kalapuikot	*kuh*-luh-pu-i-kot	fish fingers
kuumakoira	koo-muh-*koi*-rruh	hot dog
nakki/nakit	*nuhk*-ki/*nuh*-kit	small sausage
publiski	*pub*-lis-ki	kind of hot dog
ranskalaiset	*rruhn*-skuh-lai-seht	French fries

Other Meals

janssonin kiusaus   *yuhns*-son-in *kiu*-sows
   potato and herring prepared in oven
kaalikääryleet   *kah*-li-*kaa*-rrü-leeht
   minced meat covered with cabbage leaves
kesäkeitto   *ke*-sa-*kayt*-to
   vegetable soup (lit. 'summer soup')
lihamureke   *li*-huh-*mu*-rreh-keh
   seasoned minced meat prepared in the oven
metsästäjänpihvi   *mehts*-ast-ay-an-*pih*-vi
   minced meat with mushroom sauce (lit. 'Hunter's steak')
pyttipannu   *püt*-ti-*puhn*-nu
   ham and potatoes fried in butter

lihapullat	*li*-huh-*pul*-luht	meatballs
lipeäkala	*li*-peh-a-*kuh*-luh	lutefish

Local Specialities

karjalanpiirakka   *kuhrr*-yuh-luhn-*pee*-rruhk-kuh
   rye pie with rice, barley or potato filling (Eastern)
lanttusupikas   *luhnt*-tu-*su*-pik-uhs
   kind of rye pita bread with swede filling (Savo)
lörtsy   *lert*-sü
   flat doughnut with apple or meat filling (Eastern)
kukkonen   *kuk*-ko-nehn
   rice porridge on bread (Karelian)

FINNISH

leipäjuusto   *lay*-puh-*joo*-sto
   flat dessert cheese eaten with jam in the west and north of the
   country (Pohjanmaa & Kainuu)
loimulohi   *loi*-mu-lo-hi
   salmon prepared on open fire (Eastern)
mustamakkara   *mus*-tuh-*muhk*-kuh-rruh
   rice-filled black sausage (Tampere)
muurinpohjalettu   *muu*-rrin-*poh*-yuh-*leht*-tu
   thin large fried pancake (Eastern)
neulamuikut   *neh*-ul-uh-*mu*-ik-ut
   small whitefish (Karelian)
poronkäristys   po-rron-*ka*-rris-tüs
   reindeer casserole (Lapland)
rönttönen   *rrernt*-tern-ehn
   round pie with rye, potato and lingon filling (Kuhmo)
sultsina   *sult*-si-na
   kind of chappati bread stuffed with porridge (Karelian)
vatruska   *vuht*-rrus-kuh
   thick pancake made of mashed potato and wheat flour
   (Karelian)

kukko   *kuk*-ko
   large rye bread loaf with filling (Eastern)

ahvenkukko	*uh*-vehn-*kuk*-ko	pork and perch
kalakukko	*kuh*-luh-*kuk*-ko	pork and fish
lanttukukko	*luhnt*-tu-*kuk*-ko	pork and swede
muikkukukko	*muik*-ku-*kuk*-ko	pork and whitefish
perunakukko	*peh*-rru-nuh-*kuk*-ko	pork and potato

Alcoholic Drinks
kossu   *kos*-su
   another name for strong Koskenkorva spirit
kotikalja   ko-ti-*kuhl*-yuh
   lit. 'home-brewed malt drink'
lonkero   *lon*-keh-rro
   another name for a long gin and lemon
pitkä   *pit*-ka
   large glass of strong beer (lit. 'long')
huurteinen   *huurr*-tay-nehn
   cold beer, (lit. 'frosty')

FINNISH

Non-Alcoholic Drinks

berry drink	*meh*-hu	*mehu*
coffee	*kuh*-vi	*kahvi*
(drinking) water	(*juo*-muh-)*veh*-si	(*juoma*)*vesi*
fresh juice	*tuo*-rreh-*meh*-hu	*tuoremehu*
hot chocolate	*kah*-kao	*kaakao*
iced water	*yaa*-veh-si	*jäävesi*
milk	*mai*-to	*maito*
soft drink	*lim*-on-uh-di/	*limonadi/*
	li-mu/*limp*-puh-rri/	*limu/*
	lim-suh	*limppari/limsa*
soured milk	*pee*-ma	*piimä*
tea	*teeh*	*tee*

Alcoholic Drinks

beer	*o*-lut/*kuhl*-yuh	*olut/kalja*
		(lit. 'malt drink')
cocktail	*drrink*-ki	*drinkki*
light beer	*ük*-kers *o*-lut	*I-olut/ykkös olut*
medium strong beer	*kehs*-ki-*kuhl*-ya/	*keskikalja/*
	kol-mon-ehn/	*kolmonen/*
	kol-mos *o*-lut	*III-olut*
red wine	*pu*-nuh-*vee*-ni	*punaviini*
strong alcohol, vodka	*vee*-nah	*viina*
strong beer	*neh*-los-*o*-lut	*IV A-olut/*
		nelosolut
white wine	*vuhl*-ko-*vee*-ni	*valkoviini*

TIME FOR A COFFEE BREAK

A kahvila is a normal cafe, whereas a kahvio serves coffee in, say, a petrol station or a supermarket, but basically these two are similar places, also called kuppila

FINNISH

AT THE MARKET

Basics

bread	*lay*-paa	leipää
butter	*voi*	voi
cereal	*hiu*-tuh-*lay*-ta	hiualeitä
cheese	*yuus*-to	juusto
chocolate	*suk*-lah	suklaa
eggs	*kuh*-nuh-*mu*-ni-uh	kanamunia
flour	*yow*-ho-uh	jauhoa
margarine	*muhrr*-guhrr-een-i-uh	margariina
marmalade	*ap*-pehl-see-ni-	appelsiinihilloa
milk	*mai*-to	maito
macaroni	*mah*-kah-ro-ni	makaroni
olive oil	*ol*-ee-vi-*erl*-yü-uh	oliiviöljyä
rice	*ree*-si	riisi
sugar	*so*-kehrr-i	sokeri
(drinking) water	(*juo*-muh-)*veh*-si	(juoma)vesi
yoghurt	*yog*-urrt-ti	jogurtti

Meat & Poultry

beef	*now*-tuh/*harr*-ka	nauta/härkä
chicken	*kuh*-nuh/*brroy*-leh-rri	kana/broileri
ham	*kink*-ku	kinkku
pork	*porr*-sahs/*pos*-su	porsas/possu
reindeer	*po*-rron	poron
sausage	*muhk*-kuh-rruh	makkara

FINNISH

AT THE MARKET

Vegetables

cabbage	*kah*-li	kaali
carrot	*porrk*-kuh-nuh	porkkana
cucumber	*kurrk*-ku	kurkku
garlic	val-ko-*si*-pu-li	valkosipuli
mushroom	*si*-ehn-i	sieni
onion	*si*-pu-li	sipuli
pea	*hehrr*-ne	herne
potato	*peh*-rru-nuh	peruna
swede	*luhnt*-tu	lanttu
tomato	*to*-maht-ti	tomaatti
vegetable	*vi*-huhn-nehs	vihannes

Seafood

Baltic herring	*si*-luhk-kuh	silakka
fish	*kuh*-lah	kala
herring	*sil*-li	silli
salmon	*loh*-hi	lohi
seafood (not fish)	a-ü-*rri*-ai-nehn	äyriäinen
shrimp	*kuht*-kuh-rruh-pu	katkarapu

Fruit

apple	*om*-ehn-a	omena
banana	bah-*nah*-ni	banaani
grapes	vee-ni-*rü*-pa-leh	viinirypäle
lemon	si-*troo*-nah	sitruuna
orange	ap-pehl-*see*-ni	appelsiini
pear	*paa*-rü-na	päärynä
strawberry	*muhn*-sik-kuh	mansikka

FINNISH

SHOPPING

bookshop	*kirr*-yuh *kowp*-puh	*kirjakauppa*
camera shop	*vuh*-lo-*ku*-vows-*lee*-keh	*valokuvausliike*
clothing store	*vah*-the-*kowp*-puh	*vaatekauppa*
delicatessen	*hehrrk*-ku-*kowp*-puh	*herkkukauppa*
general store, shop	*kowp*-puh	*kauppa*
laundry	*peh*-su-luh	*pesula*
market	*kowp*-puh *to*-rri/	*kauppatori/*
	muhrrk-ki-nuht/	*mark-kinat/*
	buh-sah-rri	*basaari*
newsagency/	*lekh*-ti *ki*-os-ki/	*lehtikioski/*
stationers	*puh*-peh-rri-*kowp*-puh	*paperikauppa*
pharmacy	*uhp*-teehk-ki	*apteekki*
shoe shop	*kehn*-ka-*kowp*-puh	*kenkäkauppa*
souvenir shop	*muht*-kuh *mu-is*-to	*matkamuisto-*
	müü-ma-la	*myymälä*
supermarket	*su*-pehrr *muhrr*-keht	*supermarket*
vegetable shop	*vi*-huhn-nehs-*kowp*-puh	*vihanneskauppa*

I'd like to buy ...
  huh-lu-ai-sin *os*-tah ...   *Haluaisin ostaa ...*
Do you have others?
  on-ko *tayl*-la *mu-i*-tuh?   *Onko teillä muita?*
I don't like it.
  ehn oy-kayn *pi*-da *see*-ta   *En oikein pidä siitä.*
Can I look at it?
  voyn-ko mi-na *kuht*-so-uh *si*-ta?   *Voinko minä* katsoa sitä?*

I'm just looking.
mi-na *vain kuht*-seh-lehn   *Minä* vain katselen.*

How much is it?
puhl-yon-ko *seh muhk*-sah?   *Paljonko se maksaa?*

Can you write down the price?
voyt-teh-ko *kirr*-yoyt-tah   *Voitteko kirjoittaa*
hin-nuhn?   *hinnan?*

Do you accept credit cards?
voy-ko *muhk*-sah   *Voiko maksaa*
lu-ot-to-korrt-til-luh?   *luottokortilla?*

Could you lower the price?
voyt-ko *luhs*-keh-uh *hin*-tah?   *Voitko laskea hintaa?*

I don't have much money.
mul-luh *ay* o-leh
puhl-yon *rruh*-hah   *Mulla ei ole paljon rahaa.*

Can I help you?
voyn-ko *owt*-tah?   *Voinko auttaa?*

Will that be all?
yuh tu-leeh-ko *moo*-tuh?   *Ja tuleeko muuta?*

Sorry, this is the only one.
ta-ma *on may*-dan *ai*-no-uh   *Tämä on meidän ainoa.*

How much/many do you want?
puhl-yon-ko *si*-na *huh*-lu-uht?/   *Paljonko sinä* haluat?/*
ku-in-kuh *mon*-tuh *pis*-teh-taan?   *Kuinka monta pistetään?*

SAMI HANDICRAFTS

Sami handicrafts, made according to Sami traditions, make great souvenirs. They're made in the traditional way, using traditional materials such as bone, wood, metals and hides. Check for a token with the word Duodji, as this indicates that the item is genuine.

FINNISH

Essential Groceries

I'd like ...	*huh*-lu-ai-sin ...	*Haluaisin ...*
batteries	*puhrr*-is-to-ya	paristoja
bread	*lay*-paa	leipää
butter	*voi*-tuh	voita
cheese	*yuus*-to-uh	juustoa
chocolate	*suk*-lah	suklaa
eggs	*kuh*-nuh-*mu*-ni-uh	kanamunia
flour	*yow*-ho-uh	jauhoa
gas cylinder	*kah*-su-*sai*-li-er	kaasusäiliö
ham	*kink*-ku-uh	kinkkua
honey	*hun*-uh-yah	hunajaa
margarine	*muhrr*-guhrr-een-i-uh	margariinia
marmalade	*ap*-pehl-see-ni-*hil*-lo-uh	appelsiinihilloa
matches	*tu*-li-*tik*-ku-yuh	tulitikkuja
milk	*mai*-to-uh	maitoa
olive oil	*ol*-ee-vi-*erl*-yü-uh	oliiviöljyä
pepper	*pip*-pu-rri-uh	pippuria
salt	*su*-ol-ah	suolaa
shampoo	*sam*-porr-tuh	shampoota
soap	*saip*-pu-uh	saippua
sugar	*so*-kehrr-iuh	sokeria
toilet paper	*vehs*-suh-*puhp*-ehrr-iuh	vessapaperia
toothpaste	*huhm*-muhs-*tuh*-nah	hammastahnaa
washing powder	*peh*-su-*yow*-heht-tuh	pesujauhetta

Souvenirs

some earrings	*korr*-vuh-*ko*-rru-yuh	korvakoruja
some handicrafts	*ka*-si-*ter*-*i*-ta	käsitöitä
necklace	*kow*-luh-*ko*-rru	kaulakoru
pottery	*keh*-rruh-meek-kuh	keramiikka
ring	*sorr*-mus	sormus
rug	*muht*-to/*rrah*-nu	matto/raanu

FINNISH

Clothing

clothing	*vaht*-teeht	vaatteet
coat	*tuhk*-ki	takki
dress	*pu*-ku	puku
jacket	*tuhk*-ki	takki
jumper (sweater)	pu-seh-rro/ vil-luh-*pai*-tuh	pusero/ villapaita
shirt	*pai*-tuh	paita
shoes	kehng-ngat	kengät
skirt	*huh*-meh	hame
trousers	*hoh*-sut	housut

It doesn't/They don't fit.

    ta-ma/*na*-ma ay muhkh-du   *Tämä/Nämä ei mahdu.*

It's too ...   seh on lee-uhn ...   *Se on liian ...*

    big/small   *i*-so/*pi-eh*-ni   *iso/pieni*
    short/long   lü-hüt/*peet*-ka   *lyhyt/pitkä*
    tight/loose   *ki*-rreh-a/*ler-ü*-sa   *kireä/löysä*

Materials

cotton	*poo*-vil-lah	puuvillaa
handmade	ka-sin-*teh*-tüh/ ka-si-*tü-er*-ta	käsintehty/ käsityötä
leather	*nuhkh*-kah	nahkaa
brass	*mehs*-sin-ki-a	messinkiä
gold	*kul*-tah	kultaa
silver	*ho*-peh-ah	hopeaa
flax	*pehl*-luh-vah	pellavaa
pure alpaca	*uhl*-puhk-kah	alpakkaa
silk	*silk*-ki-a	silkkiä
wool	*vil*-lah	villaa

Colours

black	*mus*-tuh	*musta*
blue	*si*-ni-nehn	*sininen*
brown	*rrus*-keuh	*ruskea*
green	*vih*-rreh-a	*vihreä*
orange	*o*-rruhns-si	*oranssi*
pink	*vah*-leh-uhn-*pu*-nai-nehn (*pink*-ki)	*vaaleanpunai-nen* (*pinkki*)
purple	*vi*-o-leht-ti	*violetti*
red	*pu*-nai-nehn	*punainen*
white	*vuhl*-koy-nehn	*valkoinen*
yellow	*kel*-tai-nehn	*keltainen*

Toiletries

comb	*kuhm*-pa	*kampa*
some condoms	*kon*-do-meh-yuh	*kondomeja*
deodorant	*deh-o*-do-rruhnt-ti	*deodorantti*
hairbrush	*hi-us*-huhrr-yuh	*hiusharja*
moisturising cream	*kos*-te-us-*voy*-deh	*kosteusvoide*
razor	*puhrr*-tuh *teh*-rra	*partaterä*
sanitary napkins	*tehrr*-veh-üs-*si*-deh/ *pik*-ku-*hoh*-sun-su-o-yuh	*terveysside/ pikkuhousun-suoja*
shampoo	*suhmp*-porr	*shampoo*
shaving cream	*puhrr*-tuh-*vahh*-to	*partavaahto*
some tampons	*tuhm*-po-neh-yuh	*tamponeja*
tissues	*neh*-na-*lee*-nuh	*nenäliina*
toilet paper	*vehs*-suh-*puh*-peh-rri	*vessapaperi*
toothbrush	*huhm*-muhs-*huhrr*-yuh	*hammasharja*
toothpaste	*huhm*-muhs-*tuh*-nuh	*hammastahna*

Stationery & Publications

map	*kuhrrt*-tuh	*kartta*
newspaper	(*ehng*-luhn-nin	(*englannin*
(in English)	ki-*eh*-li-nehn)	*kielinen*)
	suh-no-muh-*lekh*-ti	*sanomalehti*
novels in English	*ehng*-luhn-nin ki-*eh*-li-si-a	*englannin kielisiä*
	rro-mah-neh-yuh	*romaaneja*
paper	*puh*-peh-rri	*paperi*
pen (ballpoint)	*kü*-na	*kynä*
	(*koo*-luh-*karr*-ki-*kü*-na)	(*kuulakärkikynä*)
scissors	*suhk*-seht	*sakset*

Photography

How much is it to process this film?
puhl-yon-ko *muhk*-sah   *Paljonko maksaa*
keh-hit-taa ta-ma fil-mi?   *kehittää tämä filmi?*

When will it be ready?
kos-kuh seh on *vuhl*-mis?   *Koska se on valmis?*

I'd like a film for this camera.
mi-na *huh*-lu-ai-sin *fil*-min   *Minä* haluaisin filmin*
ta-han *kuh*-meh-rrahn   *tähän kameraan.*

B&W (film)	*mus*-tuh-*vuhl*-koy-nehn	*mustavalkoinen*
camera	*kuh*-meh-rruh	*kamera*
colour (film)	va-rri-*fil*-mi	*värifilmi*
film	*fil*-mi	*filmi*
flash	*suh*-luh-muh	*salama*
lens	ob-yehk-tee-vi/*lins*-si	*objektiivi/linssi*
light meter	*vuh*-lo-tus-*mit*-tuh-rri	*valotusmittari*

HOLY MOLEY!

Pyhä, 'holy', is used of Sundays, religious festivals and holidays like May Day and Midsummer when nearly everything is shut and special timetables apply. The day before these events, often used for heating up the sauna and celebrating, is aatto 'eve'.

FINNISH

Smoking

A packet of cigarettes, please.
sahn-ko *tu*-puhk-kuh   *Saanko tupakka*
uhs-kin *kee*-toss   *askin, kiitos.*

Are these cigarettes strong/mild?
o-vuht-ko *na*-ma *tu*-puh-kuht   *Ovatko nämä tupakat*
vakh-vo-yuh/*mi-eh*-to-yuh?   *vahvoja/mietoja?*

Do you have a light?
on-ko *sul*-luh *tul*-tuh?   *Onko sinulla tulta?*

cigarette papers	*suh*-vu-keh-*puh*-peh-rri-uh	*savuke paperia*
some cigarettes	*tu*-puhk-kah	*tupakkaa*
filtered	*filt*-teh-rri	*filtteri*
lighter	*sü*-tü-tin/*süt*-ka	*sytytin/sytkä* (inf)
matches	*tu*-li-*ti*-kut/*ti*-kut	*tulitikut/tikut* (inf)
menthol	*menth*-torr-li	*menthol*
pipe	*peep*-pu	*piippu*
tobacco	*tu*-puhk-kuh	*tupakka*

Sizes & Comparisons

small	*pi-eh*-ni	*pieni*
big	*soo*-rri/*i*-so	*suuri/iso*
heavy	*pai*-nuh-vuh	*painava*
light	*keh*-vüt	*kevyt*
more	*eh*-nehm-man	*enemmän*
less	*va*-hehm-man	*vähemmän*
too much/many	*lee*-kah/*lee*-uhn *mon*-tuh	*liikaa/liian monta*
many	*mon*-tuh	*monta*
enough	*tuhrr*-peehk-si	*tarpeeksi*
also	*mü*-ers	*myös*
a little bit	*va*-han	*vähän*

FINNISH

ALL DAY

Finns use Päivää! (lit. 'Day!') as a general greeting during most of the day.

HEALTH

Where is the ...?	*mis-sa on ...?*	*Missä on ...?*
doctor	*la-a-ka-rri*	*lääkäri*
hospital	*sai-rrah-luh*	*sairaala*
chemist	*uhp-teehk-ki*	*apteekki*
dentist	*huhm-muhs-laa-ka-rri*	*hammaslääkäri*

I'm/My friend is sick.

o-lehn/üs-ta-va-ni on sai-rruhs   *Olen/Ystäväni on sairas.*

Could I see a female doctor?

on-ko muhkh-dol-lis-tuh   *Onko mahdollista*
saa-duh nais laa-ka-rri?   *saada naislääkäri?*

What's the matter?	*mi-ka on ha-ta-na?*	*Mikä on hätänä?*
Where does it hurt?	*mis-ta suht-too?*	*Mistä sattuu?*
My ... hurts.	*mi-nun ...*	*Minun ...*
	on ki-peh-a	*on kipeä.*

Parts of the Body

ankle	*nilk-kuh*	*nilkka*
arm	*ka-si*	*käsi*
back	*sehl-ka*	*selkä*
chest	*rrin-tuh/rrin-tuh-keh-ha*	*rinta/rintakehä*
ear	*korr-vuh*	*korva*
eye	*sil-ma*	*silmä*
finger	*sorr-mi*	*sormi*
foot	*yuhl-kuh*	*jalka*
hand	*ka-si*	*käsi*
head	*paa*	*pää*
heart	*sü-dan*	*sydän*
leg	*saa-rri*	*sääri*
mouth	*soo*	*suu*
nose	*neh-na*	*nenä*
ribs	*kül-ki-loot*	*kylkiluut*
skin	*i-ho*	*iho*
stomach	*muh-huh/vuht-suh*	*maha/vatsa*
teeth	*huhm-paht*	*hampaat*
throat	*kurrk-ku*	*kurkku*

Ailments

I have (a/an) ...	*mul*-luh *on* ...	*Minulla on* ...
allergy	*uhl*-lehrr-gi-uh	*allergia*
anaemia	*uh*-neh-mi-uh	*anemia*
blister	*rruhk*-ko	*rakko*
burn	*puh*-lo-*vuhm*-muh	*palovamma*
cold	*fluns*-suh	*flunssa*
constipation	*um*-meh-tus-tuh	*ummetusta*
cough	*üs*-ka	*yskä*
diarrhoea	*rri*-pu-li	*ripuli*
fever	*koo*-meht-tuh	*kuumetta*
headache	*paan sarr*-kü	*päänsärky*
hepatitis	*muhk*-suh-*tu*-leh-dus/	*maksatulehdus/*
	heh-puh-teet-ti	*hepatiitti*
indigestion	*rroo*-uhn-*su*-luh-tos	*ruuansulatus-*
	ha-*i*-rri-er	*häiriö*
infection	*tu*-leh-dus	*tulehdus*
influenza	*in*-flu-ehns-suh	*influenssa*
lice	*ta*-*i*-ta	*täitä*
low/high	*muh*-tuh-luh/	*matala/*
blood pressure	*korr*-keh-uh	*korkea*
	veh-rrehn-*pai*-neh	*verenpaine*
sore throat	*kurrk*-ku *ki*-peh-a	*kurkku kipeä*
sprain	*nilk*-kuh	*nilkka*
	nürr-yakh-ta-nüt	*nyrjähtänyt*
stomachache	*muh*-huh *ki*-pu	*mahakipu*
sunburn	*i*-ho *puh*-luh-nut	*iho palanut*
venereal disease	*su*-ku *pu*-*o*-li-*tow*-ti	*sukupuolitauti*

Some Useful Words & Phrases

I'm pregnant.
o-lehn *rruhs*-kah-nuh — *Olen raskaana.*

I'm on the pill.
sü-ern *eh*-pil-lehrr-ayt-a — *Syön e-pillereitä*

I haven't had my period for ... months.
mul-luh *ay* o-leh *ol*-lut *koo*-kow-ti-si-uh ... *koo*-kow-teehn — *Minulla ei ole ollut kuukautisia ...*vowel + *n kuukauteen.*

I have been vaccinated.
  min-ut *on* rro-ko-teht-tu   *Minut on rokotettu.*

I have my own syringe.
  mul-luh *on* o-muh   *Minulla on oma*
  rru-is-ku/*neh-u*-luh   *ruisku/neula.*

I feel better/worse.
  voyn-ti-ni *on* puh-rrehm-pi/   *Vointini on parempi/*
  hu-o-nom-pi   *huonompi.*

I'm ...   o-lehn ...   *Olen ...*
  asthmatic   *uhst*-mah-tik-ko   *astmaatikko*
  diabetic   *di-uh*-beeh-tik-ko   *diabeetikko*
  epileptic   *eh*-pi-lehp-tik-ko   *epileptikko*

I'm allergic to ...   *mi*-na o-lehn   *Minä* olen*
                        uhl-lehrr-gi-nehn ...   *allerginen ...*
  antibiotics   *uhn*-ti-bi-orr-tayl-leh   *antibiooteille*
  penicillin   *peh*-ni-sil-lee-nil-leh   *penisilliinille*

accident   *on*-neht-to-moos   *onnettomuus*
addiction   *rreep*-pu-voos   *riippuvuus*
antiseptic   *uhn*-ti-sehp-ti-nehn   *antiseptinen*
aspirin   *uhs*-pi-rree-ni   *aspiriini*
bandage   *si*-deh   *side*
blood test   *veh*-rri-*ko*-eh   *verikoe*
contraceptive   *ekh*-ka-i-sü-*va*-li-neh *ehkäisyväline*
injection   *rru-is*-keh   *ruiske*
injury   *vuhm*-muh   *vamma*
medicine   *laa*-keh   *lääke*
nausea   *puh*-hoyn-*voyn*-ti   *pahoinvointi*
oxygen   *huhp*-pi   *happi*
some vitamins   *vi*-tuh-mee-neh-yuh   *vitamiineja*

FINNISH

At the Chemist

I need medication for ...
    tuhrr-vit-sen *laa*-ki-tüs-ta ...-uh/   *Tarvitsen lääkitystä ...-a/*
    a *vuhrr*-tehn   *ä varten.*

I have a prescription.
    mi-nul-luh *on* rreh-sehp-ti   *Minulla on resepti.*

At the Dentist

I have a toothache.
    mi-nun *huhm*-muhs-tuh-ni   *Minun hammastani*
    sarr-keeh   *särkee.*

I've lost a filling.
    mi-nul-tuh *on*   *Minulta on irronnut*
    irr-rron-nut *paik*-kuh   *paikka.*

I've broken a tooth.
    mi-nul-tuh *on*   *Minulta on*
    loh-yehn-nut *huhm*-muhs   *lohjennut hammas.*

My gums hurt.
    i-keh-neh-ni *o*-vuht *ki*-peh-uht   *Ikeneni ovat kipeät.*

I don't want it extracted.
    ehn *huh*-lu-uh *eht*-ta   *En halua, että*
    huhm-muhs *poys*-teh-tahn   *hammas poistetaan.*

Please give me an anaesthetic.
    voyt-teh-ko *poo*-dut-tah   *Voitteko puuduttaa.*

SOCK IT TO ME COLD & STEAMY

In the traditional Finnish smoke sauna, savusauna, water is thrown over the log-heated stove to produce steam. You may see people lightly hit themselves with small, leafy birch branches, to improve circulation. Then, it's outside to jump into a lake or the sea, even in winter, when they may first cut a hole in the ice.

FINNISH

TIME & DATES

What date is it today?
   mi-ka *pa-i*-va *ta*-naan on?   *Mikä päivä tänään on?*
What time is it?
   puhl-yon-ko *kehl*-lo on?   *Paljonko kello on?*

It's in the ...	*kehl*-lo on ...	*Kello on ...*
morning	*ah*-mul-luh	*aamulla*
afternoon	*il*-tuh-*pa-i*-val-la	*iltapäivällä*
evening	*il*-luhl-luh	*illalla*

Days of the Week

Monday	*mah*-nuhn-tai	*maanantai*
Tuesday	*tees*-tai	*tiistai*
Wednesday	*kehs*-ki-*veek*-ko	*keskiviikko*
Thursday	*torrs*-tai	*torstai*
Friday	*pehrr*-yuhn-tai	*perjantai*
Saturday	*low*-uhn-tai	*lauantai*
Sunday	*sun*-nun-tai	*sunnuntai*

Months

January	*tuhm*-mi-koo	*tammikuu*
February	*hehl*-mi-koo	*helmikuu*
March	*mah*-lis-koo	*maaliskuu*
April	*huh*-ti-koo	*huhtikuu*
May	*toh*-ko-koo	*toukokuu*
June	*keh*-sa-koo	*kesäkuu*
July	*hay*-na-koo	*heinäkuu*
August	*eh*-lo-koo	*elokuu*
September	*süüs*-koo	*syyskuu*
October	*lo*-kuh-koo	*lokakuu*
November	*muhrr*-rruhs-koo	*marraskuu*
December	*yoh*-lu-koo	*joulukuu*

FINNISH

Seasons

summer	*keh*-sa	*kesä*
autumn	*sük*-sü	*syksy*
winter	*tuhl*-vi	*talvi*
spring	*keh*-vat	*kevät*

Present

today	*ta*-naan	*tänään*
this morning	*ta*-na *ah*-mu-nuh	*tänä aamuna*
tonight	*ta*-na *il*-tuh-nuh	*tänä iltana*
this week	*tal*-la *vee*-kol-luh	*tällä viikolla*
this year	*ta*-na *vu-on*-nuh	*tänä vuonna*
now	*nüt*	*nyt*

Past

yesterday	*ay*-lehn	*eilen*
day before yesterday	*toys*-suh-*pa-i*-va-na	*toissapäivänä*
yesterday morning	*ay*-lehn *ah*-mul-luh	*eilen aamulla*
last night	*vee*-meh *ü-er*-na	*viime yönä*
last week	*vee*-meh *vee*-kol-luh	*viime viikolla*
last year	*vee*-meh *vu-on*-nuh	*viime vuonna*

Future

tomorrow	*hu-o*-mehn-nuh	*huomenna*
day after tomorrow	*ü*-li *hu-o*-mehn-nuh	*ylihuomenna*
tomorrow morning	*hu-o*-mehn *ah*-mu-nuh	*huomen aamuna*
tomorrow afternoon	*hu-o*-mehn-nuh *il*-tuh-*pa-i*-val-la	*huomenna iltapäivällä*
tomorrow evening	*hu-o*-mehn *il*-tuh-nuh	*huomeniltana*
next week	*ehn*-si *vee*-kol-luh	*ensi viikolla*
next year	*ehn*-si *vu-on*-nuh	*ensi vuonna*

FINNISH

During the Day

afternoon	*il*-tuh-*pa-i*-val-la	*iltapäivällä*
dawn	*ah*-mun *koyt*-to	*aamunkoitto*
very early morning	*ah*-mul-luh *ai*-kai-sin	*aamulla aikaisin*
day	*pa-i*-va	*päivä*
early	*ai*-kai-sin	*aikaisin*
midnight	*kehs*-ki-*ü-er*	*keskiyö*
morning	*ah*-mu	*aamu*
night	*ü-er*	*yö*
noon	*kehs*-ki-*pa-i*-va	*keskipäivä*
sunset	*ow*-rring-ngon-*luhs*-ku	*auringonlasku*
sunrise	*ow*-rring-ngon-*noh*-su	*auringonnousu*

NUMBERS & AMOUNTS

0	*nol*-luh	*nolla*
1	*ük*-si	*yksi/yks* (inf)
2	*kuhk*-si	*kaksi/kaks* (inf)
3	*kol*-meh	*kolme*
4	*nehl*-ya	*neljä*
5	*vee*-si	*viisi/viis* (inf)
6	*koo*-si	*kuusi/kuus* (inf)
7	*sayt*-seh-man	*seitsemän/seittemän* (inf)
8	*kuhkh*-dehk-suhn	*kahdeksan/kasi/kaheksan* (inf)
9	*ükh*-dehk-san	*yhdeksän/ysi/yheksän* (inf)
10	*küm*-meh-nehn	*kymmenen*
11	*ük*-si-*toys*-tuh	*yksitoista*
12	*kuhk*-si-*toys*-tuh	*kaksitoista*
13	*kol*-meh-*toys*-tuh	*kolmetoista*
14	*nehl*-ya-*toys*-tuh	*neljätoista*
15	*vee*-si-*toys*-tuh	*viisitoista*
20	*kuhk*-si-*küm*-mehn-ta	*kaksikymmentä*
30	*kol*-meh-*küm*-mehn-ta	*kolmekymmentä*
40	*nehl*-ya-*küm*-mehn-ta	*neljäkymmentä*
50	*vee*-si-*küm*-mehn-ta	*viisikymmentä*
60	*koo*-si-*küm*-mehn-ta	*kuusikymmentä*
70	*sayt*-seh-man-*küm*-mehn-ta	*seitsemänkymmentä*

80	*kuhkh*-dehk-suhn-*küm*-mehn-ta	*kahdeksankymmentä*
90	*ükh*-dehk-san-*küm*-mehn-ta	*yhdeksänkymmentä*
100	*suh*-tuh	*sata*
1000	*tu*-huht	*tuhat*
one million	*mihl*-yorr-nuh	*miljoona*
1st	*ehm*-sin-ma-i-nehn/*eh*-kuh	*ensimmäinen/eka* (inf)
2nd	*toy*-nehn/*to*-kuh	*toinen/toka* (inf)
3rd	*kol*-muhs	*kolmas*
1/4	*nehl*-yas *o*-suh/*nehl*-yan-nehs	*neljäsosa/ neljännes*
1/3	*kol*-muhs *o*-suh/ *kol*-muhn-nehs	*kolmasosa/ kolmannes*
1/2	*pu-o*-leht	*puolet*
3/4	*kol*-meh *nehl*-yas *o*-sah	*kolme neljäsosaa*

Some Useful Words

Enough!	*rreet*-taa!	*Riittää!*
a little	*va*-han	*vähän*
double	*tup*-luht	*tuplat*
a dozen	*tu*-si-nuh	*tusina*
few	*huhrr*-vuh	*harva*
less	*va*-hehm-man	*vähemmän*
many	*mon*-tuh/*mo*-ni-uh	*monta/monia*
more	*eh*-nehm-man	*enemmän*
once	*kehrr*-rruhn	*kerran*
a pair	*puh*-rri	*pari*
percent	*prro*-sehnt-ti	*prosentti*
some	*yo*-tuh-kin/ *va*-han/ *yon*-kin *vehrr*-rruhn	*jotakin/ vähän/ jonkin verran*
too much	*lee*-kah/*lee*-uhn *puhl*-yon	*liikaa/liian paljon*
twice	*kuhkh*-dehs-ti/ *kuhk*-si *kehrr*-tah	*kahdesti/ kaksi kertaa*

FINNISH

ABBREVIATIONS

ALE – alennusmyynti	sale
ark – arkisin	on weekdays (Monday to Saturday)
as. – asema	station
eiL – ei lauantaisin	not on Saturdays
EP – erikoispikajuna	special express train
EU – Euroopan Unioni	European Union
FIN/fi.	Official abbreviations of Finland
Hki	Helsinki
IC	Intercity
k. – katu	Street
ke – keskiviikko	Wednesday
-kj. – -kuja	Alley
kpl – kappaletta	amount of something, or pieces
la – lauantai	Saturday
ma – maanantai	Monday
mk – markka	Finnish marks (currency)
n:o/nro – numero	number
pe – perjantai	Friday
PL – Postilokero	PO Box
puh./p. – puhelinnumero	telephone number
-t. – -tie	Road
SRM – Suomen Retkeilymajajärjestö	Finnish YHA
SS	(in timetables only) when there are two consecutive holidays, buses run on the second holiday only
su – sunnuntai	Sunday
ti – tiistai	Tuesday
Tku	Turku
to – torstai	Thursday
Tre	Tampere
v. – vuonna	year
VR – Valtion Rautatiet	National Railways

FINNISH

EMERGENCIES

Help!
uh-pu-uh!
Apua!

It's an emergency!
ta-ma on ha-ta-tuh-pows!
Tämä on hätätapaus!

There's been an accident!
nüt on *tuh*-puh-tu-nut
on-neht-to-moos!
Nyt on tapahtunut onnettomuus!

Call a doctor!
kut-su-kah *laa*-ka-rri!
Kutsukaa lääkäri!

Call an ambulance!
soyt-tuh-kah *uhm*-bu-luhns-si!
Soittakaa ambulanssi!

I've been raped.
mi-nut on rrais-kuht-tu
Minut on raiskattu.

I've been robbed.
mi-nut on *rrü-ers*-teht-tü
Minut on ryöstetty.

Call the police!
soyt-tuh-kah po-lee-si!
Soittakaa poliisi!

Where is the police station?
mis-sa on po-lee-si *uh*-seh-muh?
Missä on poliisiasema?

Go away!
meh-neh *poys!//ha-i*-vü!
Mene pois!/Häivy! (inf)

I'll call the police!
mi-na *kut*-sun po-lee-sin!
Minä* kutsun poliisin!

Thief!
vuh-rruhs!
Varas!

I'm/My friend is ill.
mi-na o-lehn/
mun *üs*-ta-va on *sai*-rruhs
Minä* olen/
Minun ystäväni on sairas.

I'm lost.
mi-na o-lehn *ehk*-sü-nüt
Minä* olen eksynyt.

SIGNS

POLIISI
POLICE

POLIISIASEMA
POLICE STATION

FINNISH

Where are the toilets?
mis-sa *on vehs*-suh?   *Missä on vessa?*

Could you help me please?
voyt-teh-ko (*voyt*-ko) *owt*-tah   *Voitteko (voitko) auttaa.*

Could I please use the telephone?
sahn-ko *ka-üt*-taa   *Saanko käyttää*
pu-heh-lin-tuh?   *puhelinta?*

I'm sorry. I apologise.
oh-lehn *puh*-hoyl-luh-ni.   *Olen pahoillani.*
püü-dan *uhn*-teehk-si   *Pyydän anteeksi.*

I didn't realise I was doing
anything wrong.
ehn tuh-yun-nut *teh*-keh-va-ni   *En tajunnut tekeväni*
mi-taan *vaa*-rrin   *mitään väärin.*

I didn't do it.
ehn teh-nüt *si*-ta   *En tehnyt sitä.*

I wish to contact my
embassy/consulate.
huh-lu-uhn *ot*-tah *ükh*-teh-üt-ta   *Haluan ottaa yhteyttä*
soorr-*la*-heh-tüs-ter-ni/   *suurlä-hetystööni/*
kon-su-laht-teen   *konsulaattiin.*

I speak English.
pu-hun *ehng*-luhn-ti-uh   *Puhun englantia.*

I have medical insurance.
mi-nul-luh *on vuh*-koo-tus   *Minulla on vakuutus.*

FINNISH

My possessions are insured.
    tuh-vuh-rruh-ni *on*   *Tavarani on*
    vuh-koo-teht-tu   *vakuutettu.*

My ... was stolen.
    mi-nul-tuh *on*   *Minulta on*
    vuh-rruhs-teht-tu   *varastettu ...*

I've lost my...	*mi*-na *o*-lehn	*Minä* olen*
	hu-kuhn-nut ...	*hukannut ...*
bag	*lowk*-ku-ni	*laukkuni*
handbag	*ka*-si -*owk*-ku-ni	*käsilaukkuni*
money	*rruh*-huh-ni	*rahani*
travellers	*muht*-kuh-*shehk*-ki-ni	*matkashekkini*
cheques		
passport	*puhs*-si-ni	*passini*

ICELANDIC

ICELANDIC

QUICK REFERENCE

Hello.	hahl-loh	Halló.
Goodbye.	blehs	Bless.
Yes./No.	yow/nay	Já./Nei.
Excuse me. (forgive me)	ahf-sahk-ith	Afsakið.
Sorry.	myehrr thi-kirr thahth layht	Mér þykir það leitt.
Please.	gyer-thö svo vehl	Gjörðu svo vel.
Thank you.	tahk firr-irr	Takk fyrir.
You're welcome.	ehk-ehrrt ahth thahk-ah	Ekkert að þakka.
I'd like ...	gyai-ti yehkk fayn-khith ...	Gæti ég fengið ...
a one-way ticket	mith-ah/ahth-rrah layth-in-ah	miða/aðra leiðina
a return ticket	mith-ah/bowth-ahrr layth-irr	miða/báðar leiðir

I (don't) understand.
 yehkk skil (ehk-i)   Ég skil (ekki).
Do you speak English?
 tah-lahrr thoo ehn-skö?   Talar þú ensku?
Where is ...?
 kvahrr ehrr ...?   Hvar er ...?
Go straight ahead.
 fahrr-thö baynt owfrram   Farðu beint áfram.
Turn left/right.
 baykh-thö til vinst-rri/haikh-rri. Beygðu til vinstri/hægri.
Do you have any rooms available?
 ehrr-ö hehrr-behrr-khi leörs?   Eru herbergi laus?
I'm looking for a public toilet.
 yehkh ehrr ahth lay-tah ahth   Ég er að leita að
 ahl-mehn-inkhs-sahl-ehrr-dni   almenningssalerni.

1	aydn	einn	6	sehks	sex
2	tvayrr	tveir	7	syer	sjö
3	thrreer	þrír	8	owt-dah	átta
4	fyoh-rrirr	fjórir	9	nee-ö	níu
5	fimm	fimm	10	tee-ö	tíu

ICELANDIC

Icelandic is a North Germanic language. Iceland was settled primarily by Norwegians in the 9th and 10th centuries. By the 14th century Icelandic (Old Norse) and Norwegian had grown apart considerably. This was due to changes in Norwegian, while Icelandic changed remarkably little through the centuries. In fact, it has an unbroken literary tradition, dating from about 1100. The treasures of the Sagas and the poetic Edda, written about 700 years ago, can be enjoyed by a modern-day speaker of Icelandic.

Icelanders are proud of their literary heritage. They are particularly conservative when it comes to the written word. Borrowed vocabulary is ill tolerated and the policy of keeping the language pure is very strong. After all, Icelandic is spoken by a mere 280,000 people, and outside pressures on the language, in these times of easy travel and worldwide communications, are enormous.

The practice of creating neologisms (new words) instead of adopting foreign words is well established in Iceland. Neologisms, such as útvarp, 'radio', sjónvarp, 'television', tölva, 'computer', and þota, 'jet', are just a few that have become part of the Icelandic vocabulary in the last 50 years.

Icelanders are a rather informal people. A person is very rarely addressed by title and/or surname. Icelanders use the ancient patronymic system, where son, 'son' or dóttir, 'daughter' is attached to the genitive form of the father's or, less commonly, the mother's, first name. The telephone book entries are listed according to first names.

As one might expect, most Icelanders speak English, and often as many as three or four other languages, although among themselves they only converse in Icelandic. Your efforts to speak Icelandic will most certainly be met with great enthusiasm.

STRESS

Stress is generally on the first syllable.

ICELANDIC

PRONUNCIATION

Double consonants are pronounced as such. The Icelandic alphabet consists of 33 letters: a, á, b, d, ð, e, é, f, g, h, i, í, j, k, l, m, n, o, ó, p, r, s, t, u, ú, v, x, y, ý, z, þ, æ, ö.

Pronunciation is given in the general pronunciation guide at the front of this book, with the following exceptions:

Diphthongs

ICELANDIC	GUIDE	SOUNDS
au	eör	there is no equivalent sound in English

Semiconsonants

é	yeh	as in the 'ye' in 'yes'

Consonants

f	f	as in English. When between vowels or at the end of a word it's pronounced as 'v'. When followed by *l* or *n* it's pronounced as 'b'.
g	g	as the 'g' in 'get'
	kh	between vowels or before *r* or *ð*, *g* has a guttural sound, as the 'ch' in Scottish 'loch'
h	h	as in English, except when followed by *v*, when it's pronounced as 'k'
þ	th	as the 'th' in 'thin'
ð	th	as the 'th' in 'lather'

PRONOUNS		
SG		
I	yehkh	ég
you	<u>th</u>oo	þú
she/he/it		
	hoon/hahn/<u>th</u>ah<u>th</u>	hún/hann/það
PL		
we	vith	við
you (pol)	<u>th</u>oo	þú
you (pl)	<u>th</u>ith	þið
they	<u>th</u>ayrr/<u>th</u>airr/<u>th</u>eör	þeir/þær/þau

MIND YOUR þ's & ð's

Remember, the Icelandic letter þ, represented as <u>th</u> in the pronunciation guide, is pronounced as the 'th' in 'thin', while ð, represented as th, is pronounced as the 'th' in 'lather'.

ICELANDIC

GREETINGS & CIVILITIES
Top Useful Phrases

Hello.	hahl-loh	*Halló.*
Goodbye.	blehs	*Bless.*
Yes./No.	yow/nay	*Já./Nei.*
Excuse me. (forgive me)	ahf-sahk-ith	*Afsakið.*
Sorry.	myehrr <u>th</u>i-kirr <u>th</u>ahth layht	*Mér þykir það leitt.*
Please.	gyer-thö svo vehl	*Gjörðu svo vel.*
Thank you.	tahk firr-irr	*Takk fyrir.*
That's fine.	ahlt ee lai-i	*Allt í lagi.*
You're welcome.	ehk-ehrrt ahth <u>th</u>ahk-ah	*Ekkert að þakka.*

Forms of Address

Madam/Mrs	frroo	*frú*
Sir/Mr	hehrr-rrah	*herra*
Miss	frrer-kehn	*fröken*
companion/friend	vin-ko-nah/vin-örr	*vinkona/vinur* (f/m)

Greetings

Good morning.	gohth-ahn dai-in	*Góðan daginn.*
Good afternoon.	gohth-ahn dai-in	*Góðan daginn.*

Good evening/night.
khot kverld/khoh-th-ah noht   *Gott kvöld./Góða nótt.*
How are you?
kvehrr-dnikh heh-vörr <u>th</u>oo <u>th</u>ahth?   *Hvernig hefur þú það?*

Well, thanks.	khot tahk	*Gott, takk.*

ICELANDIC

SMALL TALK
Meeting People

What's your name?	kvahth hay-tirr-<u>thoo</u>?	*Hvað heitir þú?*
My name is ...	yehkh hay-ti ...	*Ég heiti ...*
I'm pleased to meet you.	kon-dö sail/saidl	*Komdu sæll/sæll.* (f/m)

> **DID YOU KNOW ...** Family names are illegal in Iceland, unless they were adopted before the Personal Names Act which was passed by Iceland's parliament, Alþing, in 1925.

Nationalities

Where are you from? kvahth-ahn ehrrt <u>thoo</u>? *Hvaðan ert þú?*

I'm from ...	yehkh ehrr frrow ...	*Ég er frá ...*
Australia	owst-rrah-lee-ö	*Ástralíu*
Canada	kaha-nah-dah	*Kanada*
England	aynkh-lahn-di	*Englandi*
Ireland	eer-lahn-di	*Írlandi*
New Zealand	nee-ah syow-lahn-di	*Nýa Sjálandi*
Scotland	skot-lahn-di	*Skotlandi*
the USA	bahnd-ah-rree-kyö-nöm	*Bandaríkjunum*

Age

How old are you?
    kvahth ehrr-dö ger-möl/gahm-ahdl?   *Hvað ertu gömul/gamall?* (f/m)
I'm ... years old.
    yehkh ehrr ... ow-rrah   *Ég er ... ára.*

ICELANDIC

Occupations

What do you do?	kvahth gehrr-irr thoo?	*Hvað gerir þú?*
I'm (a/an) ...	yehkh ehrr ...	*Ég er ...*
in business	ee vith-skift-öm	*í viðskiptum*
journalist	frryeht-ah-mahth-örr	*fréttamaður*
manual worker	vehrrk-ah-mahth-örr	*verkamaður*
nurse	hyook-rrön-ahrr-frraith-ing-örr	*hjúkrunarfræðingur*
office worker	skrrif-stof-ö-mahth-örr	*skrifstofumaður*
scientist	vee-sin-dah-mahth-örr	*vísindamaður*
student	nowms-mahth-örr	*námsmaður*
teacher	kehn-ah-rri	*kennari*
waiter	thyohdn/ thyohn-ös-dö-stool-kah	*þjónn/ þjónustustúlka*
writer	rrit-hehrf-önd-örr	*rithöfundur*

Religion

What is your religion?
kvehrr-ahrr trroo-ahrr ehrrt thoo? — *Hverrar trúar ert þú?*

I'm not religious.
yehkh ehrr ehk-i trroo-öth/ trroo-ahth-örr — *Ég er ekki trúuð/ trúaður.* (f/m)

I'm ...	yehkh ehrr ...	*Ég er ...*
Buddhist	boo-dah-trroo-ahrr	*búddatrúar*
Catholic	kah-tholsk/ kah-thol-skörr	*kaþólsk/ kaþólskur* (f/m)
Christian	krrist-in-ahrr trroo-ahrr	*kristinnar trúar*
Hindu	hin-doo trroo-ahrr	*hindú trúar*
Jewish	gith-ing-örr	*gyðingur*
Muslim	moo-hah-mehths-trroo-ahrr	*múhameðstrúar*

ICELANDIC

Family

Are you married?
    ehrrt-ö gift/gift-örr?

Ert þú gift/giftur? (f/m)

I'm single.
    yehkh ehrr ayn-hlayp/
    ayn-hlayp-örr

*Ég er einhleyp/
einhleypur.* (f/m)

I'm married.
    yehkh ehrr gift/gift-örr

Ég er gift/giftur. (f/m)

How many children do you have?
    kvahth owt thoo merg berdn?

Hvað átt þú mörg börn?

I don't have any children.
    yehkh ow ayn-gin berdn

Ég á engin börn.

Do you have a boyfriend/girlfriend?
    owt thoo kairr-ahs-dah/
    kairr-ös-dö?

*Átt þú kærasta/
kærustu?*

brother	brroh-thirr	*bróðir*
children	berdn	*börn*
daughter	doht-irr	*dóttir*
family	fyerl-skil-dah	*fjölskylda*
father	fahth-irr	*faðir*
grandfather	ah-vi	*afi*
grandmother	ahm-mah	*amma*
husband	ay-in-mahth-örr	*eiginmaður*
mother	mohth-irr	*móðir*
sister	sist-irr	*systir*
son	son-örr	*sonur*
wife	ay-in-ko-nah	*eiginkona*

Kids' Talk

How old are you?
    kvahth ehrr-tö ger-möl/
    gahm-ahdl?

*Hvað ertu gömul/
gamall?* (f/m)

When's your birthday?
    kveh-nayrr owh-tö ahm-mai-li?

Hvenær áttu afmæli?

What do you do after school?
    kvath geh-rrirr-thoo ehf-tirr skoh-la?

Hvað gerirðu eftir skóla?

Do you have a pet at home?
owt-tö gyai-lö-deer hehi-ma?   *Áttu gæludýr heima?*

I have a ...	yehkh ow ...	*Ég á ...*
bird	fögl	*fugl*
budgerigar	pow-va-geörk	*páfagauk*
canary	kah-nah-rree-fögl	*kanarífugl*
cat	kerht	*kött*
dog	hönd	*hund*
frog	frrosk	*frosk*

Feelings

I (don't) like ...
yehkh ehrr (ehk-i) hrri-vin ahv ...   *Ég er (ekki) hrifinn af...*
I'm cold/hot.
myehrr ehrr kahlt/hayt   *Mér er kalt/heitt.*

I'm ...	yehkh ehrr ...	*Ég er ...*
angry	rrayth/rrayth-örr	*reið/reiður* (f/m)
grateful	<u>th</u>ahk-lowt/ <u>th</u>ahk-law-törr	*þakklát/* *þakklátur* (f/m)
happy	ow-naikhth/ aw-naikhth-örr	*ánægð/* *ánægður* (f/m)
hungry	sveörnkh/svown-görr	*vöng/svangur* (f/m)
sad	hrrig/hrrig-görr	*hrygg/hryggur* (f/m)
tired	<u>th</u>rrayt/<u>th</u>rrayt-örr	*þreytt/þreyttur* (f/m)
well	frreesk/frrees-görr	*frísk/frískur* (f/m)

I'm worried.
yehkh hehf ow-hig-yörr   *Ég hef áhyggjur.*
I'm sorry. (condolence)
myehrr <u>th</u>ik-irr <u>th</u>ahth layht   *Mér þykir það leitt.*

Some Useful Phrases

Sure.	viss-ö-lehkh-ah	*Vissulega.*
Just a minute.	bee-dö ahth-ayns	*Bíddu aðeins.*
Good luck!	gown-gi <u>th</u>yehrr vehl!	*Gangi þér vel!*

ICELANDIC

ICELANDIC

BREAKING THE LANGUAGE BARRIER

Do you speak English?
    tah-lahrr <u>th</u>oo ehn-skö?   *Talar þú ensku?*
Does anyone speak English?
    tah-lahrr ayn-kvehrr ehn-skö?   *Talar einhver ensku?*
I speak a little Icelandic.
    yehkh tah-lah svoh lit-lah   *Ég tala svolitla*
    ees-lehn-skö   *íslensku.*
I don't speak ...
    yehkh tah-lah ehki ...   *Ég tala ekki ...*
I (don't) understand.
    yehkh skil (ehk-i)   *Ég skil (ekki).*
Could you speak more slowly please?
    gyai-tirr <u>th</u>oo tah-lah<u>th</u>   *Gætir þú talað*
    svo-lee-tith haikh-ahrr?   *svolítið hægar?*

Could you repeat that?
    gyai-tirr <u>th</u>oo   *Gætir þú*
    ehn-dörr-tehk-ith <u>th</u>eht-ah?   *endurtekið þetta?*
How do you say ...?
    kvehrr-dnikh say-irr   *Hvernig segir*
    mah<u>th</u>-örr ...?   *maður ...?*
What does ... mean?
    kvahth <u>th</u>eeth-irr?   *Hvað þýðir ...?*

I speak ...	yehkh tah-lah ...	*Ég tala ...*
English	ehn-skö	*ensku*
French	frrern-skö	*frönsku*
German	<u>th</u>ees-kö	*þýsku*
Italian	ee-terl-skö	*ítölsku*
Spanish	spern-skö	*spönsku*

BODY LANGUAGE

Icelandic society is small and it's possible to recognise Icelanders abroad because of the way they watch people directly, even in a big city, as if they expect to meet someone they know. Icelanders also tend – or at least used to, they're becoming more sophisticated now – to stare at foreigners.

Possibly the reason Icelanders crowd each other is that they have a different sense of bodily space from other westerners. An interesting idea, which may also account for the large number of automobile collisions, is that they have a different sense of 'car space' – a sense that there is much more space around themselves and their cars than in fact there is.

In the old Icelandic rural culture, people used to kiss a lot when they met. Nowadays most people only shake hands or put a little kiss on one cheek only. Icelanders are rather reserved and it takes time to get to know them, but they're known for their hospitality and they're used to fixing things (for themselves or anyone who needs it), so even if they don't seem very friendly you may experience their helpfulness all the same.

SIGNS

AÐGANGUR BANNAÐUR	NO ENTRY
BANNAÐ	PROHIBITED
FARANGUR	BAGGAGE COUNTER
FRÁTEKIÐ	RESERVED
INNGANGUR/INN	ENTRANCE
INNRITUN	CHECK-IN COUNTER
KONUR/KARLAR	LADIES/GENTLEMEN
NEYÐARÚTGANGUR	EMERGENCY EXIT
OPIÐ/LOKAÐ	OPEN/CLOSED
ÓKEYPIS	FREE ADMISSION
REYKINGAR BANNAÐAR	NO SMOKING
SÍMI	TELEPHONE
SNYRTING	TOILETS
TOLLUR	CUSTOMS
UPPLÝSINGAR	INFORMATION
ÚTGANGUR/ÚT	EXIT

ICELANDIC

PAPERWORK

address	hay-mil-is-fowng	*heimilisfang*
age	ahld-örr	*aldur*
birth certificate	faith-ing-ahrr-vot-orrth	*fæðingarvottorð*
car owner's title	ayg-nahrr-voth-orrth	*eignarvottorð*
car registration	biv-rrayth-ah-skoth-ön	*bifreiðaskoðun*
customs	todl-skoth-ö	*tollskoðun*
date of birth	faith-ing-ahrr-dahkh-örr	*fæðingardagur*
driver's licence	er-kö-skeer-tay-ni	*ökuskírteini*
identification	skil-rree-ki	*skilríki*
immigration	vehkh-ah-brryehvs-skoth-ön	*vegabréfsskoðun*
name	nahbn	*nafn*
nationality	thyohth-ehrr-dni	*þjóðerni*
passport	vehkh-ah-brryehv	*vegabréf*
(number)	(s-noo-ehrr)	*(snúmer)*
place of birth	faith-ing-ahrr-stahth-örr	*fæðingarstaður*
profession	aht-vin-ah	*atvinna*
reason for travel	ow-staith-ah fehrrth-ah-lahkhs-ins	*ástæða ferðalagsins*
religion	trroo	*trú*
sex	kin	*kyn*
tourist card	fehrrth-ah-mahn-ah-spyahld	*ferðamannaspjald*
visa	vehkh-ah-brryehvs-ow-rrit-ön	*vegabréfsáritun*

GETTING AROUND

What time does the ... leave/arrive?	kveh-nayrr fehrr/ keh-mörr ...?	*Hvenær fer/ kemur ...?*
aeroplane	flökh-vyehl-in	*flugvélin*
boat	bow-törr-in	*báturinn*
(city)bus	vahgn-in	*vagninn*
tram	sporr-vahgn-in	*sporvagninn*

ICELANDIC

Directions

Where is ...?
    kvahrr ehrr ...?   *Hvar er ...?*
How do I get to ...?
    kvehrr-dnikh kyehmst   *Hvernig kemst*
    yehkh til ...?   *ég til ...?*
Is it far from here?
    ehrr thahth lowngt hyehth-ahn? *Er það langt héðan?*
Can I walk there?
    ehrr thahth ee gern-gö fai-rri? *Er það í göngufæri?*
Can you show me (on the map)?
    geh-törr thoo seent myehrr   *Getur þú sýnt mér*
    (ow korrt-in-ö)?   *(á kortinu)?*
I want to go to ...
    migh lown-gahrr ahth   *Mig langar að*
    fah-rrah til ...   *fara til ...*
Go straight ahead.
    fahrr-thö baynt owfrram   *Farðu beint áfram.*
It's two blocks down.
    thahth ehrr tvaym-örr   *það er tveimur*
    gert-öm nehth-ahrr   *götum neðar.*

Turn left/right	baykh-thö til	*Beygðu til*
at the ...	vinst-rri/haikh-rri vith ...	*vinstri/hægri við ...*
next corner	nais-dah horrdn	*næsta horn*
traffic lights	öm-fehrrth-ahrr-ljohs-in	*umferðarljósin*
behind	firr-irr ahft-ahn	*fyrir aftan*
in front of	firr-irr frrahm-ahn	*fyrir framan*
far	lownkht ee börr-dö	*langt í burtu*
near	now-laikht	*nálægt*
opposite	ow moh-ti	*á móti*

ICELANDIC

Booking Tickets

Where can I buy a ticket?
kvahrr geht yehkh kayft mith-ah? *Hvar get ég keypt miða?*

I want to go to ...
yehkh vil fah-rrah til ... *Ég vil fara til ...*

Do I need to book?
<u>thahrrf</u> yehkh ahth pahn-tah? *Parf ég að panta?*

I'd like to book a seat to ...
gyai-ti yehkh pahn-tahth fahrr til ... *Gæti ég pantað far til ...*

I'd like ...	gyai-ti yehkh fayn-khith ...	*Gæti ég fengið ...*
a one-way ticket	mith-ah/	*miða/*
	ahth-rrah layth-in-ah	*aðra leiðina*
a return ticket	mith-ah/	*miða/*
	bowth-ahrr layth-irr	*báðar leiðir*
two tickets	tvo mith-ah	*tvo miða*
a student's fare	nowms-mahn-	*námsmanna-*
	ah-mith-ah	*miða*
1st class	firrst-ah fahrr-rreem-i	*fyrsta farrými*
2nd class	ahn-ahth fahrr-rreem-i	*annað farrými*

Is it completely full?
ehrr ahl-vehkh fölt? *Er alveg fullt?*

Can I get a stand-by ticket?
gyeht yehkh fayn-gith *Get ég fengið*
forr-fahd-lah-mith-ah? *forfallamiða?*

Can I have a refund?
gyeht yehkh fayn-gith *Get ég fengið*
ehnd-örr-grrayths-lö? *endurgreiðslu?*

DID YOU KNOW ... There are no trains in Iceland, but there are plenty of buses!

SIGNS

BROTTFÖR	DEPARTURES
KOMA	ARRIVALS
MIÐASALA	TICKET OFFICE
STRÆTISVAGNABIÐSTÖÐ	BUS STOP
STÖÐ	STATION
TÍMAÁÆTLUN	TIMETABLE

Air

Is there a flight to ...?
    ehrr flo-yith til ...?   *Er flogið til ...?*
How long does the flight take?
    kvahth ehrr <u>the</u>h-tah lowngt flüg? *Hvað er þetta langt flug?*

airport tax	flü-vadla-skah-türr	*fluhvallaskattur*
boarding pass	brroht-fah-rrahrr-spyald	*brottfaraspjald*

Bus

Where is the bus stop?
    kvahrr ehrr bith-sterth-in?   *Hvar er biðstöðin?*
Which bus goes to ...?
    kvahth-ah vahkhn fehrr til ...?   *Hvaða vagn fer til ...?*
Could you let me know
when we get to ...?
    gyai-tirr <u>thoo</u> low-tith mikh   *Gætir þú látið mig*
    vi-tah <u>the</u>hkh-ahrr   *vita þegar*
    vith kom-öm til ...?   *við komum til ...?*
I want to get off!
    yehkh vil fah-rrah oot!   *Ég vil fara út!*

What time is	kveh-nairr	*Hvenær*
the ... bus?	kehm-örr ... vahgn-in?	*kemur ... vagninn?*
first	firrst	*fyrst*
next	naist	*næst*
last	seeth-ahst	*síðast*

ICELANDIC

Taxi

Please take me to ...
gyai-tir thoo ehkith myehrr til ...?   *Gætir þú ekið mér til ...?*

How much does it cost to go to ...?
kvahth kost-ahrr aht   *Hvað kostar að*
fah-rrah til ...?   *fara til ...?*

Here is fine, thank you.
hyehrr-dnah ehrr ow-gyait tahk   *Hérna er ágætt, takk.*

The next street to the left/right.
nais-tah gah-tah til   *Næsta gata til*
vinst-rri/haikh-rri   *vinstri/hægri.*

Continue.	hahl-dö ow-frrahm	*Haltu áfram.*
Stop here!	stahn-sah hyehrr-dnah!	*Stansa hérna!*

Car

Where's the next petrol station?
kvahrr ehrr nais-dah   *Hvar er næsta*
behn-seen-sterth?   *bensínstöð?*

The battery is flat.
gaym-irr-in ehrr   *Geymirinn er*
rahv-mahgns-leös   *rafmagnslaus.*

The radiator is leaking.
vahs-kahs-in leh-körr   *Vatnskassinn lekur.*

I have a flat tyre.
thahth ehrr   *Það er*
sprroon-ghith hyow myer   *sprungið hjá mér.*

It's overheating.
hahn heh-vör of-hit-nath   *Hann hefur ofhitnað.*

It's not working.
hahn virrk-ahrr ehk-i   *Hann virkar ekki.*

ICELANDIC

air (for tyres)	loft (ee dehk)	*loft (í dekk)*
battery	rrahf-gay-mirr	*rafgeymir*
brakes	brrehm-sörr	*bremsur*
clutch	koop-leeng	*kúpling*
driver's licence	ehr-kö-skeer-tay-ni	*ökuskírteini*
engine	vyehl	*vél*
lights	lyohs	*ljós*
radiator	vahss-kahss-i	*vatnskassi*
road map	vehkh-ah-korrt	*vegakort*
tyres	dehk	*dekk*
windscreen	frrahm-rrooth-ah	*framrúða*

SIGNS

ALLUR AKSTUR BANNAÐUR	NO ENTRY
BIÐSKYLDA	GIVE WAY
BLÝLAUST	UNLEADED
EÐLILEGT	NORMAL
EINSTEFNA	ONE WAY
ENGIN BÍLASTÆÐI	NO PARKING
SJÁLFSAFGREIÐSLA	SELF SERVICE
STANS	STOP
SUPER	SUPER
VERKSTÆÐI	GARAGE
VÉLVIRKI	MECHANIC
VIÐGERÐIR	REPAIRS

ACCOMMODATION

Where is a ...	kvahrr ehr ...	*Hvar er ...*
hotel?	ho-tehl?	*hótel?*
cheap	oh-deert	*ódýrt*
nearby	now-laikht	*nálægt*
clean	hrraynt	*hreint*

What is the address?
kvahth ehrr hay-mil-is-fown-gith? *Hvað er heimilisfangið?*
Could you write the address, please?
gyai-tirr <u>thoo</u> skrrif-ahth *Gætir þú skrifað*
nith-örr hay-mil-is fown-gith? *niður heimilisfangið?*

At the Hotel

ICELANDIC

Do you have any rooms available?
ehrr-ö hehrr-behrr-khi leörs? *Eru herbergi laus?*

I'd like ...	gyai-ti yehkh fayn-khith ...	*Gæti ég fengið ...*
a single room	ayn-stahk-lings-hehrr-behrr-khi	*einstaklingsherbergi*
a double room	tvehg-yah-mahn-ah-hehrr-behrr-gi	*tveggjamannaherbergi*
a room with a bathroom	hehrr-behrr-khi mehth bahth-i	*herbergi með baði*
to share a dorm	ahth day-lah hehrr-behrr-khi mehth erth-rröm	*að deila herbergi með öðrum*
a bed	rroom	*rúm*

I'm going to stay for ...	yehkh vehrrth ee ...	*Ég verð í ...*
one day	aydn dahkh	*einn dag*
two days	tvo dahkh-ah	*tvo daga*
one week	ay-nah vi-kö	*eina viku*

Sorry, we're full.
myehrr thi-kirr thahth layt thahth ehrr födl boh-kahth *Mér þykir það leitt, það er fullbókað.*

How long will you be staying?
kvahth ait-lahrr thoo ahth veh-rra layn-gi? *Hvað ætlar þú að vera lengi?*

How many nights?
kvahth mahrr-gahrr nai-törr? *Hvað margar nætur?*

How much is it per night/ per person?
kvahth kost-ahrr noht-in firr-irr mahn-in? *Hvað kostar nóttin fyrir manninn?*

Requests & Complaints

Can I see it?
mow yehkh syow thahth?
Má ég sjá það?

Are there any other/cheaper rooms?
eh-rrö nok-örr ern-örr/
oh-deer-ah-rri hehrr-behrr-gi?
*Eru nokkur önnur/
ódýrari herbergi?*

Is there a reduction for
students/children?
ehrr ahf-slowt-örr firr-irr
nowms-mehn/berdn?
*Er afsláttur fyrir
námsmenn/börn?*

Does it include breakfast?
ehrr morrkh-ön-maht-örr
in-i-fahl-in?
*Er morgunmatur
innifalinn?*

It's fine, I'll take it.
thahth ehrr ow-gyait
yehkh fai thahth
*Það er ágætt,
ég fæ það.*

I'm not sure how long I'm staying.
yehkh ehrr ehk-i viss öm
kvahth yehkh vehrrth layn-gi
*Ég er ekki viss um
hvað ég verð lengi.*

Where is the bathroom?
kvahrr ehrr
bahth-hehrr-behrr-gith?
*Hvar er
baðherbergið?*

May I leave these in your safe?
mow yehkh gay-mah theh-dah
ee er-ikh-is-hohl-vi?
*Má ég geyma þetta
í öryggishólfi?*

Is there somewhere to wash clothes?
ehrr ayn-kvehrrs-stahth-ahrr
haikht ahth thvo thvoht?
*Er einhversstaðar
hægt að þvo þvott?*

Can I use the kitchen?
mow yehkh no-tah
ehld-hoo-sith?
*Má ég nota
eldhúsið?*

Can I use the telephone?
mow yehkh no-tah
see-mahn?
*Má ég nota
símann?*

ICELANDIC

Some Useful Words & Phrases

We're leaving now/tomorrow.

vith ehrr-öm aht fah-rrah
noo-nah/ow morr-goon

*Við erum að fara
núna/á morgun.*

I'd like to pay the bill.

yehkh vil borr-khah
rraykn-inkh-in

*Ég vil borga
reikninginn.*

bathroom	bahth-hehrr-behrr-gi	*baðherbergi*
bed	rroom	*rúm*
blanket	teh-bi	*teppi*
clean	hrraydn	*hreinn*
dirty	ow-hrraydn	*óhreinn*
double bed	tvee-brrayt rroom	*tvíbreitt rúm*
electricity	rrahv-mahgn	*rafmagn*
excluded	firr-irr öt-ahn	*fyrir utan*
fan	vif-dah	*vifta*
included	in-i-fahl-ith	*innifalið*
key	li-kidl	*lykill*
lift (elevator)	lif-dah	*lyfta*
light bulb	lyow-sah-peh-rrah	*ljósapera*
a lock	lows	*lás*
mirror	spay-idl	*spegill*
pillow	kod-di	*koddi*
quiet	hlyoht	*hljótt*
sheet	lahk	*lak*
shower	störr-dah	*sturta*
soap	sow-pah	*sápa*
toilet	kloh-seht/sahl-ehrr-dni	*klósett/salerni*
toilet paper	klow-seht-pah-peer	*klósettpappír*
towel	hahnd-klai-thi	*handklæði*
(cold/hot) water	(kahlt/hayt) vahtn	*(kalt/heitt) vatn*
window	khlö-khi	*gluggi*

AROUND TOWN

English	Pronunciation	Icelandic
I'm looking for a/the ...	yehkh ehrr ahth lay-tah ahth ...	*Ég er að leita að ...*
bank	bown-kah	*banka*
city centre	mith-bai-nöm	*miðbænum*
... embassy	... sehn-di-rrow-thi-nö	*... sendiráðinu*
hotel	hoh-tehl-i-nö mee-nö	*hótelinu mínu*
market	mahrrk-ahth-nöm	*markaðnum*
police	lerkh-rrehgl-ö-ni	*lögreglunni*
post office	pohst-hoos-i-nö	*pósthúsinu*
public toilet	ahl-mehn-inkhs-sahl-ehrr-dni	*almennings-salerni*
telephone centre	seem-sterthin-i	*símstöðinni*
tourist information office	öp-lees-een-gah-thjohn-öst-ö firr-irr fehrrth-ah-fohlk	*upplýsinga-þjónustu fyrir ferðafólk*

What time does it open/close?
  kveh-nairr ehrr op-nahth/
  lo-kahth?

*Hvenær er opnað/
lokað?*

What street/suburb is this?
  kvahth-ah gah-tah/
  kvehrr-vi ehrr <u>th</u>eh-dah?

*Hvaða gata/
hverfi er þetta?*

For directions, see the Getting Around section, page 207.

SIGNS

FARFUGLAHEIMILI	YOUTH HOSTEL
GISTIHEIMILI	GUESTHOUSE
GISTIHÚS	MOTEL
HÓTEL	HOTEL

ICELANDIC

ICELANDIC

At the Post Office

I'd like	yehkh ait-lah	*Ég ætla*
to send a ...	ahth sehn-dah ...	*að senda ...*
letter	brreef	*bréf*
postcard	korrt	*kort*
parcel	pahk-ah	*pakka*
telegram	skay-ti	*skeyti*

I'd like some stamps.
   yehkh aid-lah ahth fow   *Ég ætla að fá*
   nok örr frree-mehrr-gi   *nokkur frímerki.*

How much does it cost
to send this to ...?
   kvahth kos-dahrr ahth   *Hvað kostar að*
   sehn-dah <u>th</u>eh-dah til ...?   *senda þetta til ...?*

an aerogram	flökh-brreef	*flugbréf*
airmail	flookh-pohst-örr	*flugpóstur*
envelope	öm-slahkh	*umslag*
mailbox	pohst-kahss-i	*póstkassi*
registered mail	ow-birrth-ahrr-pohst-örr	*ábyrgðarpóstur*
surface mail/sea mail	syoh-pohst-örr	*sjópóstur*

Telephone & Internet

I want to ring ...
   yehkh <u>th</u>ahrrv ahth hrreen-gya ...   *Ég þarf að hringja ...*
The number is ...
   noo-mehrr-ith ehrr ...   *Númerið er ...*
How much does a three-minute
call cost?
   kvahth kos-dahrr   *Hvað kostar*
   <u>th</u>rri-khjah-meen-oot-nah   *þriggja mínútna*
   sahm-tahl?   *samtal?*
How much does each extra minute cost?
   kvahth kos-dahrr   *Hvað kostar*
   kvehrr meen-oo-tah?   *hver mínúta?*

ICELANDIC

I'd like to speak to (Jón Pálsson).
    gyai-ti yehkh fayn-gith aht   *Gæti ég fengið að*
    tahlah vith (yohn powls-sohn)?   *tala við (Jón Pálsson)?*
I want to make a reverse-charges
phone call.
    yehkh ait-lah aht hrreen-khyah   *Ég ætla að hringja*
    okh vith-tahk-ahn-di borr-gahrr   *og viðtakandi borgar.*

It's engaged.   <u>th</u>ahth ehrr ow tah-li   *Það er á tali.*
I've been cut off.   <u>th</u>ahth slit-nahth-i   *Það slitnaði.*

Where can I get Internet access?
    kvahr gyeht yehkh fayn-gyith   *Hvar get ég fengið*
    aht noh-tah in-tehrr-neh-tith?   *að nota internetið?*
I'd like to send an email.
    Mig lown-guhrr til aht   *Mig langar til að*
    sen-duh terl-vü-pohst   *senda tölvupóst.*

At the Bank

I want to exchange some money/
travellers cheques.
    yehkh <u>th</u>ahrrf aht skif-dah   *Ég þarf að skipta*
    pehn-inkh-öm/fehrrth-ah-tyehköm   *peningum/ferðatékkum.*
What is the exchange rate?
    kvehrrt ehrr gehngith?   *Hvert er gengið?*
How many kronas per dollar?
    kvahth ehrr-ö mahrr-gahrr   *Hvað eru margar*
    krrohn-örr ee dol-ah-rrah-nöm?   *krónur í dollaranum?*

bank notes	sehth-lahrr	*seðlar*
cashier	gyahld-kehrr-i	*gjaldkeri*
coins	smow-mint	*smámynt*
credit card	grrayth-slö-korrt	*greiðslukort*
exchange	skif-dah	*skipta*
loose change	rrayth-ö-fyeh	*reiðufé*
signature	ön-dirr-skrrift	*undirskrift*

ICELANDIC

INTERESTS & ENTERTAINMENT
Sightseeing

Do you have a guidebook/local map?
owt-ö fehrrth-ah-hahnd-bohk/   *Áttu ferðahandbók/*
korrt ahv stahth-nöm?   *kort af staðnum?*

What are the main attractions?
kvahth ehrr mahrrk-vehrrt   *Hvað er markvert*
ahth syow?   *að sjá?*

What is that?
kvahth ehrr <u>th</u>eh-dah?   *Hvað er þetta?*

How old is it?
kvahth ehrr <u>th</u>ahth gahm-ahlt?   *Hvað er það gamalt?*

Can I take photographs?
mow yehkh tah-kah mind-irr?   *Má ég taka myndir?*

What time does it open/close?
klök-ahn kvahth op-nahrr/   *Klukkan hvað opnar/*
lok-ahrr?   *lokar?*

Going Out

What's there to do in the evenings?
kvahth ehrr haikht ahth   *Hvað er hægt að*
gyeh-rra ow kverl-din?   *gera á kvöldin?*

Is there a local entertainment guide?
ehrr til baik-leen-görr öm   *Er til bæklingur um*
skiehm-tah-nirr hyehrr   *skemmtanir hér*
ow stahth-nöm?   *á staðnum?*

I feel like	mig lowngarr	*Mig langar*
going to a/the ...	til ahth fahrrah ...	*til að fara ...*
cinema	ee bee-oh	*í bíó*
opera	ee oh-peh-rrö-nah	*í óperuna*
theatre	ee layk-hoo-sith	*í leikhúsið*
bar	ow bahrr	*á bar*
cafe	ow kahffi-hoos	*á kaffihús*
concert/gig	ow tohn-lay-kah	*á tónleika*
disco	ow diskoh-tehk	*á diskótek*
nightclub	ow nai-törr-kloobb	*á næturklúbb*
restaurant	ow vay-teen-gah-hoos	*á veitingahús*

ICELANDIC

Sports & Interests

What sports do you play?
    kvah-thah ee-<u>th</u>rroh-tirr   *Hvaða íþróttir*
    stön-dahrr <u>th</u>oo?   *stundar þú?*

What are your interests?
    kvehrr eh-rrö <u>th</u>een   *Hver eru þín*
    ow-högah-mowl?   *áhugamál?*

art	lis-tirr	*listir*
basketball	ker-fö-bol-ti	*körfubolti*
chess	skowk	*skák*
collecting things	ahth sab-nah hlö-töm	*að safna hlutum*
dancing	ahth dahnsah	*að dansa*
food	mah-törr	*matur*
football	fohd-bol-ti	*fótbolti*
hiking	geörn-gö-fehrr-thirr	*gönguferðir*
martial arts	bahrr-dahgah-ee-<u>th</u>rroh-tirr	*bardagaíþróttir*
meeting friends	ahth hih-tah vi-ni	*að hitta vini*
movies	kvik-min-dirr	*kvikmyndir*
music	tohn-list	*tónlist*
nightclubs	nai-törr-kloob-bahrr	*næturklúbbar*
photography	lyohs-min-dön	*ljósmyndun*
reading	lehs-törr	*lestur*
shopping	ahth fah-rrah ee boo-thirr	*að fara í búðir*
skiing	ahth fah-rrah ow skee-thi	*að fara á skíði*
swimming	sönd	*sund*
tennis	tehn-nis	*tennis*
travelling	ahth fehrr-thahst	*að ferðast*
TV/videos	syohn-vahrrp/	*sjónvarp/*
	mind-bernd	*myndbönd*
visiting friends	ahth haym-sai-kyah vi-ni	*að heimsækja vini*

Festivals

During Þorri, the fourth month of winter (from mid-January to mid-February), it's common to hold a party called þorrablót, where people gather to sing and eat traditional Icelandic food.

Seven weeks before Easter is bolludagur 'bun-day', so-called because people are supposed to have all kinds of buns on this day. Children wake their parents in the morning with bolluvöndur, a decorated birch-rod. The last day before the beginning of the traditional Lenten fast (Shrove Tuesday) is sprengidagur. The name refers to sprenging (explosion) because people are supposed to eat as much saltkjöt og baunir (salted lamb/mutton, served with split pea soup) as they can, even so much that they may 'explode'.

A very old tradition in Iceland is celebrating the first day of summer, sumardagurinn fyrsti. It's an old custom to give sumargjöf (a summer gift) to close relatives.

Sautjándi júní, 17 June, is Iceland's National Independence Day. It's celebrated in front of the Parliament where the fjallkona, a female symbol of Iceland (usually a young actress in national costume), recites a poem.

The most important day of preparation for Jólin (Christmas), is 23 December, called þorláksmessa after the only officially canonised Icelandic saint. The main Christmas celebration starts with a Christmas church service on Christmas Eve, aðfangadagskvöld, followed by a family dinner. To wish someone a merry Christmas you say gleðileg jól

ICELANDIC

IN THE COUNTRY
Weather

What's the weather like?
kvehrr-dnikh ehrr vehth-rrith?
Hvernig er veðrið?

It's ... today.	vehth-rrith ehrr ... ee dahkh	*Veðrið er ... í dag.*
Will it be ... tomorrow?	vehrrth-örr ... ow morr-khön?	*Verður ... á morgun?*
cloudy	skee-yahth	*skýjað*
cold	kahlt	*kalt*
hot	hayt	*heitt*
raining	rrikh-neenkh	*rigning*
snowing	snyohrr	*snjór*
sunny	sohl-skin	*sólskin*
windy	kvahst	*hvasst*

Camping

Am I allowed to camp here?
mow yehk tyahl-dah hyehrr? *Má ég tjalda hér?*
Is there a campsite nearby?
ehrr tyahld-staith-i hyehrr *Er tjaldstæði hér*
now-laikht? *nálægt?*

backpack	bahk-po-ki	*bakpoki*
can opener	doh-sah-op-nah-rri	*dósaopnari*
firewood	ehld-i-vith-örr	*eldiviður*
gas cartridge	gahs-koo-törr	*gaskútur*
mattress	dee-nah	*dýna*
penknife	vah-sah-hneev-örr	*vasahnífur*
rope	snai-rri	*snæri*
tent (pegs)	tyahld(-hai-lahrr)	*tjald(hælar)*
torch/flashlight	vah-sah-lyohs	*vasaljós*
sleeping bag	svehbn-po-ki	*svefnpoki*
stove	ehld-ah-veel	*eldavél*
water bottle	vahs-flahs-ga	*vatnsflaska*

ICELANDIC

FOOD

breakfast	morr-gön-mah-törr	*morgunmatur*
lunch	how-day-is-maht-örr	*hádegismatur*
dinner	kverld-maht-örr	*kvöldmatur*

Table for ..., please.
gyeht yehkh fayn-gith ...	*Get ég fengið ...*
mah-nah borrth?	*manna borð?*

Can I see the menu please?
gyeht-yehkh fayn-gith ahth	*Get ég fengið að*
syow maht-sehth-il-in?	*sjá matseðilinn?*

What does it include?
kvahth ehrr in-i-fahl-ith?	*Hvað er innifalið?*

Is service included in the bill?
ehrr thyoh-nös-dah in-i-fahl-in?	*Er þjónusta innifalin?*

ashtray	ers-kö-bah-khi	*öskubakki*
the bill	rrayk-ninkh-örr-in	*reikningurinn*
a cup	bod-li	*bolli*
a drink	drrik-örr	*drykkur*
a fork	khahf-adl	*gaffall*
a glass	khlahs	*glas*
a knife	hnee-vörr	*hnífur*
a plate	disk-örr	*diskur*
a spoon	skayth	*skeið*
teaspoon	teh-skayth	*teskeið*

Vegetarian Meals

I'm a vegetarian.
yehkh ehrr grrain-meht-is-ai-tah	*Ég er grænmetisæta.*

I don't eat meat.
yehkh borr-thah ehk-i kyert	*Ég borða ekki kjöt.*

Staple Foods & Condiments

bread	brreörth	*brauð*
cream	rryoh-mi	*rjómi*
eggs	ehg	*egg*

ICELANDIC

fish	fis-körr	*fiskur*
fruit	ow-vehg-stirr	*ávextir*
ketchup	toh-mahts-soh-sah	*tómatsósa*
meat	kyert	*kjöt*
mustard	sin-nehp	*sinnep*
pepper	pi-pahrr	*pipar*
potatoes	kahrr-ter-blörr	*kartöflur*
rice	hrrees-grryohn	*hrísgrjón*
salt	sahlt	*salt*
sauce	soh-sah	*sósa*
seasoning	krridd	*krydd*
sugar	si-görr	*sykur*
vegetables	grrain-meh-ti	*grænmeti*

Breakfast Menu

boiled egg	so-thith ehg	*soðið egg*
bread	brreörth	*brauð*
bread roll	rroon-stih-kyi	*rúnstykki*
butter	smyeörrr	*smjör*
cereal	morr-gün-korrdn	*morgunkorn*
cheese	ostörr	*ostur*
coffee	kahf-fi	*kaffi*
fruit juice	ow-vahgs-tah-sah-vi	*ávaxtasafi*
honey	hö-nowng	*hunang*
jam	söl-tah	*sulta*
marmalade	mahrr-meh-lah-thi	*marmelaði*
milk	myohlk	*mjólk*
muesli	müsl	*müsl*
oatmeal	hahv-rrah-grrehü-türr	*hafragrautur*
orange juice	ah-pehl-see-n-sah-vi	*appelsínsafi*
sour milk	soorr-myohlk	*súrmjólk*
(type of yoghurt)		
sugar	si-görr	*sykur*
tea	teh	*te*
toast	rris-tahth brrehüth	*ristað brauð*
yoghurt	yoh-goorrt	*jógúrt*

ICELANDIC

Meat & Poultry

beef	neör-tah-kyert	*nautakjöt*
chicken	kyooh-kleen-görr	*kjúklingur*
ham	skin-kah	*skinka*
lamb	lahm-bah-kyert	*lambakjöt*
pork	svee-nah-kyert	*svínakjöt*
reindeer	hrrayn-dee-rrah-kyert	*hreindýrakjöt*
sausage	pil-sah	*pylsa*
turkey	kahl-koodn	*kalkúnn*

Fish

cod	thorr-skörr	*þorskur*
haddock	ee-sah	*ýsa*
halibut	loo-thah	*lúða*
herring	seeld	*síld*
lobster	hö-mahrr	*humar*
(smoked) salmon	(rraykh-dörr) lahks	*(reyktur) lax*
scallop	her-rr-pö-dis-körr	*hörpudiskur*
shrimp	rrai-kyah	*rækja*

Fruit

apples	ehb-li	*epli*
apricots	ah-prree-koh-sörr	*apríkósur*
bananas	bah-nah-nahrr	*bananar*
blueberries	blow-behrr	*bláber*
crowberries	krrai-kyi-behrr	*krækiber*
grapes	veen-behrr	*vínber*
lemon	see-trroh-nah	*sítróna*
oranges	ah-pehl-see-nörr	*appelsínur*
peaches	fehrrs-kyörr	*ferskjur*
pears	peh-rrörr	*perur*
pineapple	ah-nah-nahs	*ananas*
strawberries	yahrr-thahrr-behrr	*jarðarber*

ICELANDIC

Vegetables

cabbage	kveet-kowl	*hvítkál*
carrots	göl-rrai-törr	*gulrætur*
cauliflower	blohm-kowl	*blómkál*
cucumber	goorr-kah	*gúrka*
garlic	kveet-leör-körr	*hvítlaukur*
green peas	grrai-nahrr beör-nirr	*grænar baunir*
green pepper	grrain pah-prri-kah	*græn paprika*
lettuce	sah-lahd	*salat*
mushrooms	sveh-pirr	*sveppir*
onion	leör-körr	*laukur*
potatoes	kahrr-ter-blörr	*kartöflur*

Desserts

biscuits	smow-ker-körr/kehgs	*smákökur/kex*
cake	kahkah	*kaka*
fruit	ow-vehgs-tirr	*ávextir*
ice cream	ees/rryoh-mah-ees	*ís/rjómaís*
pancakes	per-nö-ker-körr	*pönnukökur*
pudding	boo-theen-görr	*búðingur*
chocolate	sooh-kö-lah-thi	*súkkulaði*
stewed fruit	ow-vahg-stah-grreör-törr	*ávaxtagrautur*

Drinks

coffee	kahf-fi	*kaffi*
(white/black)	(mehth myolk/svahrrt)	*(með mjólk/svart)*
fruit juice	ow-vahgs-tah-sah-vi	*ávaxtasafi*
ice	klah-kyi	*klaki*
soft drinks	gos-drrih-kyirr	*gosdrykkir*
tea	teh	*te*
water	vahdn	*vatn*

> **DID YOU KNOW ...** Alcohol was prohibited in Iceland in 1912. Beer wasn't legalised again until 1 March 1989, now known as Bjórdagurinn, 'beer day'.

ICELANDIC

MENU DECODER

Starters

flatkökur	flahd-ker-körr	thin unsweet bread
og *hangikjöt*	og hown-gyi-kyert	made of rye flour, eaten with butter and slices of smoked lamb
grafinn lax	grrahv-inn lahks	grav lax
harðfiskur	harrth-fis-görr	dried fish, stockfish

Main Meals

bjúgu   byoo-ö
   smoked minced meat sausage. Served hot or cold with
   potatoes in white sauce.

flatkökur   flaht-ker-körr
   rye pancakes, also popular with *hangikjöt*

hangikjöt   hown-gyi-kyert
   smoked lamb, leg or shoulder. Served hot or cold, with
   potatoes in bechamel sauce and green peas. Also popular
   as a luncheon meat.

harðfiskur   hahrrth-fis-körr
   dried fish; haddock, cod or catfish. It does not require
   cooking but is enjoyed as snack food, often spread with a
   little butter.

kjötsúpa   kyert-soo-pah
   soup, made of a small quantity of vegetables and a large
   quantity of lamb meat and rice. Always served hot.

ICELANDIC

saltkjöt   sahlt-kyert
   salted lamb/mutton, served with potatoes or swede turnips
   and often accompanied by split pea soup
slátur   slow-törr
   blood and liver puddings. Prepared in the months of Sep-
   tember and October, when slaughtering is at its peak. Blood
   pudding, blóðmör (blohth-mehrr), and liver pudding,
   lifrarpylsa (liv-rrahrr-pil-sah), are eaten sliced hot or cold.
   Traditionally, the *slátur* that could not be eaten fresh was
   pickled in whey and enjoyed throughout the winter months.
svið   svith
   singed sheep heads. Eaten hot or cold, with either plain
   boiled potatoes, mashed potatoes or swede turnips. The
   pressed and gelled variety is popular for packed lunches.
   seytt rúgbrauð saiht rroo-brreörth cooked rye bread,
   moist and chewy. Popular with hangikjöt.

Desserts
pönnukökur með   pern-nö-ker-körr mehth
sykri eða   si-grri ehth
með sultu og rjóma   mehth söl-tö og rryo-mah
   pancakes with sugar or with jam and cream
skyr   skyirr
   dairy product similar to yoghurt, it's very low in fat. Eaten
   as dessert with sugar and milk and with fresh berries,
   when in season.

Alcoholic Drinks

aqua vitae (brandy)	brreh-ni-veen	*brennivín*
beer	byohrr	*bjór*
cognac	ko-nee-ahk	*koníak*
liqueur	lee-kyer	*líkjör*
whisky	vis-kee	*whisky*
red/ white wine	rreörth-veen/ kveet-veen	*rauðvín/ hvítvín*

ICELANDIC

SHOPPING

general store, shop booth		*búð*
laundry	thvo-hdah-hoos	*þvottahús*
market	mahrr-kahth-örr	*markaður*
newsagency/	blah-thah-sah-lah/	*blaðasala/*
stationers	boh-kah-booth	*bókabúð*
pharmacy	ahp-oh-tehk	*apótek*
shoe shop	skoh-booth	*skóbúð*
supermarket	stohrr-mahrr-kahth-örr	*stórmarkaður*
vegetable shop	grrain-meht-is-booth	*grænmetisbúð*

I'd like to buy ...
mikh lown-khahrr   *Mig langar*
ahth keör-pah ...   *að kaupa ...*
Can you write down the price?
gyeht-örr-ö skrri-vahth   *Gætir þú skrifað*
nith-örr vehrrthith?   *niður verðið?*

Essential Groceries

batteries	rrahv-hler-thör	*rafhlöður*
bread	brreörth	*brauð*
butter	smyer-rr	*smjör*
cheese	os-törr	*ostur*
chocolate	sooh-kö-lah-thi	*súkkulaði*
eggs	ehg	*egg*
flour	kvay-ti	*hveiti*
gas cylinder	gahs-hihl-kyi	*gashylki*
honey	hö-nowng	*hunang*
marmalade	mahrr-meh-lah-thi	*marmelaði*
matches	ehld-spee-törr	*eldspýtur*
milk	myohlk	*mjólk*
olive oil	oh-lee-vö-o-lee-ö	*ólífuolíu*
pepper	pi-pahrr	*pipar*
salt	sahlt	*salt*
shampoo	syahm-poh	*sjampó*

ICELANDIC

soap	sow-pö	*sápu*
sugar	si-körr	*sykur*
toilet paper	kloh-seht-pah-pirr	*klósettpappír*
toothbrush	tahn-bös-di	*tannbursti*
washing powder	tvoh-tah-dooft	*þottaduft*

Souvenirs

Typically Icelandic souvenirs include lopapeysur (lo-pah-pay-sör), woollen sweaters and all kinds of woollen articles; pieces of jewellery made of icelandic resources, such as chains with a lava cube covered with gold; body lotion and other cosmetics made of the clay from the Blue Lagoon; Icelandic brennivín (brrehn-ni-veen), schnapps, not least hvannarótar-brennivín (kvahn-nah-rroh-tahrr-brrehn-ni-veen), schnapps flavoured with angelica.

Clothing

clothing	fert	*föt*
coat	kow-pah	*kápa*
dress	kyohdl	*kjóll*
jacket	yah-kyi	*jakki*
jumper/sweater	pay-sah	*peysa*
shirt	skyirr-tah	*skyrta*
shoes	skohrr	*skór*
skirt	pils	*pils*
trousers	bög-sörr	*buxur*

Materials

cotton	boh-mödl	*bómull*
handmade	hahnd-gyehrrt	*handgert*
leather	leh-thörr	*leður*
brass	oorr mehs-eeng	*messing*
gold	oorr göd-li	*gulli*
silver	oorr sil-vrri	*silfri*
flax	herrr	*hör*
silk	sil-kyi	*silki*
wool	ödl	*ull*

ICELANDIC

Colours

black	svahrrt	*svart*
blue	blowt	*blátt*
brown	brroont	*brúnt*
green	grraint	*grænt*
red	rreört	*rautt*
white	kveet	*hvítt*
yellow	gölt	*gult*

Toiletries

comb	grray-thah	*greiða*
condoms	smok-ahrr	*smokkar*
deodorant	svi-tah-likt-ahrr-ay-thirr	*svitalyktareyðir*
razor	rrahk-vyehl	*rakvél*
sanitary napkins	der-mö-bin-di	*dömubindi*
shampoo	syahm-poh	*sjampó*
shaving cream	rrahk-krrehm	*rakkrem*
soap	sow-pah	*sápa*
tampons	vaht-tahp-ahrr/	*vatttappar/*
	tahm-poh-nahrr	*tampónar*
tissues	brryehv-thörr-körr	*bréfþurkur*
toilet paper	kloh-seht-pah-peer	*klósettpappír*
toothpaste	tahn-krrehm	*tannkrem*

Stationery & Publications

map	korrt	*kort*
newspaper	dakh-blahth	*dagblað*
(in English)	(ow ehn-skö)	*(á ensku)*
paper	pah-peer	*pappír*
pen (ballpoint)	pehn-ni/koo-lö-pehn-ni	*penni/kúlupenni*

ICELANDIC

Photography

How much is it to process this film?
kvahht kos-tahrr ath
frrahm-kahdlah thehs-sah fil-mö? *Hvað kostar að framkalla þessa filmu?*

When will it be ready?
kveh-nairr vehrr- thörr
hoon til-boo-in? *Hvenær verður hún tilbúin?*

I'd like a film for this camera.
mikh vahn-tahrr fil-mö ee
thehs-sah min-dah-vyehl *Mig vantar filmu í þessa myndavél.*

camera	min-dah-vyehl	*myndavél*
develop	frrahm-kad-lah	*framkalla*
film	fil-mah	*filma*
ready	til-boo-ith	*tilbúið*

Smoking

A packet of cigarettes, please.
aydn see-gahrr-eh-dö-pahk-ah
tahk *Einn sígarettupakka, takk.*

Do you have a light?
ow-dö ehld? *Áttu eld?*

cigarette papers	see-gahrr-eh-dö-brryehv	*sígarettubréf*
cigarettes	see-gahrr-eh-dörr	*sígarettur*
filtered	mehht see-ö/fil-tehrr	*með síu/filter*
lighter	kvay-kyah-rri	*kveikjari*
matches	ehld-speet-örr	*eldspýtur*
menthol	mehnt-ohl	*mentól*
tobacco	toh-bahk	*tóbak*

Sizes & Comparisons

big	stohrrt	*stórt*
small	lee-tith	*lítið*
heavy	thoont	*þungt*
light	lyeht	*létt*
less	mi-nah	*minna*
more	may-rrah	*meira*

ICELANDIC

HEALTH

Where is a ...?	kvahrr ehrr ...?	*Hvar er ...?*
doctor	laik-nirr	*læknir*
hospital	syook-rrah-hoos	*sjúkrahús*
chemist	ah-poh-tehk	*apótek*
dentist	tahn-laik-nirr	*tannlæknir*

Could I see a female doctor?
gyai-ti yehkh fayn-gith ahth   *Gæti ég fengið að*
tah-lah vith kvehn layk-ni?   *tala við kvenlækni?*
What's the matter?
kvahth ehrr ahth?   *Hvað er að?*
Where does it hurt?
kvahrr fin-örr thoo til?   *Hvar finnur þú til?*
It hurts here.
mikh vehrrk-yahrr hyehrr   *Mig verkjar hér.*

Parts of the Body

ankle	erh-kli	*ökkli*
arm	hahnd-lehg-görr	*handleggur*
back	bahk	*bak*
chest	brreeng-gah	*bringa*
ear	ay-rrah	*eyra*
eye	eör-gah	*auga*
finger	feen-görr	*fingur*
feet/legs	fai-törr	*fætur*
hands	hehn-dörr	*hendur*
head	her-völh	*höfuð*
heart	hyarr-tah	*hjarta*
hips	myath-mirr	*mjaðmir*
mouth	mön-nörr	*munnur*
neck	howls	*háls*
ribs	rriv-bayn	*rifbein*
skin	hooth	*húð*
stomach	mai-i	*magi*
teeth	tehn-nörr	*tennur*
thighs	lai-rri	*læri*

ICELANDIC

Ailments

I have (a)...	yehkh ehrr mehth ...	*Ég er með ...*
cold	kvehf	*kvef*
constipation	hahrrth-lee-vi	*harðlífi*
diarrhoea	nith-örr-gowng	*niðurgang*
fever	hi-tah	*hita*
headache	her-vöth-vehrrk	*höfuðverk*
indigestion	mehlt-eeng-ahrr-trröb-lön	*meltingartruflun*
influenza	flehn-sö	*flensu*
low/high	low-ahn/how-ahn	*lágan/háan*
blood pressure	blohth-<u>thr</u>reest-eeng	*blóðþrýsting*
sore throat	howls-bohl-gö	*hálsbólgu*
sprain	tokh-nön	*tognun*
stomachache	mahkh-ah-vehrrk	*magaverk*
sunburn	sohl-brrö-ni	*sólbruni*

| I'm sunburnt. | yehk hehrr sohl-brrön-in | *Ég er sólbrunninn.* |

Some Useful Words & Phrases

I'm ...	yehkh ehrr ...	*Ég er ...*
asthmatic	mehth ahs-mah	*með asma*
diabetic	sik-örr-syoo-körr	*sykursjúkur*
epileptic	flokh-ah-vay-körr	*flogaveikur*

I'm allergic to antibiotics/penicillin.
yehkh ehrr mehth ov-nai-mi   *Ég er með ofnæmi*
firr-irr foo-kah-liv-yöm/   *fyrir fúkalyfjum/*
pehn-si-lee-ni   *pensilíni.*

I'm pregnant.
yehkh ehrr oh-frreesk   *Ég er ófrísk.*

ICELANDIC

I've been vaccinated.
    yehkh fyehk oh-nai-mis-sprreör-tö *Ég fékk ónæmisprautu.*
I feel better/worse.
    myehrr leeth-örr beh-törr/vehrr *Mér líður betur/verr.*

antibiotics	foo-kah-lif	*fúkalyf*
antiseptic	soht-hrrayns-ahndi	*sótthreinsandi*
blood pressure	blohth-<u>th</u>rreest-ing-örr	*blóðþrýstingur*
blood test	blohth-prrövah	*blóðprufa*
contraceptive	gyeht-nahth-ahrr-verdn	*getnaðarvörn*
injection	sprreör-tah	*sprauta*
medicine	lif	*lyf*
menstruation	blaith-eeng-ahrr	*blæðingar*
nausea	oh-khleh-thi	*ógleði*
toothache	tahn-pee-nah	*tannpína*

At the Chemist

I need medication for ...
    yehkh <u>th</u>ahrrf lif vith ... *Ég þarf lyf við ...*
I have a prescription.
    yehkh ehrr mehth lif-sehth-il *Ég er með lyfseðil.*

At the Dentist

I have a toothache.
    yehkh ehrr mehth tahn-pee-nö *Ég er með tannpínu.*
I've lost a filling.
    yehkh hehv misst fid-leen-gö *Ég hef misst fyllingu.*
I've broken a tooth.
    yehkh hehv brro-tith tern *Ég hef brotið tönn.*
My gums hurt.
    mikh vehrr-kyarr ee *Mig verkjar í*
    tahn-hol-dith *tannholdið.*
Please give me an anaesthetic.
    gyehrr-thö svo vehl *Gerðu svo vel*
    ath day-vah mikh *að deyfa mig.*

ICELANDIC

TIME & DATES

What date is it today?
kvahth-ah dahkh-örr *Hvaða dagur*
ehrr ee dahkh? *er í dag?*

What time is it?
kvahth ehrr klök-ahn? *Hvað er klukkan?*

It's ... am/pm.
hoon ehrr ... firr-irr how-day-i/ *Hún er ... fyrir hádegi/*
ehf-dirr how-day-i *eftir hádegi.*

in the morning	ahth mo-dni	*að morgni*
in the evening	ahth kverl-di	*að kvöldi*

Days of the Week

Monday	mow-nö-dahkh-örr	*mánudagur*
Tuesday	thrrith-yö-dahkh-örr	*þriðjudagur*
Wednesday	mith-vik-ö-dahkh-örr	*miðvikudagur*
Thursday	fim-tö-dahkh-örr	*fimmtudagur*
Friday	fers-dö-dahkh-örr	*föstudagur*
Saturday	leörkh-ah-dahkh-örr	*laugardagur*
Sunday	sön-ö-dahkh-örr	*sunnudagur*

Months

January	yah-noo-ahrr	*janúar*
February	fehb-rroo-ahrr	*febrúar*
March	mahrrs	*mars*
April	ah-prreel	*apríl*
May	mai	*maí*
June	yoo-nee	*júní*
July	yoo-lee	*júlí*
August	ow-goost	*ágúst*
September	sehft-ehm-behrr	*september*
October	okt-oh-behrr	*október*
November	noh-vehm-behrr	*nóvember*
December	dehs-ehm-behrr	*desember*

ICELANDIC

Seasons

summer	sö-mahrr	*sumar*
autumn	heörst	*haust*
winter	veh-törr	*vetur*
spring	vorr	*vor*

Present

today	ee dahkh	*í dag*
this morning	ee morr-gön	*í morgun*
tonight	ee kverld	*í kvöld*
this week	<u>th</u>ehs-ah vi-kö	*þessa viku*
this year	<u>th</u>eht-ah owrr	*þetta ár*
now	noo-nah	*núna*

Past

yesterday	ee gyairr	*í gær*
two days ago	firr-irr tvay-mörr derkh-öm	*fyrir tveimur dögum*
last night	seeth-öst-ö noht	*síðustu nótt*
last week	(ee) seeth-öst-ö vi-kö	*(í) síðustu viku*
last year	seeth-ast-lith-ith owrr	*síðastliðið ár*

Future

tomorrow	ow morr-gön	*á morgun*
in two days	ehf-dirr tvo dahg-ah	*eftir tvo daga*
next week	(ee) nais-tö vi-kö	*(í) næstu viku*
next month	(ee) nais-tah mown-öthi	*(í) næsta máuði*
next year	(ow) nais-tah ow-rri	*(á) næsta ár*

During the Day

afternoon	ehf-dirr how-day-i	*eftir hádegi*
day	dahkh-örr	*dagur*
midnight	mithnait-i	*miðnætti*
morning	morr-gön	*morgunn*
night	noht	*nótt*
noon	how-day-i	*hádegi*

NUMBERS & AMOUNTS

0	nool	*núll*
1	aydn	*einn*
2	tvayrr	*tveir*
3	<u>th</u>rreer	*þrír*
4	fyoh-rrirr	*fjórir*
5	fimm	*fimm*
6	sehks	*sex*
7	syer	*sjö*
8	owt-dah	*átta*
9	nee-ö	*níu*
10	tee-ö	*tíu*
20	tö-tökh-ö	*tuttugu*
21	tö-tö-gö og aydn	*tuttugu og einn*
30	<u>th</u>rryow-tee-ö	*þrjátíu*
40	fyer-tee-ö	*fjörutíu*
50	fim-tee-ö	*fimmtíu*
60	sehks-tee-ö	*sextíu*
70	syer-tee-ö	*sjötíu*
80	ow-tah-tee-ö	*áttatíu*
90	nee-tee-ö	*níutíu*
100	ayt hön-drrahth	*eitt hundrað*
1000	ayt <u>th</u>oos-önd	*eitt þúsund*
one million	ayn mil-yohn	*ein milljón*

ICELANDIC

Some Useful Words

a little (amount)	lee-tith	*lítið*
few	fow-irr	*fáir*
more	may-rrah	*meira*
some	nok-rrirr	*nokkrir*
too much/many	ov mi-kith/mahrr-girr	*of mikið/margir*

ICELANDIC

ABBREVIATIONS

f.h./e.h. – fyrir hádegi/eftir hádegi	am/pm
h.f. – hlutafélag	Ltd./Inc.
S.V.R. – Strætisvagnar Reykjavíkur	Reykjavík Municipal Bus Company
f.kr./e.kr.	BC/AD
frk. – fröken	Miss
frú	Mrs
hr. – herra	Mr/Sir
Rvk. – Reykjavík	Reykjavík
FÍB – Félag íslenskra bifreiðaeigenda	The Icelandic Automobile Association
kl. – klukkan	o'clock
km/klst. – kílómetrar á klukkustund	kilometres per hour
kr. – króna	crown (Icelandic monetary unit)
v. – við	at
vsk. – virðisaukaskattur	tax (included in the price on all goods and services)
t.h. – til hægri	to the right (used in addresses)
hs. – heimasími	telephone at home
vs. – vinnusími	telephone at work
t.v. – til vinstri	to the left (used in addresses)
(1.) h. – hæð	(1st) floor

EMERGENCIES

Help!	hyowlp!	*Hjálp!*
Go away!	fahrr-thö!	*Farðu!*
Thief!	thyoh-vörr!	*þjófur!*

SIGNS

LÖGREGLA
POLICE

LÖGREGLUSTÖÐ
POLICE STATION

There's been an accident!
 thahth hehf-örr orrth-ith slis! — *Það hefur orðið slys!*

Call a doctor/an ambulance!
 now-ith ee laik-ni/
 syook-rrah beel! — *Náið í lækni/
sjúkrabíl!*

I've been raped.
 myehrr vahrr neörth-gahth — *Mér var nauðgað.*

I've been robbed!
 yehkh vahrr rraind/rrain-dörr! — *Ég var rænd/-ur!* (f/m)

Call the police!
 nowith ee lerg-rrehgl-ön-ah! — *Náið í lögregluna!*

Where is the police station?
 kvahrr ehrr
 lerkh-rrehkh-lö-sterth-in? — *Hvar er
lögreglustöðin?*

I'm/My friend is ill.
 yehkh ehrr/vin-örr min
 ehrr vay-körr — *Ég er/vinur minn
er veikur.*

I'm lost.
 yehkh ehrr vilt/vilt-örr — *Ég er villt/-ur.* (f/m)

Where are the toilets?
 kvahrr ehrr snirrt-inkh-in?/
 kvahrr ehrr kloh-seht-ith? — *Hvar er snyrtingin?/
Hvar er klósettið?*

Could you help me please?
 gyai-tirr thoo hyowlp-ahth myehrr? — *Gætir þú hjálpað mér?*

Could I please use the telephone?
 gyai-ti yehkh fayn-khith
 ahth hrrin-gyah? — *Gæti ég fengið
að hringja?*

I'm sorry.
 myehrr thik-irr thahth layht — *Mér þykir það leitt.*

ICELANDIC

I didn't realise I was doing
anything wrong.

  yehkh vi-si ehk-i ahth yehkh   *Ég vissi ekki að ég*
  vai-rri ahth gyeh-rrah rrow-nt   *væri að gera rangt.*

I didn't do it.

  yehkh gyehrr-thi thahth ehk-i   *Ég gerði það ekki.*

I wish to contact my embassy/consulate.

  yehkh vil hah-vah sahm-bahnd   *Ég vil hafa samband*
  vith sehndi-rrowth mit/   *við sendiráð mitt/*
  rraith-is -mahn min   *ræðismann minn.*

I speak English.

  yehkh tah-lah ehn-skö   *Ég tala ensku.*

I have medical insurance.

  yehkh hehf   *Ég hef*
  syook-rrah-trrikh-een-gö   *sjúkratryggingu.*

My possessions are insured.

  aykh-örr meen-ahrr   *Eigur mínar*
  ehrr-ö trrikhth-arr   *eru tryggðar.*

My... was stolen.	... vahrr sto-lith	*... var stolið.*
I've lost my ...	yehkh teen-di ...	*Ég týndi ...*
bags	ter-skö-nöm mee-nöm	*töskunum mínum*
handbag	hahnd-tersk-ön-i	*handtöskunni*
	mi-ni	*minni*
money	pehn-eeng-ön-öm	*peningunum*
	mee-nöm	*mínum*
travellers	fehrrth-ah-tyeh-kö-nöm	*ferðatékkunum*
cheques	mee-nöm	*mínum*
passport	vehg-ah-brryeh-vi-nö	*vegabréfinu*
	mee-nö	*mínu*

NORWEGIAN

NORWEGIAN

QUICK REFERENCE

English	Pronunciation	Norwegian
Hello.	gud-*dahg*	Goddag.
Goodbye.	*huh*-deh	Ha det.
Yes./No.	yah/nay	Ja./Nei.
Excuse me.	*un*-shül	Unnskyld.
Sorry.	*beh-klah*-gehrr	Beklager,
	til-yi mai	tilgi meg.
Please.	va sho *snil*	Vær så snill.
Thank you.	tuhk	Takk.
You're welcome.	*ing*-ön *or*-shahk	Ingen årsak.

I'd like a ...	yay vil *ya*-rrnö hah ...	Jeg vil gjerne ha ...
one-way ticket	*ehn*-kehlt-bi-*leht*	enkelt billett
return ticket	*too*-rrö-*toorr*	tur-retur

I (don't) understand.
  yay fosh-*tor-rr* (ik-kö)   Jeg forstår (ikke).
Do you speak English?
  snuh-kö du *ehng*-ölsk?   Snakker du engelsk?
Where is ...?
  voor arr ...?   Hvor er ...?
Go straight ahead.
  deh arr *rreht* frruhm   Det er rett fram.
Turn left/right.
  tah til *vehns*-trrö/*höy*-rrö. Ta til venstre/høyre.
Do you have any rooms available?
  hah du *lay*-di-ö *rrum*?   Har du ledige rom?
I'm looking for a public toilet.
  yay *leh*-törr eht-törr eht   Jeg leter etter et
  of-föntli too-a-*leht*   offentlig toalett.

1	ehn	en	6	sehks	seks
2	too	to	7	shu/süv	sju/syv
3	trreh	tre	8	*ot*-tö	åtte
4	*fee*-rrö	fire	9	nee	ni
5	fehm	fem	10	tee	ti

NORWEGIAN

Norway has two official written language forms. They are very similar, and every Norwegian learns both at school. Bokmål (BM), literally 'book-language', is the urban-Norwegian variety of Danish, the language of the former rulers of Norway. It's the written language of 80 percent of the population. Although many Norwegians speak a local dialect in the private sphere, most of them speak BM in the public sphere. BM is therefore very appropriate for the traveller who wants to communicate with Norwegians all over the country.

The other written language is Nynorsk (NN), or 'New Norwegian' – as opposed to Old Norwegian, the language in Norway before 1500 AD, that is, before Danish rule. It's an important part of Norwegian cultural heritage as it's the truly 'Norwegian' language, as opposed to the Danish-based BM. In order to preserve the language, Norway has a NN theatre in Oslo – Det Norske Teater. Traditionally, many NN writers also produce their works to be performed in the NN tongue; the language lends itself to theatre and song as it can be very lyrical. By law the national TV and radio channels also broadcast a certain percentage of their text in NN.

In speech the distinction between BM and NN is no problem since Norwegians understand either. Although both are used in the media, BM is predominant in the daily papers, television and radio. Many people are put off trying to speak Norwegian because of the two languages, but in reality, BM is the ruling language. This book uses BM only.

A striking feature of both written languages is that many words have two or more officially authorised forms of spelling in either language. One can choose according to one's speech or social aspirations. In many cases it's possible to choose spellings which are common to either language.

In the rural areas you may come across people who hardly speak a word of English, and if you show an effort to speak Norwegian, it will help a great deal to establish contact. Many Norwegians will answer you in English, as they are only too eager to show off their knowledge. Their use of English is usually very good.

PRONUNCIATION
Vowels

Length, as a distinctive feature of vowels, is very important in the pronunciation of Norwegian. Almost every vowel has a (very) long and a (very) short counterpart, when appearing in a stressed syllable. Generally, it's long when followed by one consonant, and short when followed by two or more consonants.

A few words, mainly function words like pronouns and auxilliaries, are 'mispronounced': the vowel is short in spite of the fact that it's followed by only one consonant.

Pronunciation is given in the pronunciation guide in the front of the book.

PRONOUNS		
SG		
I	yay	*jeg*
you	du	*du*
he/she/it		
PL	hun/hahn/deh	*hun/han/det*
we	vi	*vi*
you (pol)	*deh*-rreh	*Dere*
you (pl)	*deh*-rreh	*dere*
they	dem	*dem*

GREETINGS & CIVILITIES
Top Useful Phrases

Hello.	gud-*dahg*	*Goddag.*
Goodbye.	*hah*-deh	*Ha det.*
Yes.	yah	*Ja.*
No.	nay	*Nei.*
Excuse me.	*un*-shül	*Unnskyld. meg.*
Please.	va sho *snil*	*Vær så snill.*
Thank you.	tuhk	*Takk.*
Many thanks.	*tusn* tuhk	*Tusen takk.*
That's fine.	*ing*-ön *or*-shahk	*Ingen årsak.*
You're welcome.		

May I? Do you mind?
  for-rr yay *lorv*? hah du   *Får jeg lov? Har du*
  noo-ö i-*moot* deh?   *noe imot det?*

Sorry. (excuse me, forgive me)
  behk-lah-gehrr til-yi mai   *Beklager, tilgi meg.*

Good morning.	gu *morr*-gon	*God morgen.*
Good afternoon.	gud-*dahg*	*Goddag.*
Good evening/night.	gu *kvehl*/*nuht*	*God kveld/natt.*
How are you?	voorr-duhn *hah* du deh?	*Hvordan har du det?*
Well, thanks.	brrah tuhk	*Bra, takk.*

NORWEGIAN

Forms of Address

Madam/Mrs	frru	*fru*
Sir/Mr	harr	*herr*
Miss	*frrayrr*-kön	*frøken*
companion	kuh-muh-*rraht*	*kamerat*
friend	vehn-*nin*-nö/vehn	*venninne/venn* (f/m)

NORWEGIAN

SMALL TALK
Meeting People

What is your name?	vah *hay*-tö du?	*Hva heter du?*
My name is ...	yay *hay*-törr ...	*Jeg heter ...*

I'd like to introduce you to ...
    deh-tö arr ...   *Dette er ...*
I'm pleased to meet you.
    hü-gö-li o *trreh*-fö day   *Hyggelig å treffe deg.*

Nationalities

Where are you from?	voorr *arr* du frrah?	*Hvor er du fra?*

I'm from ...	yay *arr* frruh ...	*Jeg er fra ...*
Australia	ow-*strrah*-li-uh	*Australia*
Canada	*kuh*-nuh-duh	*Kanada*
England	*ehng*-luhn	*England*
Ireland	ee-*rrluhn*	*Irland*
New Zealand	nü *say*-luhn	*Ny Zealand*
Norway	*norr*-gö	*Norge*
Scotland	*skot*-luhn	*Skottland*
the USA	a-*mehrr*-rrik-uha/	*Amerika/*
	ü-wehs-*sah*	*USA*
Wales	vehls	*Wales*

Age

How old are you?
    voor *guhm*-muhl arr du?   *Hvor gammel er du?*
I'm ... years old.
    yay arr ...   *Jeg er ...*

Occupations

What do you do?

vah *dree-vö* du may? *Hva driver du med?*

I'm a/an ...	yay arr ...	*Jeg er ...*
artist	*kunst*-nörr	*kunstner*
businesswoman/ man	fo-*rreht*-nings-kvin-nö/ fo-*rreht*-nings-muhn	*foretnings kvinne/ forretnings mann*
doctor	*lay*-gö	*lege*
engineer	in-shön-*yayrr*-rr	*ingeniør*
farmer	*gahrr*-brru-körr	*gardbruker*
journalist	shoo-rrnuh-*list*	*journalist*
lawyer	uhd-vo-*kuht*	*advokat*
manual worker	uhrr-*bay*-dörr	*arbeider*
mechanic	meh-*kah*-ni-körr	*mekaniker*
nurse	*sy*-kö-play-örr	*sykepleier*
office worker	koon-*toorr*-uhrr-bay-dörr	*kontor-arbeider*
scientist	*vee*-tön-skahps-muhn	*vitenskapsmann*
student	stu-*deh*-nt	*student*
teacher	*la*-rrörr	*lærer*
waiter	*kehl*-nörr/sehrr-*vay*-rrings-dah-mö	*kelner/ serveringsdame*
writer	fo-rr-*fuht*-törr	*forfatter*

NORWEGIAN

THE LONG AND THE SHORT OF IT

Nearly all vowels in Norwegian have short and long versions. This can affect the meaning, so look at the word carefully.

NORWEGIAN

Religion

What is your religion?
    vah arr din rreh-li-*gyoon?*   *Hva er din religion?*
I'm not religious.
    yay arr *ik*-kö rreh-li-*yers*   *Jeg er ikke religiøs.*

I'm ...	yay arr ...	Jeg er ...
Buddhist	bud-*dist*	buddhist
Catholic	kuh-*tolsk*	katolsk
Hindu	*hin*-du	hindu
Jewish	*yayrr*-dö	jøde
Muslim	*mus*-lim	muslim
Protestant	prro-teh-*stuhnt*	protestant

Family

Are you married?   arr du *yift?*   *Er du gift?*

I'm...	yay arr ...	Jeg er ...
single	ehns-li	enslig
married	*yift*	gift

How many children do you have?
    voor muhng-ö *bah-rrn* hah du?   *Hvor mange barn har du?*
I don't have any children.
    yay *huh ik*-kö noon bah-rrn   *Jeg har ikke noen barn.*
I have a daughter/a son.
    yay hahrr ehn *duht-törr/sern*   *Jeg har en datter/sønn.*
How many brothers/sisters
do you have?
    voor muhng-ö *sers*-kön hah du?   *Hvor mange søsken har du?*
Is your husband/wife here?
    arr *muhn-n* din harr/   *Er mannen din her?/*
    arr koo-nuh di harr?   *Er kona di her?*
Do you have a boyfriend/girlfriend?
    hah du *fuhst* ferl-lö?   *Har du fast følge?*

brother	brroorr	*bror*
children	bah-rrn	*barn*
daughter	*duht*-törr	*datter*
family	fuh-*mee*-li-ö	*familie*
father	fahrr	*far*
grandfather	*behs*-tö-fahrr	*bestefar*
grandmother	*behs*-tö-moorr	*bestemor*
husband	muhn	*mann*
mother	moorr	*mor*
sister	*sers*-törr	*søster*
son	sern	*sønn*
wife	*koo*-nö	*kone*

Kids' Talk

How old are you?
   voorr guh-mehl arr du?   *Hvor gammel er du?*
When's your birthday?
   norr hahrr du *bush*-dahg?   *Når har du bursdag?*
What do you do after school?
   vah *yer* du eh-tehrr skoo-leh-tid?   *Hva gjør du etter skoletid?*
Do you have a pet at home?
   hahrr du eht *cha*-leh-dürr   *Har du et kjæledyr*
   yeh-meh?   *hjemme?*

I have a ...	yay hahrr ehn ...	*Jeg har en ...*
bird	fool	*fugl*
budgerigar	un-du-*luht*	*undulat*
canary	kuh-*nuh*-rri-fool	*kanarifugl*
cat	kuht	*katt*
dog	hun	*hund*
frog	frrorsk	*frosk*

NORWEGIAN

Feelings

I (don't) like ...
yay *lee*-körr (*ik*-kö) ...   *Jeg liker (ikke) ...*
I feel cold/hot.
yay *früs*-örr/yay arr *vuh*-rrm   *Jeg fryser/Jeg er varm.*
I'm in a hurry.
yay hahrr *huhst*-varrk   *Jeg har hastverk.*
You're right.
du hah *rreht*   *Du har rett.*

I'm ...	*yay arr ...*	*Jeg er ...*
angry	*sin*-nuh	*sinna*
happy	*lük*-kö-li	*lykkelig*
hungry/thirsty	*shul*-tön/ter-sht	*sulten/tørst*
tired	trrer-t	*trøtt*
sad	oo-*lük*-kö-li/*nay*-forr	*ulykkelig/nedfor*
sleepy	*sherv*-ni	*søvnig*
well	brrah	*bra*
worried	oo-*rroo*-li	*urolig*

I'm sorry. (condolence)
kon-doo-*lay*-rrörr   *Kondolerer.*
I'm grateful.
yay arr *tuhk*-nehm-li   *Jeg er takknemlig.*

BREAKING THE LANGUAGE BARRIER

Do you speak English?
snuh-kö du *ehng*-ölsk?   *Snakker du engelsk?*
Does anyone speak English?
arr deh noon som snuh-körr   *Er det noen som snakker*
ehng-ölsk harr?   *engelsk her?*
I speak a little ...
yay snuh-kö *lit* ...   *Jeg snakker litt ...*
I don't speak ...
yay snuh-körr *ik*-kö ...   *Jeg snakker ikke ...*

I (don't) understand.
    yay fosh-*tor*-rr (*ik*-kö)   *Jeg forstår (ikke)*.

Could you speak more slowly please?
    kuhn du snuh-kö luhng-   *Kan du snakke langsommere?*
    som-mö-rrö?

Could you repeat that?
    kuhn du *yehn*-tuh day?   *Kan du gjenta det?*

How do you say ...?
    vah hay-törr ... por noshk?   *Hva heter ... på norsk?*

What does ... mean?
    vah bö-*türr* ...?   *Hva betyr ...?*

I speak ...	yay snuh-kuhrr ...	*Jeg snakker ...*
English	*ehng*-ehlsk	*engelsk*
French	frruhnsk	*fransk*
German	tüsk	*tysk*
Norwegian	noshk	*norsk*
Spanish	spuhnsk	*spansk*

Some Useful Phrases

Of course./Sure.	sehl-*ferrl*-geh-li/vist	*Selvfølgelig./Visst.*
Just a minute.	vehnt lit;	*Vent litt;*
	eht öy-eh-blik	*Et øyeblikk.*
It's (not) important.	deh arr (*ik*-kö)	*Det er (ikke)*
	vik-ti	*viktig.*
It's (not) possible.	deh arr (*ik*-kö)	*Det er (ikke)*
	moo-li	*mulig.*
Wait!	vehnt!	*Vent!*
Good luck!	*lük*-kö *til*!	*Lykke til!*

BODY LANGUAGE

It's considered good manners to shake hands with Norwegians when you meet. Remember, this includes both men and women; many Norwegian women feel ignored in English-speaking nations where usually only the men shake hands.

After having met a few times, a friendly hug or a peck on the cheek is common – this includes both women and men.

PAPERWORK

address	uh-*drreh*-sö	*adresse*
age	*uhl*-dörr	*alder*
birth certificate	*ferts*-ls-uht-tehst	*fødselsattest*
border	*grrehn*-sö	*grense*
car owner's title	*vongn*-ko-rt	*vognkort*
car registration	*chehn*-nö-tayn	*kjennetegn*
customs	*tol*	*toll*
date of birth	*fert*-söls-dah-tu	*fødselsdato*
driver's licence	*fayrr*-rrörr-kort	*førerkort*
identification	lay-gay-ti-*muh*-shon	*legitimasjon*
immigration	*in*-vuhn-drring	*innvandring*
marital status	si-*veel*-stuhn	*sivilstand*
name	nuhvn	*navn*
nationality	nuh-shu-nuh-li-*tayt*	*nasjonalitet*
passport (number)	*puhs*(-num-mörr)	*pass(nummer)*
place of birth	*fayrr*-dö-stay	*fødested*
profession	*ürr*-kö	*yrke*
reason for travel	*hehn*-sikt meh *rray*-sn	*hensikt med reisen*
religion	rreh-li-*gyoon*	*religion*
sex	chern	*kjønn*
tourist card	tu-*rrist*-kort	*turistkort*
visa	*vee*-sum	*visum*

GETTING AROUND

What time does ... leave/arrive?	*norr* gor-rr/ kom-mörr ...?	*Når går/ kommer ...?*
the (aero)plane	*flü*-yö	*flyet*
the boat	*bor*-tn	*båten*
the (city) bus	(*bü*-)busn	*(by)bussen*
the (intercity) bus	(*lin*-yö-)busn	*(linje-)bussen*
the train	*tor*-gö	*toget*
the tram	*trrik*-kön	*trikken*

Directions

Where is ...?		
voor arr ...?		*Hvor er ...?*
How do I get to ...?		
voor-duhn kom-mörr yay til ...?		*Hvordan kommer jeg til ...?*
Is it far from/near here?		
arr deh *luhngt harr*-frruh?		*Er det langt herfra?*

NORWEGIAN

SIGNS

BAGASJEINNLEVERING	**CHECK-IN COUNTER**
DAMER/HERRER	**LADIES/GENTLEMEN**
FORBUDT	**PROHIBITED**
GRATIS ADGANG	**FREE ADMISSION**
INFORMASJON/ OPPLYSNINGER	**INFORMATION**
INGEN ADGANG	**NO ENTRY**
INNGANG	**ENTRANCE**
NØDUTGANG	**EMERGENCY EXIT**
REISEGODS	**BAGGAGE COUNTER**
RESERVERT	**RESERVED**
RØYKING FORBUDT	**NO SMOKING**
TELEFON	**TELEPHONE**
TOLL	**CUSTOMS**
UTGANG	**EXIT**
WC/TOALETTER	**TOILETS**
ÅPEN/STENGT	**OPEN/CLOSED**

Can I walk there?
  kuhn yay *gor* deet?   *Kan jeg gå dit?*

Can you show me (on the map)?
  kuhn du *vee*-sö ma   *Kan du vise meg*
  (po *kuh*-rtö)?   *(på kartet)?*

Are there other means
of getting there?
  arr deh ehn *ahn*-ön mor-tö or   *Er det en annen måte å*
  kom-mö *deet* po?   *komme dit på?*

I want to go to ...
  yay skuhl til ...   *Jeg skal til ...*

Go straight ahead.
  deh arr *rreht* frruhm   *Det er rett fram.*

It's two blocks down.
  deh arr *too* kvuh-rtahl *vee*-dö-rrö   *Det er to kvartal videre.*

Turn left/right at the ...	*tah* til *vehns*-trrö/	*Ta til venstre/*
	höy-rrö veh ...	*høyre ved ...*
next corner	*nehs*-tö *yayrr*-nö	*neste hjørne*
traffic lights	*lüs*-krrüs-sö	*lyskrysset*

behind	bak	*bak*
in front of	fo-rruhn	*foran*
far	luhngt	*langt*
near	narr	*nær*
opposite	or-vörr-*forr*	*overfor*
next to	*veh*-si-dehn-*uhv*	*ved siden av*

SIGNS

ANKOMST	**ARRIVALS**
AVGANG	**DEPARTURES**
BILLETTKONTOR	**TICKET OFFICE**
JERNBANESTASJON	**TRAIN STATION**
RUTEPLAN	**TIMETABLE**
STASJON	**STATION**
T-BANE	**SUBWAY**

NORWEGIAN

Booking Tickets

Excuse me, where is the
ticket office?
    un-shül voor *arr*   *Unnskyld, hvor er*
    bi-leht-lu-kuh?   *billettluka?*

Where can I buy a ticket?
    voor kuhn yay   *Hvor kan jeg*
    sher-peh bi-*leht?*   *kjøpe billett?*

I want to go to ...
    yay skuhl til ...   *Jeg skal til ...*

Do I need to book?
    arr deh nerd-*vehn*-di o   *Er det nødvendig å*
    bö-*stil*-lö pluhs?   *bestille plass?*

I'd like to book a seat to ...
    yay vil *ya*-rrnö bö-*stil*-lö   *Jeg vil gjerne bestille*
    si-tö-pluhs til ...   *sitte-plass til ...*

I'd like ...	yay vil *ya*-rrnö hah ...	*Jeg vil gjerne ha ...*
a one-way ticket	*ehn*-kehlt-bi-*leht*	*enkelt billett*
a return ticket	*too*-rrö-*toorr*	*tur-retur*
two tickets	*too* bi-*leht*-tehrr	*to billetter*
tickets for all of us	bi-*leh*-tehrr til os	*billetter til oss*
	uhl-lö *suh*-mehn	*alle sammen*
a student's fare	stu-*dehnt*-rruh-buht	*studentrabatt*
a child's fare	*bah*-rrnö-bi-*leht*	*barnebillett*
a pensioner's fare	ho-*nayrr*-bi-*leht*	*honnør-billett*
1st class	*fersh*-tö kluhs-sö	*første klasse*
2nd class	*ahn*-ön kluhs-sö	*annen klasse*

Is it completely full?
    arr deh *halt* fult?   *Er det helt fullt?*

Can I get a stand-by ticket?
    kuhn yay for ehn   *Kan jeg få en*
    shuhn-sö-bi-*leht?*   *sjansebillett?*

NORWEGIAN

NORWEGIAN

Air

Is there a flight to ...?
  arr deh eht flü til ...?
  Er det et fly til ...?

When is the next flight to ...?
  norr gor *nehs*-tö flü-yö til ...?
  Når går neste flyet til ...?

How long does the flight take?
  voor *luhng*-ö tid tahrr
  flüv-ning-ehn?
  Hvor lang tid tar
  flyvningen?

What is the flight number?
  vah arr *flait*-nu-mö-rrö?
  Hva er flightnummeret?

You must check in at ...
  du mor shehk-kö *in* veh ...
  Du må sjekke inn ved ...

check-in desk	*in*-shehk-*in*-skrruhn-keh	*innsjekking skranke*
airport tax	*luft*-huhvn-*ahv*-yift	*lufthavnavgift*
boarding pass	um-*boorr*-steeg-(n)ing-sko-rt	*ombord-stig(n)ings-kort*
customs	tol	*toll*

Bus

Where is the bus/tram stop?
  voor arr *bus*-hol-lö-pluhsn/
  trrik-hol-lö-pluhsn?
  Hvor er busholdeplassen/
  trikkholdeplassen?

Which bus goes to ...?
  vil-kön bus gor rtil ...?
  Hvilken buss går til ...?

Does this bus go to ...?
  gor *rdehn*-nö busn til ...?
  Går denne bussen til ...?

How often do buses pass by?
  voor muhng-ö *bus*-sörr gor-rdeh? *Hvor mange busser går det?*

What time is the	no-rr kom-mör	*Når kommer*
... bus?	... busn?	*... bussen?*
next	*nehs*-tö	*neste*
first	*fer*-shtö	*første*
last	*sis*-tö	*siste*

NORWEGIAN

Train

Is this the right platform for ...?
    arr *deht*-tö *rreht*-tö
    pluht-forr-muh forr
    tor-gö til ...?
    Er dette rette plattforma
    for toget til ...?

SIGNS
SPOR
PLATFORM

The train leaves from platform ...
    tor-gö gor-rr frra spoorr ...   *Toget går fra spor ...*

Passengers must ...	rray-sön-dö mor ...	*Reisende må ...*
change trains	*büt*-tö torg	*bytte tog*
change platforms	gor til spoorr ...	*gå til spor ...*

dining car	*spee*-sö-vongn	*spisevogn*
express	ehks-*prrehs*-torg	*ekspresstog*
local	lu-*kahl*-torg	*lokaltog*
sleeping/	*sor*-vö-vongn/	*sovevogn/*
couchette car	*lig*-gö-vongn	*ligge-vogn*

NORWEGIAN

Metro

Which line takes me to ...?
vil-kön *lin*-yö/*bah*-nö
mor yay tah til ...?

*Hvilken linje/bane
må jeg ta til ...?*

What is the next station?
vah arr *nehs*-tö stuh-*shoon?*

Hva er neste stasjon?

SIGNS	
T-BANE	METRO/UNDERGROUND
UTGANG	WAY OUT
VEKSLING	CHANGE (for coins)

Taxi

Where can I get hold of a taxi?
vorr kuhn yay for
tahk i ehn drro-shö?

*Hvor kan jeg få
tak i en drosje?*

Please take me to ...
vil du *chayrr*-rrö ma teel ...?

Vil du kjøre meg til ...?

How much does it cost to go to ...?
vorr *mü*-yö *kos*-törr deh
o *chayrr*-rrö til ...?

*Hvor mye koster det
å kjøre til ...?*

Here is fine, thank you.
du kuhn *stop*-pö *harr tuhk*

Du kan stoppe her, takk.

Continue!
buh-rrö *furrt*-sheht!

Bare fortsett!

The next street to the left/right.
nehs-tö gah-teh til
vehn-strrö/*höy*-rrö

*Neste gate til
venstre/høyre.*

Stop here!
stop harr!

Stopp her!

Please slow down.
va sho snil o cher-rr
lit *suhk*-teh-rreh

*Vær så snill og kjør
litt saktere.*

Please wait here.
varr sor snil o *vehn*-tö harr

Vær så snill å vente her.

Car

Where can I rent a car?
    voor kuhn yay *lay*-ö ehn *beel?*   *Hvor kan jeg leie en bil?*

How much is it daily/weekly?
    vorr mü-yö *kos*-törr deh   *Hvor mye koster det*
    parr *dahg/u*-kö?   *pr. dag/uke?*

Does that include insurance/mileage?
    arr deh *in*-kloo-*dehrrt*   *Er det inkludert*
    fo-*shik*-rring/frree   *forsikring/fri*
    chayrr-rrö-ah-stuhn?   *kjøreavstand?*

Where's the next petrol station?
    voor *arr* narr-mös-tö   *Hvor er nærmeste*
    behn-seen-stuh-*shoon?*   *bensinstasjon?*

How long can I park here?
    voor *lehng*-ö kan   *Hvor lenge kan*
    beel-n min *stor* harr?   *bilen min stå her?*

Does this road lead to ...?
    arr deh-tö *vay*-yön til ...?   *Er dette veien til ...?*

air (for tyres)	luft	*luft*
battery	buht-tö-*rree*	*batteri*
brakes	*brrehm*-sörr	*bremser*
clutch	klerch	*kløtsj*
driver's licence	*fayrr*-rrörr-kort	*førerkort*
engine	*moo*-turr	*motor*
lights	*lük*-törr	*lykter*
oil	*ul*-yö	*olje*
puncture	pung-*tay*-rring	*punktering*
radiator	rruh-di-*yah*-turr	*radiator*
road map	kuhrt	*kart*
tyres	dehk	*dekk*
windscreen	*frront*-rru-tö	*frontrute*

NORWEGIAN

NORWEGIAN

SIGNS

BILVERKSTED	REPAIRS
BLYFRI	UNLEADED
ENVEISKJØRNING	ONE WAY
GARASJE	GARAGE
INNKJØRNING FORBUDT	NO ENTRY
MEKANIKER	MECHANIC
MOTORVEI	FREEWAY
NORMAL	NORMAL
OMKJØRNING	DETOUR
PARKERING FORBUDT	NO PARKING
SELVBETJENING	SELF SERVICE
STOPP	STOP
SUPER	SUPER
VIKEPLIKT	GIVE WAY

I need a mechanic.
    yay *trrehng*-ehrr ehn
    bil-meh-*kah*-ni-körr   *Jeg trenger en
                                    bilmekaniker.*

The battery is flat.
    buht-tö-*rree*-ö arr *fluht*   *Batteriet er flatt.*

The radiator is leaking.
    rruh-di-*ah*-toorrn arr *lehk* *Radiatoren er lekk.*

I have a flat tyre.
    yu-lö arr pung-*tayrt*   *Hjulet er punktert.*

It's overheating.
    moo-toorrn *koo*-körr   *Motoren koker.*

It's not working.
    deh fung-*gay*-rrörr ik-kö   *Det fungerer ikke.*

Some Useful Phrases

The train is delayed/cancelled.
tor-gö arr fo-*shing*-keht/*in*-stilt   *Toget er forsinket/innstilt.*

How long will it be delayed?
voor *mü*-yö arr deh fo-*shing*-keht?   *Hvor mye er det forsinket?*

There is a delay of ... hours.
tor-gö arr ... *tee*-mörr   *Toget er ... timer*
eht-törr *rru*-tö   *etter rute.*

How long does the trip take?
voor *lehng*-ö tahrr rray-suh?   *Hvor lenge tar reisa?*

Is it a direct route?
arr deh eht di-*rrehk*-tö torg?   *Er det et direkte tog?*

Is that seat taken?
arr *dehn*-nö *stoo*-ln *up*-tuht?   *Er denne stolen opptatt?*

I want to get off at ...
yay vil gor *ahv* i ...   *Jeg vil gå av i ...*

Where can I hire a bicycle?
voor kuhn yay *lay*-ö   *Hvor kan jeg leie*
ehn *sük*-köl?   *en sykkel?*

ACCOMMODATION

Where is a ...?	voor arr eht ...?	*Hvor er et ...?*
cheap hotel	*bil*-li hu-*tehl*	*billig hotell*
good hotel	got hu-*tehl*	*godt hotell*
nearby hotel	hu-*tehl* i *narr*-haytn	*hotell i nærheten*
nice/quaint hotel	*koo*-shli/*guhm*-muhl-duhks hu-*tehl*	*koselig/gammel-dags hotell*

What is the address?
vah arr uh-*drrehs*-ehn?   *Hva er adressen?*

Could you write the
address, please?
kuhn du *va*-rrö so snil   *Kan du være så snill*
o *skrree*-vö up uh-*drrehs*-ehn? *å skrive opp adressen?*

NORWEGIAN

At the Hotel

Do you have any rooms available?
   hah du *lay*-di-ö *rrum*?   *Har du ledige rom?*

I'd like ...	yay vil *ya*-rrnö ...	*Jeg vil gjerne ...*
a single room	hah eht *ehng*-költ-rrum	*ha et enkeltrom*
a double room	hah eht *dob*-ölt-rrum	*ha et dobbeltrom*
to share a dorm	*lig*-gö por *sor*-vö-sah-lön	*ligge på sovesalen*

NORWEGIAN

SIGNS

GJESTGIVERI/PENSJONAT	GUESTHOUSE
HOTELL	HOTEL
VANDRERHJEM	YOUTH HOSTEL

Do you have identification?
   hah du lay-gi-ti-muh-*shoon*?   *Har du legitimasjon?*
Your membership card, please.
   may-lehms-ko-rtö dit *tuhk*   *Medlemskortet ditt, takk.*
Sorry, we're full.
   beh-*klah*-görr deh arr *fült*   *Beklager, det er fullt.*
How long will you be staying?
   voor *lehng*-ö *blee*-rr du harr?   *Hvor lenge blir du her?*
How many nights?
   voor muhng-ö *neht*-törr?   *Hvor mange netter?*
It's ... per day/per person.
   deh arr ... pa r*dahg*/parr pa-*shoon*   *Det er ... pr. dag/pr. person.*
There are (four) of us.
   vi arr (*fee*-rrö) stük-körr   *Vi er (fire) stykker.*

I want a room	yay vil *ya*-rrnö hah	*Jeg vil gjerne ha*
with a ...	eht *rrum* meh ...	*et rom med ...*
bathroom	bahd	*bad*
shower	dush	*dusj*
television	*teh*-veh	*tv*
window	*vin*-du	*vindu*

I'm going to stay for ...	yay hah *tehnkt* o blee harr i ...	*Jeg har tenkt å bli her i ...*
one day	*ehn dahg*	*en dag*
two days	*too dah*-gehrr	*to dager*
one week	*an u*-kö	*en uke*

How much is it per night/per person?
  voor *mü-yö* arr deh parr dahg/ parr pa-*shoon*?
  Hvor mye er det pr. dag/ pr. person?

Can I see it?
  kuhn yay for *se* deh?
  Kan jeg få se det?

Are there any others?
  hah du *uhn*-drrö?
  Har du andre?

Are there any cheaper rooms?
  hah du *bil*-li-ö-rrö *rrum*?
  Har du billigere rom?

Can I see the bathroom?
  kuhn yay fo *se bah*-dö?
  Kan jeg få se badet?

Is there a reduction for students/children?
  yee du stu-*dehmt*-rruh-*buht*/ *bah*-rrnö-rruh-*buht*?
  Gir du studentrabatt/ barnerabatt?

Does it include breakfast?
  in-kloo-*deh*-rrehrr deh *frroo*-kostn?
  Inkluderer det frokosten?

It's fine, I'll take it.
  brrah yay tah rdeh.
  Bra, jeg tar det.

I'm not sure how long I'm staying.
  yay *veht* ik-kö voor *leh*-ngö yay skuh blee harr
  Jeg vet ikke hvor lenge jeg skal bli her.

Is there a lift?
  fins deh ehn *hays* harr?
  Finnes det en heis her?

Where is the bathroom?
  voor arr *bah*-dö?
  Hvor er badet?

Is there hot water all day?
  arr deh *vuh-rrnt* vuhn *döy*-nö *rrunt*?
  Er det varmt vann døgnet rundt?

Do you have a safe where
I can leave my valuables?
    hah du ehn sayf darr yay
    kan *lehg*-gö va-*rdee*-sah-kö-nö
    mee-nö?
Is there somewhere to wash clothes?
    kuhn yay vuhs-kö *kla*-rrnö
    mee-nö noo-eh *steh*?
Can I use the kitchen?
    arr deh *lorv* o *brru*-kö
    cherk-kö-nö?
Can I use the telephone?
    kuhn yay for *lor-nö*
    tay-lay-*foon*-n?

*Har du en safe der jeg
kan legge verdisakene
mine?*

*Kan jeg vaske klærne
mine noe sted?*

*Er det lov å bruke
kjøkkenet?*

*Kan jeg få låne
telefonen?*

Requests & Complaints

Please wake me up at ...
    va sho *snil* o *vehk*-kö ma ...
The room needs to be cleaned.
    deht-tö *rrum*-mö bayrr
    yayrr-rrös *rraynt*
Please change the sheets.
    va sho snil o *shift*-ö
    sehng-ö-töy
I can't open/close the window.
    yay *grray*-örr ik-kö *orp*-nö/
    luk-kö *vin*-du-ö
I've locked myself out of my room.
    yay hah *lor-st* ma *oo*-tö
    ah *rrum*-mö mit
The toilet won't flush.
    yay for-rr *ik*-kö spült
    nay po too-a-*leht*-tö
I don't like this room.
    yay *lee*-körr ik-kö
    deht-tö *rrum*-ö

Vær så snill å vekke meg ...

*Dette rommet bør
gjøres reint.*

*Vær så snill å skifte
sengetøy.*

*Jeg greier ikke åpne/
lukke vinduet.*

*Jeg har låst meg ute
av rommet mitt.*

*Jeg får ikke spylt
ned på toalettet.*

*Jeg liker ikke
dette rommet.*

It's ...	deh arr ...	*Det er ...*
expensive	*dürt*	*dyrt*
noisy	fo mü-yö *brrork*	*for mye bråk*
too dark	forr *mer-rrt*	*for mørkt*
too small	fo *lee-*tö	*for lite*

Some Useful Words & Phrases

I'm leaving now/tomorrow.
  yay *rray-*sörr nor/i-*mo-*rn   *Jeg reiser nå/i morgen.*
I'd like to pay the bill.
  kuhn yay for *rrehng-*ning-ehn   *Kan jeg få regningen,*
  tuhk?   *takk?*

name	nuhvn	*navn*
surname	*eht-*tö-nuhvn	*etternavn*
address	uh-*drrehs-*sö	*adresse*
room number	*rrum-*num-mörr	*romnummer*
air-conditioning	*klee-*muh-uhn-lehg	*klimaanlegg*
balcony	buhl-*kong*	*balkong*
bathroom	bahd	*bad*
bed	sehng	*seng*
bill	*rray-*ning	*regning*
blanket	*tehp-*pö	*teppe*
chair	stool	*stol*
clean	rrayn	*rein*
cupboard	skahp	*skap*
dirty	*shit-*n	*skitten*
double bed	*dob-*bölt-sehng	*dobbeltseng*
electricity	strrerm	*strøm*
fan	*vif-*tö	*vifte*
key	nerk-köl	*nøkkel*
lift (elevator)	hays	*heis*
light bulb	*lüs-*pa-rrö	*lyspære*
a lock	lors	*lås*
mattress	muh-*drruhs*	*madrass*
mirror	spayl	*speil*
padlock	*hehng-*ö-lors	*hengelås*
pillow	*pu-*tö	*pute*

NORWEGIAN

NORWEGIAN

quiet	*stil*-lö	stille
room (in hotel)	rrum/*va*-rröl-sö	rom/værelse
sheet	*lah*-kön	laken
shower	dush	dusj
soap	*sor*-pö	såpe
suitcase	*kuf*-först	koffert
swimming pool (indoor)	*sverm*-mö-huhl	svømmehall
table	boo-rr	bord
toilet	doo	do
toilet paper	*doo*-puh-*peerr*	dopapir
towel	*hong*-klö	håndkle
water	vuhn	vann
hot/cold water	*vuh*-rrnt/*kuhlt* vuhn	varmt/kaldt vann
window	*vin*-du	vindu

AROUND TOWN

I'm looking for ...	yay *leh*-törr eht-törr ...	Jeg leter etter ...
the art gallery	*kunst*-guhl-lö-*rree*-ö	kunstgalleriet
a bank	*buhng*-kön	banken
the church	*chirr*-kehn	kirken
the city centre	*sehn*-trrum	sentrum
the ... embassy	den ...	den ...
	uhm-buhs-*sah*-dö	ambassade
my hotel	hu-*tehl*-lö mit	hotellet mitt
the market	*to*-rr-gö	torget
the museum	mu-*say*-ö	museet
the police	pu-li-*ti*-ö	politiet
the post office	*post*-kun-*too*-rrö	postkontoret
the chemist	*uh*-po-*tehk*	apotek
a public toilet	eht *of*-fönt-li too-a-*leht*	et offentlig toalett
the telephone centre	*tay*-lö-*varr*-kö	televerket
the tourist information office	tu-*rrist*-in-fo-rr-muh-*shoon*	turistinformasjon

What time does it open/close?
    norr orp-nö/*stehng*-ö rdehn?   *Når åpner/stenger den?*
What street/suburb is this?
    vilk-ön *gah*-tö/*forr*-stahd arr deh? *Hvilken gate/forstad er det?*

For directions, see the Getting Around section, page 253.

NORWEGIAN

At the Post Office

I'd like to send a ... yay skuh *sehn*-nö ...   *Jeg skal sende ...*
    letter   eht *brrayv*   *et brev*
    postcard   eht *post*-kort   *et postkort*
    parcel   ehn *puhk*-kö   *en pakke*
    telegram   eht tay-lö-*grruhm* *et telegram*

I'd like some stamps.
    yay vil *ya*-rrnö *hah* noon   *Jeg vil gjerne ha noen*
    free-marr-kö   *frimerker.*
How much does it cost
to send this to ...?
    voor *mü*-yö kos-törr deh   *Hvor mye koster det*
    o *sehn*-nö deh-tö til ...?   *å sende dette til ...?*

air mail	*luft*-post	*luftpost*
envelope	kon-vu-*lut*	*konvolutt*
mail box	*post*-kuhs-sö	*postkasse*
registered mail	rreh-kom-muhn-*dayrt* post	*rekommandert post*
surface mail	or-vörr-flah-tö-*post*	*overflatepost*

NORWEGIAN

Telephone & Internet

I want to ring ...
    yay vil *rring*-ö til ...   *Jeg vil ringe til ...*
The number is ...
    num-mö-rrö arr ...   *Nummeret er ...*
How much does a
three-minute call cost?
    voor *mü*-yö *kos*-törr ehn   *Hvor mye koster en*
    trray mi-*nut*-tehsh *suhm*-tah-lö? *tre minutters samtale?*
How much does each
extra minute cost?
    voor *mü*-yö *kos*-törr *vart*   *Hvor mye koster hvert*
    ehks-trruh mi-*nut*?   *ekstra minutt?*
I'd like to speak to (Mr Olsen).
    yay skul-lö *ya*-rrnö for   *Jeg skulle gjerne få*
    snuhk-kö may (harr *ol*-sehn) *snakke med (herr Olsen).*
I want to make a reverse-charges
phone call.
    yay vil bö-*stil*-lö ehn   *Jeg vil bestille en*
    suhm-tah-lö meh   *samtale med*
    noo-*tay*-rrings-or-vörr-*fay*-rring *noteringsoverføring.*
It's engaged.
    deh arr *upp*-tuht   *Det er opptatt.*
I've been cut off.
    suhm-tah-lön blay *brrut*   *Samtalen ble brutt.*

Where can I get Internet access?
    voor kuhn yay for *ahd*-gang til *Hvor kan jeg få adgang til*
    in-tehrr-neht?   *Internet?*
I'd like to send an email.
    yay vil *ya*-rrnö sehn-deh   *Jeg vil gjerne sende*
    ehn *ee*-mayl   *en email.*

At the Bank

I want to exchange some money/
travellers cheques.

  yay vil *ya*-rrnö *vehks*-lö
  pehng-örr/*heh-vö* noon
  rray-sö-shehk-körr

*Jeg vil gjerne veksle
penger/heve noen
reisesjekker.*

What is the exchange rate?

  vah arr vuh-*loo*-tuh-ku-shön?

Hva er valutakursen?

How many Norwegian
kroner per dollar?

  voor *muhng*-ö *krroo*-nörr
  forr *ehn* dol-luhrr?

*Hvor mange kroner
for en dollar?*

Can I have money transferred
here from my bank?

  kuhn yay for or-vörr-fayrr-rt
  pehng-örr *heet* frrah
  buhng-kön min?

*Kan jeg få overført
penger hit fra
banken min?*

How long will it take to arrive?

  voor *lehng*-ö vil deh *tah*?

Hvor lenge vil det ta?

Has my money arrived yet?

  hahrr *pehng*-ö-nö mee-nö
  kom-möt nor?

*Har pengene mine
kommet nå?*

autobank	*mi*-ni-buhnk	*minibank*
bank draft	*vehk*-sl/rreh-*mis*-sö	*veksel/remisse*
bank notes	*pehng*-ö-sehd-lörr	*pengesedler*
cashier	kuh-*say*-rrörr	*kasserer*
coins	*mün*-törr	*mynter*
credit card	krreh-*dit*-kort	*kredittkort*
exchange	*vehk*-sling	*veksling*
loose change	*vehk*-slö-pehng-örr	*vekslepenger*
signature	*un*-nörr-skrrift	*underskrift*

INTERESTS & ENTERTAINMENT
Sightseeing

Do you have a guidebook/local map?
   hah du ehn *gaid*/eht   *Har du en guide/et*
   lo-kuhl-kuhrt?   *lokalkart?*

What are the main attractions?
   vah arr di *vik*-ti-stö   *Hva er de viktigste*
   say-*varr*-di-hay-törr?   *severdigheter?*

What is that?
   vah arr *deh*?   *Hva er det?*

How old is it?
   voor *guhm*-mölt arr deh?   *Hvor gammelt er det?*

Can I take photographs?
   kuhn yay tah *bil*-dörr?   *Kan jeg ta bilder?*

What time does it open/close?
   norr orp-nö/*stehng*-ö dehn?   *Når åpner/stenger den?*

ancient	*guhm*-mehl	*gammel*
beach	strruhn	*strand*
castle	slot	*slott*
cathedral	kuh-teh-*drrahl*	*katedral*
church	*chirr*-kö	*kirke*
concert hall	kon-*sart*-hus	*konserthus*
library	bi-bli-yu-*tayk*	*bibliotek*
main square	(*stoo-rr*)-to-rrgö	*(stor)torget*
market	*to*-rrgö	*torget*
town hall	*rrord*-hus	*rådhus*
monastery	*klos*-törr	*kloster*
monument	his-*too*-rrisk *büg*-ning	*historisk bygning*
mosque	mos-*kay*	*moské*
old town	guhm-möl *bü*	*gammel by*
the old city	*guhm*-lö-bü-yön	*gamlebyen*
opera house	*oo*-pö-rruh-hus	*operahus*
palace	slot	*slott*
ruins	rroo-*ee*-nörr	*ruiner*

NORWEGIAN

stadium	*stah*-di-on	*stadion*
statues	*bil*-löd-ster-törr	*billedstøtter*
synagogue	sü-nuh-*goo*-gö	*synagoge*
temple	*hor-v/tehm*-pöl	*hov/tempel*
university	u-ni-va-shi-*tayt*	*universitet*

NORWEGIAN

Going Out

What's there to do in the evenings?
vah kuhn muhn *yer*-rrö   *Hva kan man gjøre*
om *kvehl*-n?   *om kvelden?*
Are there any discos?
arr deh noon dis-ku-*tayk*?   *Er det noen diskotek?*
Are there places where you
can hear local folk music?
arr deh noo-ön stay-dörr darr   *Er det noen steder der*
ehn kuhn *her*-rrö po noshk   *en kan høre på norsk*
fol-kö-mu-*sik*?   *folkemusikk?*
How much does it cost to get in?
voor *mü*-yö kost-örr deh   *Hvor mye koster det*
forr o ko-mö *in*?   *for å komme inn?*

cinema	*chee*-nu	*kino*
concert	kon-*sart*	*konsert*
discotheque	dis-ku-*tayk*	*diskotek*
theatre	tay-*ah*-törr	*teater*

NORWEGIAN

Sports & Interests

What do you do in your spare time?
    vah yer rdu i frree-ti-dehn?   *Hva gjør du i fritiden?*
What sport do you play?
    vah shluhgs id-rreht   *Hva slags idrett*
    drri-vehrr du?   *driver du?*

art	kunst	*kunst*
basketball	*buh*-skeht-*buhl*	*basketball*
boxing	*buk*-sing	*boksing*
cooking	*muht-luhg*-ing	*matlaging*
fishing	*fee*-sking	*fisking*
football/soccer	*fut*-buhl	*fotball*
going out	gor ut	*gå ut*
going to the cinema	gor por *chee*-nu	*gå på kino*
music	mu-*sik*	*musikk*
photography	foo-too-grruh-*fee*-rring	*fotografering*
reading	*lehs*-ning	*lesning*
shopping	*huhn*-dlay	*handle*
sport	sport/*i*-drreht	*sport/idrett*
the theatre	ti-*uh*-tehrr	*teater*
travelling	*rray*-sehrr	*reiser*
writing	*skrri*-vehrr	*skriver*

Festivals

Santa Lucia is celebrated on 13 December. Children dressed in white, the boys wearing cone-shaped hats and the girls with tinsel and glitter in their hair, take part in candlelight processions.

Jul (Christmas) is celebrated on the evening of 24 December, when gifts are exchanged. In the countryside, people mount sheaves of oats, julenek, on poles for the birds, and many people leave a bowl of porridge out for the nisse, a type of Christmas gnome traditionally thought to bring good luck to farmers.

At Easter, påske, the Sami people hold colourful celebrations in Karasjok and Kautokeino with concerts, joik (traditional chanting), reindeer races and other festivities.

Syttende maj (17 May) is Norway's Constitution Day. Everybody celebrates, and many wear traditional costume. In every city and town there are marching bands and parades of school children. The biggest celebrations take place in Oslo where you'll see thousands of school children march up Karl Johans gate to the palace, where they're greeted by the royal family.

Midsummer's Eve (Jonsok), is celebrated throughout the country, with bonfires and parties.

NORWEGIAN

IN THE COUNTRY
Weather

What's the weather forecast?
vah arr *varr*-mehl-ling-uh?   *Hva er værmeldinga?*

The weather is ...	va-rrö arr ...	*Været er ...*
today.	i-dahg	*i dag.*
Will it be ...	blee rdeh ...	*Blir det ...*
tomorrow?	i-*mo-rrn*?	*i morgen?*
cloudy	or-vö-shü-yeht	*overskyet*
cold	kuhlt	*kaldt*
foggy	tor-kö	*tåke*
frosty	*frost*-va-rr	*frostvær*
hot	vuh-rnt	*varmt*
raining	rrayn	*regn*
snowing	sner	*snø*
sunny	mü-yö *sool*	*mye sol*
windy	mü-yö *vin*	*mye vind*

Camping

SIGNS	
KAMPING/LEIRPLASS	CAMPING GROUND

Am I allowed to camp here?
for-rr yay lorv til o *shlor* op
tehl-tö mit harr?

*Får jeg lov til å slå opp
teltet mitt her?*

Is there a campsite nearby?
fins deh ehn *kam*-ping
plass i *narr-hay*-tön?

*Finnes det en camping-
plass i nærheten?*

backpack	*rrüg*-sehk	ryggsekk
can opener	*boks*-or-pnörr	boksåpner
compass	kom-*puhs*	kompass
crampons	*brrod*-dör	brodder
firewood	veh	ved
gas cartridge	prru-*pahn*-bö-*hol*-lörr	propanbeholder
ice axe	*ees*-erks	isøks
mattress	muh-*drruhs*	madrass
penknife	*lum*-mö-kneev	lommekniv
rope	tohv	tau
tent	tehlt	telt
tent pegs	*tehlt*-plug-görr	teltplugger
torch (flashlight)	*lum*-mö-lükt	lommelykt
sleeping bag	sor-vö-poo-sö	sovepose
stove	*koo*-kö-uhp-puh-*rraht*	kokeapparat
water bottle	*vuhn*-fluhs-kö	vannflaske

FOOD
Some Useful Words & Phrases

breakfast	*frroo*-kost	*frokost*
lunch	lernsh	*lunsj*
dinner	*mid*-dahg	*middag*

Table for ..., please.
    eht *boo-rr* til ... tuhk   *Et bord til ..., takk.*
Can I see the menu please?
    kuhn yay for meh-*nü*-yön tuhk   *Kan jeg få menyen, takk.*
I'd like today's special, please.
    yay vil *ya*-rrnö hah   *Jeg vil gjerne ha*
    dah-göns rreht takk   *dagens rett, takk.*
What does it include?
    vah in-kloo-*deh*-rreh rdeh?   *Hva inkluderer det?*
Is service included in the bill?
    arr bö-*vart*-ning-uh   *Er bevertninga*
    ee-bö-rray-nöt?   *iberegnet?*
Not too spicy please.
    ik-kö fo *shtarrkt*   *Ikke for sterkt*
    krrüd-*drruh* tuhk   *krydra, takk.*

ashtray	*uhs*-kö-bay-görr	*askebeger*
the bill	*rray*-ning-ön	*regningen*
a cup	ehn *kop*	*en kopp*
dessert	deh-*sehrr*	*dessert*
a drink	ehn *drringk*	*en drink*
a fork	ehn *guhf*-föl	*en gaffel*
a glass	eht *gluhs*	*et glass*
a knife	ehn *kneev*	*en kniv*
a plate	ehn tuhl-larr-kön	*en tallerken*
spicy	starrkt (*krrüd*-rruh)	*sterkt (krydra)*
a spoon	ehn *shay*	*en skje*
stale	*dor*-vönt	*dovent*
starter	forr-reht	*forrett*
sweet	sayrr-t	*søt*
teaspoon	*tay*-sheh	*teskjed*
toothpick	*tuhn*-pirr-körr	*tannpirker*

Vegetarian Meals

I'm a vegetarian.

yay arr veh-geh-tuh-rri-*ah*-nörr   *Jeg er vegetarianer.*

I don't eat meat.

yay *spi*-sörr ik-kö *cher-t*   *Jeg spiser ikke kjøtt.*

I don't eat chicken or fish or ham.

yay spee-sörr *varr*-kön *chül*-ling   *Jeg spiser verken kylling*
ehl-lörr *fisk* ehl-lö *shing*-kö   *eller fisk eller skinke.*

Breakfasts & Breads

biscuit	chehks	kjeks
brown bread	*grrorv*-brrer	grovbrød
crisp-bread	*kneh*-keh-brrer	knekkebrød
cured ham	*speh*-keh-shin-keh	spekeskinke
food on top of a sandwich, like cold cuts	*por*-lehg	pålegg
fried egg (sunny side up)	*spayl*-ehg	speilegg
hard-boiled	*hahrr*-kukt	hardkokt
honey	*hun*-ning	honning
jam	*sül*-teh-töy	syltetøy
oatmeal biscuits	*huh*-vrreh-*chehks*	havrekjeks
oatmeal porridge	*huh*-vrreh-*grrert*	havregrøt
open sandwich	smer-brrer	smørbrød
peanut butter	*pi-a*-nert-smer-rr	peanøttsmør
porridge, cereal	grrert	grøt
roll	*rrun*-stü-keh	rundstykke
rusk	*kuh*-vrring	kavring
scrambled eggs	*ehg*-eh-*rreh*-rreh	eggerøre
slice	*shi*-veh	skive
soft-boiled	*blert*-kukt	bløtkokt
white bread	loof	loff
wholemeal bread	*hehl*-koorrn-brrer	helkornbrød

MENU DECODER

Dairy Products

gammalost	*guh*-muhl-ust	semi-hard brown cheese with strong flavour
geitost	*yayt*-ust	sweet brown goat cheese
gudbrands dalsost	*gud*-brruhns-duhls-ust	cheese similar to geitost
mysost	*müs*-ust	brown whey cheese
normannaost	nor-*man*-nuh-ust	Danish Blue
pultost	*pült*-ust	soft fermented cheese, often with caraway seeds
riddarost	*rrid*-ehrr-ust	Munster cheese
remuladesaus	*rrehm*-u-luh-deh-sows	cream mayonnaise with chopped gherkins and parsley

Soups & Mixed Dishes

dagens rett	dah-gehns-*rreht*	today's special
fårikål	forr-ih-*korl*	lamb in cabbage stew
flatbrød	*fluht*-brrer	thin wafer of rye/barley
gryte(rett)	*grrü*-teh-(reht)	casserole
italiensk salat	it-uhl-i-*ehnsk*-sah-*luht*	salad of diced cold meat, potatoes, apples and vegetables in mayonnaise
lapskaus	*luhp*-skows	thick stew of diced meat, potatoes, onions and other vegetables
koldtbord	*korlt*-boorr	buffet of cold dishes (fish, meat, cheese, salad and a sweet)
pyttipanne	*püt*-i-*puh*-nö	chunks of meat and potatoes, fried with onions, etc
suppe	*su*-pö	soup
surkål	*surr*-korl	boiled cabbage flavoured with caraway seeds, sugar and vinegar

NORWEGIAN

NORWEGIAN

Meat

bankebiff	ban-keh-bif	slices/chunks of beef simmered in gravy
benløse fugler	behn-lor-sö-foo-lehrr	rolled slices of veal stuffed with minced meat
blodpudding	bloo-pud-ing	black pudding
bris/brissel	brris/brri-söl	sweetbread
dyrestek	dü-rreh-stayk	roast venison
fenalår	feh-nuh-lor-rr	cured leg of lamb
fleske pannekake	fleh-skeh-puh-neh kah-keh	thick pancake with bacon, baked in the oven
fleskepølse	fleh-skeh-perl-seh	pork sandwich spread
fyll	fül	stuffing, forcemeat
kålruletter	korl-rru-leht-ehrr	minced meat in cabbage leaves
kalvetunge	kuhl-veh-tung-eh	calf's tongue
kjøttdeig	chert-day	minced meat
kjøttkake	chert-kah-keh	small hamburger steak
kjøttpålegg	chert-por-lehg	cold meat cuts
kjøttpudding	chert-pud-ing	meat loaf
lam(mebog)	luh-meh-boog	(shoulder of) lamb
lever(postei)	leh-vehrr pu-stay	liver (pate)
medaljong	mehd-uhl-yong	small round fillet
pai	pai	pie
pinnekjøtt	pi-neh-chert	salted and fried lamb ribs
postei	pu-stay	meat pie
spekemat	speh-keh-maht	cured meat (lamb, beef, pork, reindeer, often served with scrambled eggs)
spekepølse	speh-keh-perl-seh	air-dried sausage
syltelabb	sül-teh-lahb	boiled, salt-cured pig's trotter

Seafood

fiskebolle	fis-keh-bol-eh	fish ball
fiskegrateng	fis-keh-grruh-teng	fish casserole
fiskekake	fis-keh-kah-keh	fried fishball

fiskepudding	*fis*-keh-pud-ing	fish pate fried in a pan
gaffelbitar	*guh*-fehl-*bee*-tehrr	salt- and sugar-cured sprat/herring fillets
gravlaks	*grrahv-luhks*	salt- and sugar-cured salmon with dill and a creamy sauce
kaviar	kuh-vi-*uhrr*	smoked cod-roe spread
klippfisk	*klip*-fisk	salted and dried cod
lutefisk	*lu*-teh-*fisk*	stockfish treated in lye solution, boiled
plukkfisk	*pluk*-fisk	poached fish in white sauce
rakefisk	*rrahk*-fisk	cured and fermented fish (often trout)
sildesalat	*sil*-deh-suh-*laht*	salad with slices of herring, cucumber, onions, etc
spekesild	*speh*-keh-*sild*	salted herring, often served with pickled beetroot, potatoes and cabbage

Desserts

arme riddere	*uhrr*-meh-*rri*-deh-rreh	slices of bread dipped in batter, fried and served with jam
bløtkake	*blert*-kah-keh	rich sponge layer cake with whipped cream
fløteis	*fler*-teh-*ees*	ice cream made of cream
fløtevaffel	*fler*-teh-*vuh*-fehl	cream-enriched waffle with jam
fromasj	frroo-*muhsh*	mousse/blancmange
fruktis	*frrukt*-ees/sorr-*beh*	sorbet/water ice
julekake	*yu*-leh-*kah*-keh	rich fruit cake
hvetebolle	*veh*-teh-*bor*-leh	bun; sweet roll
kransekake	*krruhn*-seh-*kah*-keh	pile of almond-macaroon rings
kringle	*krring*-leh	ring-twisted bread with raisins
lefse	*lehf*-seh	thin pancake (without eggs)
napoleonskake	*nuh*-pool-eh-uns-*kah*-keh	custard slice

NORWEGIAN

riskrem	*rrees*-krrehm	boiled rice with whipped cream and raspberry jam
rislapp	*rrees*-luhp	small sweet rice cake
rødgrøt	*rrer*-grrert	fruit pudding with vanilla cream
rømmegrøt	*rrer*-meh-grrert	boiled sour cream porridge with cinnamon and sugar
rørte tyttebær	*rreh*-teh-tü-teh-*barr*	mashed uncooked cranberries
sirupsnipp	*si*-rrup-*snip*	ginger cookie
tilslørte bonde-piker	*til*-sler-teh-bon-deh-*pee*-kehrr	layers of apple sauce and breadcrumbs, topped with whipped cream
vannbakkels	*vuhn-buh*-kehls	cream puff
vørterkake	*ver-rr*-teh-*kah*-keh	spiced malt bread
wienerbrød	*wee*-nehrr-*brrer*	Danish pastry

Non-Alcoholic Drinks

brus	brrus	fizzy fruit drink
kefir	*keh*-firr	fermented milk
kulturmelk	kul-*turr*-*møhlk*	cultured thick milk
vørterøl	ver-tehrr-*erl*	non-alcoholic beer

Alcoholic Drinks

akevitt	uh-*keh*-vit	kind of gin flavoured with spices
bokkøl	*buk*-erl	bock beer
dram	drrahm	drink/tot/shot
exportøl	ehks-*purt*-erl	strong, light-coloured beer
gløgg	glerg	kind of mulled wine, with schnapps and spices
hjemmebrent	*yeh*-meh-*brrøhnt*	home-made brandy
lett-	leht	with little/less alcohol or sugar
pils	pils	lager
pjolter	*pyorl*-tehrr	long drink of whisky and soda water
toddi	to-di	mulled wine

Dairy Products

butter	smer-rr	smør
cheese	ust	ost
cream	*fler*-teh	fløte
cream cheese	*fler*-teh-ust	fløteost
sour cream	rrer-mö	rømme
whipped cream	krrehm; *pis*-keht-krrehm	krem; pisket krem

Meat

beef	*uk*-seh-*chert*	oksekjøtt
fillet of beef	*uk*-seh-fi-*leh*	oksefilet
game	vilt	vilt
ham	*shin*-keh	skinke
kidney	*nü*-rreh	nyre
lamb/mutton	sow-eh-chert	sauekjøtt
meat	chert	kjøtt
meatball	*chert-bor*-leh	kjøttbolle
pork	*svi*-neh-*chert*	svinekjøtt
pork chop	*svi*-neh-kort-eh-*leht*	svinekotelett
roast beef	*uk*-seh-stayk	oksestek
roast pork	*svi*-neh-stayk	svinestek
roast reindeer	*rrayns*-dürr-stayk	reinsdyrstek
rump steak	*mer*-brrahd	mørbrad
sausage	*perl*-seh	pølse
spare rib	*svi*-neh-*rri*-beh	svineribbe
veal	*kuhl*-veh-*chert*	kalvekjøtt

Seafood

anchovy	uhn-*shoos*	ansjos
catfish	*stayn*-bit	steinbit
coalfish	say	sei
cod	torshk	torsk
crab	*krruh*-beh	krabbe
crayfish	krrehps	kreps
eel	orl	ål

NORWEGIAN

NORWEGIAN

fish	*flün*-drreh	*fisk*
flounder	*flün*-drreh	*flyndre*
frog fish/ angler fish	*brray*-fluhb	*breiflabb*
haddock	*hü*-seh/*korl*-yeh	*hyse/kolje*
herring	sil	*sild*
lobster	*hu*-mehrr	*hummer*
mackerel	muh-*krrel*	*makrell*
mussel	*blor*-shehl	*blåskjel(l)*
pickled/ marinated herring	*krrüd*-ehrr-sil/*sürr*-sil	*kryddersild/sursild*
plaice	*rrer*-speh-teh	*rødspette*
(rainbow) trout	(*rrayng*-büeh-)*er*-eht	*(regnbue)ørret*
roe	rrorrrgn	*rogn*
sea trout	*sher-er*-rreht	*sjøørret*
shellfish	*skuhl*-dürr	*skaldyr*
shrimps	*rray*-kehrr	*reker*
(smoked) salmon	(*rrer-keh*-)*luhks*	*(røyke)laks*
sole	*sher-tun*-geh	*sjøtunge*
sprat/sardine	*brris*-ling	*brisling*
tuna	*tun*-fisk	*tunfisk*
whale steak	*vahl*-bif	*hvalbiff*

Poultry & Wildfowl

black grouse	*orr*-fool	*orrfugl*
chicken	*chül*-ling	*kylling*
chicken fricassee	*hern*-seh-*frri*-kuh-*seh*	*hønsefrikasse*
duck	uhn	*and*
goose	gors	*gås*
partridge	*rrap-hern*-eh	*rapphøne*
ptarmigan	*rrü*-peh	*rype*
quail	*vuhk*-tehl	*vaktel*
turkey	kuhl-*kun*	*kalkun*

Vegetables

beans	*bern-nehrr*	bønner
beetroot	rrrr-*beh*-tehrr	rødbeter
Brussels sprouts	*rroo*-sehn-*korl*	rosenkål
button mushroom	sham-pin-*yong*	sjampinjong
cabbage	korl	kål
carrots	*gu*-leh-rrer-tehrr	gulrøtter
cauliflower	*blorm-korl*	blomkål
chives	*grrehs*-lerk	gressløk
cucumber	uh-*gurrk*	agurk
horseradish	*peh*-pehrr-*rroot*	pepperrot
leek	*pu*-rreh	purre
lentils	*lin*-sehrr	linser
marrow/squash	*grrehs*-kahrr	gresskar
mashed potatoes	por-*teht*-mos	potetmos
mushroom	sop	sopp
onion	lerk	løk
peas	*at*-tehrr	erter
pickled gherkin	*sül*-teh-uh-*gurrk*	sylteagurk
potato dumplings	rruh-speh-*buh*-lehrr	raspeballer
potato pancake	*lum*-peh	lompe
radish	rreh-*dik*	reddik
red cabbage	*rror*-korl	rødkål
spinach	spi-*naht*	spinat
sugar peas	*su*-kehrr-at-tehrr	sukkererter
swede	korl-rah-*bi*	kålrabi
tomato	too-*maht*	tomat
vegetables	*grrern*-suh-kehrr	grøn(n)saker

Spices, Herbs & Condiments

caraway seeds	*kuhrr*-veh	karve
cardamom	kuhrr-deh-*mum*-meh	kardemomme
cinnamon	kuh-*nehl*	kanel
curry	*kuh*-rri	karri
garlic	*veet*-lerk	hvitløk

NORWEGIAN

NORWEGIAN

mustard	*sehn*-ehp	*sennep*
parsley	pa-*shi*-leh	*persille*
pepper	*peh*-pehrr	*pepper*
spices/herbs	krrü-*dehrr*	*krydder*
sugar	su-*kehrr*	*sukker*
tarragon	ehs-trruh-*gon*	*estragon*
thyme	*ti*-mi-uhn	*timian*
vinegar	*eh*-dik	*eddik*

Fruit

apple	*ehp*-leh	*eple*
apricot	uh-prri-*kus*	*aprikos*
banana	buh-*nahn*	*banan*
bilberries	*blor*-barr	*blåbær*
blackberries	*byer*-neh-*barr*	*bjørnebær*
blackcurrants	*sool*-barr	*solbær*
cherry	*shi*-sheh-*barr*	*kirsebær*
cranberries	*tü*-teh-*barr*	*tyttebær*
currant	*kor*-int	*korint*
fruit	frrukt	*frukt*
fruit salad	frrukt-suh-*laht*	*fruktsalat*
gooseberries	*sti*-kehls-*barr*	*stikkelsbær*
grapes	*drroo*-ehr	*druer*
lemon	si-*trroon*	*sitron*
orange	uh-pehl-*seen*	*appelsin*
peach	*fa*-shkehn	*fersken*
pear	*pah*-rreh	*pære*
pineapple	uh-nuh-*nuhs*	*ananas*
plum	*plu*-meh	*plomme*
raisin	rroo-*sin*	*rosin*
raspberries	*brring*-eh-*barr*	*bringebær*
redcurrants	rrips	*rips*
rhubarb	rruh-*buhrr*-brruh	*rabarbra*
stewed plums	*plu*-meh-*grrert*	*plommegrøt*
stewed prunes	*svi*-skeh-*grrert*	*sviskegrøt*
strawberries	*yoorr*-barr	*jordbær*

Desserts, Cakes & Cookies

apple cake	*eh*-pleh-*kah*-keh	eplekake
biscuit/cookie	*smor*-*kah*-keh	småkake
cake	*kah*-keh	kake
chocolate	shoo-kor-*luh*-deh	sjokolade
ice cream	ees	is
meringue	muh-*rrehngs*	marengs
pancake	*puh*-neh-*kah*-keh	pannekake
sponge cake	*suk*-kehrr-*brrer*	sukkerbrød
tart	*tahrr*-teh	terte

Non-Alcoholic Drinks

apple juice	*eh*-pleh-*must*	eplemost
cocoa	kuh-*kuh*-oo	kakao
coffee	*kuh*-feh	kaffe
fruit juice	yoos	jus
ice	ees	is
milk	mehlk	melk
mineral water	*fuhrr*-is	farris
non-alcoholic	*uhl*-ku-hool-*frri*	alkoholfri
orangeade	*uh*-pehl-seen-*brrus*	appelsinbrus
squash	suhft	saft
tea	teh	te
water	vuhn	vann

Alcoholic Drinks

beer	erl	øl
brandy	*brrehn*-eh-vin	brennevin
cognac	*kon*-yuhk	konjakk
dark beer	*bah*-yehrr	bayer
double	*dor*-behl	dobbel
dry	ter-rr	tørr
liqueur	li-*ker*-rr	likør
port	*purrt*-vin	portvin
red/white wine	*rrer*-vin/*veet*-vin	rødvin/hvitvin
rum	rroom	rom
sparkling	mus-*sehrr*-ehn-deh	musserende

NORWEGIAN

AT THE MARKET

Basics
bread	brrer	*brød*
butter	smer-rr	*smør*
cheese	ust	*ost*
chocolate	shoo-kor-*luh*-deh	*sjokolade*
cooking oil	*ol*-yeh	*olje*
eggs	ehg	*egg*
flour (plain)	mehl	*mel*
jam	*sül*-teh-töy	*syltetøy*
milk	mehlk	*melk*
rice	rrees	*ris*
sugar	*su*-kehrr	*sukker*
mineral water	*fuhrr*-is	*farris*

Meat & Poultry
beef	*uk*-seh-*chert*	*oksekjøtt*
chicken	*chül*-ling	*kylling*
duck	uhn	*and*
ham	*shin*-keh	*skinke*
lamb/mutton	sow-eh-chert	*sauekjøtt*
meat	chert	*kjøtt*
pork	*svi*-neh-*chert*	*svinekjøtt*
sausage	*perl*-seh	*pølse*
turkey	kuhl-*kun*	*kalkun*
veal	*kuhl*-veh-*chert*	*kalvekjøtt*

Vegetables
beans	*bern*-nehrr	*bønner*
beetroot	rrrr-*beh*-tehrr	*rødbeter*
Brussels sprouts	*rroo*-sehn-*korl*	*rosenkål*
cabbage	korl	*kål*
carrots	*gu*-leh-rrer-tehrr	*gulrøtter*
cauliflower	*blorm*-korl	*blomkål*
cucumber	uh-*gurrk*	*agurk*
mushroom	sop	*sopp*

AT THE MARKET

onion	lerk	*løk*
peas	*at*-tehrr	erter
potato	por-*teht*	potet
red cabbage	*rror*-korl	*rødkål*
spinach	spi-*naht*	spinat
tomato	too-*maht*	tomat
vegetables	*grrern*-suh-kehrr	grøn(n)saker

Seafood

cod	torshk	*torsk*
crab	*krruh*-beh	krabbe
crayfish	krrehps	kreps
fish	fisk	*fisk*
herring	sil	*sild*
lobster	*hu*-mehrr	hummer
mackerel	muh-*krrel*	makrell
mussel	*blor*-shehl	*blåskjel(l)*
salmon	*luhks*	laks
shrimps	*rray*-kehrr	reker
whale steak	*vahl*-bif	hvalbiff

Fruit

apple	*ehp*-leh	eple
apricot	uh-prri-*kus*	aprikos
banana	buh-*nahn*	banan
bilberries	*blor*-barr	*blåbær*
fruit	frrukt	frukt
grapes	*drroo*-ehrr	druer
lemon	si-*trroon*	sitron
orange	uh-pehl-*seen*	appelsin
peach	*fa*-shkehn	fersken
pear	*pah*-rreh	*pære*
plum	*plu*-meh	plomme
strawberries	*yoorr*-barr	*jordbær*

NORWEGIAN

SHOPPING

How much is it ...?

vorr mü-yö *kos-törr* deh ...?   *Hvor mye koster det ...?*

bookshop	*book*-huhn-dl	bokhandel
camera shop	foo-tu-fo-*rreht*-ning	fotoforretning
clothing store	klays-bu-*tik*	klesbutikk
delicatessen	deh-li-kuh-*tehs*-sö-fo-*rreht*-ning	delikatesse-forretning
general store; shop	*dah*-lig-vah-rrö-fo-*rreht*-ning	dagligvare-forretning
green grocer	grrern-sahks-*huhn*-dlörr	grøn(n)sakshandler
laundry	rrehn-sö-*rree*	renseri
market	*muhrr*-köd	marked
newsagency/ stationers	chyosk	kiosk
pharmacy	uh-pu-*tayk*	apotek
shoeshop	skoo-töy-fo-*rreht*-ning	skotøyforretning
souvenir shop	su-vö-*neerr*-shuhp	suvenirsjapp
supermarket	snahrr-cherp(s-bu-*tik*)	snarkjøp(sbutikk)

I'd like to buy ...

yay kuhn *for* ...   *Jeg kan få ...*

Do you have others?

hah du uhn-drreh?   *Har du andre?*

I don't like it.

deh *lee*-körr yay *ik*-kö   *Det liker jeg ikke.*

Can I look at it?

kuhn yay for *say* po deh?   *Kan jeg få se på det?*

I'm just looking.

yay bah-rrö *sayrr* ma rrünt   *Jeg bare ser meg rundt.*

Can you write down the price?

kuhn du *skrree*-vö *up* prree-sn?   *Kan du skrive opp prisen?*

Do you accept credit cards?

tah du i-*moot* krray-*dit*-kort?   *Tar du imot kredittkort?*

Could you lower the price?
    kun-nö du seht-tö *ned prree*-sn?   *Kunne du sette ned prisen?*
I don't have much money.
    yay *hahrr* ik-kö mü-yö *pehng*-örr   *Jeg har ikke mye penger.*

Can I help you?
    kuhn yay *yehl*-pö day?   *Kan jeg hjelpe deg?*
Will that be all?
    vah rdeh sor noo *ahnt*?   *Var det så noe annet?*
Would you like it wrapped?
    skuhl yay puhk-kö deh   *Skal jeg pakke det*
    in forr *day*?   *inn for deg?*
Sorry, this is the only one.
    bö-*klah*-görr deht-tö arr   *Beklager, dette er*
    dehn *ay*-nehs-tö   *den eneste.*
How much/many do you want?
    voor *mü-yö*/*muhng*-ö   *Hvor mye/mange*
    vil du *hah*?   *veel du ha?*

NORWEGIAN

Essential Groceries

batteries	buh-teh-*ri*	*batteri*
bread	brrer	*brød*
butter	smer-rr	*smør*
cheese	ust	*ost*
chocolate	shoo-kor-*luh*-deh	*sjokolade*
cooking oil	*ol*-yeh	*olje*
eggs	ehg	*egg*
flour (plain)	mehl	*mel*
ham	*shin*-keh	*skinke*
honey	*hun*-ning	*honning*
jam	*sül*-teh-töy	*syltetøy*
matches	*für*-sti-kehr	*fyrstikker*
milk	mehlk	*melk*
pepper	*peh*-pehrr	*pepper*
rice	rrees	*ris*
salt	suhlt	*salt*

NORWEGIAN

shampoo	*shuhm*-poo	sjampo
soap	*sor*-pö	såpe
sugar	*su*-kehrr	sukker
toilet paper	*doo*-puh-pee-rr	dopapir
toothbrush	*tuhn*-ber-shtö	tannbørste

Souvenirs

earrings	*ohrr*-rrö-*dob*-börr	øredobber
glasswork	*gluhs*-töy	glasstøy
handicraft	*kunst*-huhn-varrk	kunsthandverk
necklace	*huhls*-chay-dö	halskjede
Norwegian vest	*kuf*-tö	kofte
pottery	*stayn*-töy	steintøy
ring	*rring*	ring
rug	*rrü*-yö	rye

Clothing

clothing	klarr	klær
coat	frruhk	frakk
dress	*choo*-lö	kjole
jacket	*yuhk*-kö	jakke
jumper (sweater, jersey)	*gehn*-sörr	genser
shirt	*shu*-rtö	skjorte
shoes	skoo	sko
skirt	sher-rt	skjørt
trousers	*buk*-sörr	bukser

It doesn't fit.	deh *puhs*-sörr ik-kö	Det passer ikke.

It's too ...	deh arr forr ...	Det er for ...
big	*shtoort*	stort
small	*lee*-tö	lite
short	kort	kort
long	*luhngt*	langt
tight	*teht*-sit-tuhn-nö	tettsittande
loose	lowst	laust

Materials

cotton	*bum*-ul	bomull
handmade	*hon-lah*-göt	håndlaget
leather	larr	lær
brass	*mehs*-sing	messing
gold	gul	gull
silver	serlv	sølv
silk	sil-kö	silke
wool	ul	ull

Toiletries

comb	kuhm	kam
condoms	kun-*doom*	kondom
deodorant	day-yu-du-*rruhnt*	deodorant
hairbrush	*hor-rr*-ber-shteh	hårbørste
razor	buhrr-*bayrr*-her-völ	barberhøvel
sanitary napkins	*dah*-mö-bin	damebind
shampoo	*shuhm*-poo	sjampo
shaving cream	buhrr-*bayrr*-krraym	barberkrem
soap	*sor*-pö	såpe
sunblock cream	*sern*-blok-ul-yö	sunblock-olje
tampons	tuhm-*pong*-örr	tamponger
tissues	puh-*peerr*-lum-mö-ter-rr-klö	papirlommetørkle
toilet paper	*doo*-puh-peerr	dopapir
toothpaste	*tuhm*-krraym	tannkrem

NORWEGIAN

Stationery & Publications

map	kuhrt	kart
newspaper	uh-*vees*	avis
newspaper in English	*ehng*-ölsk-sprror-kli uh-*vees*	engelskspråklig avis
novels in English	*ehng*-öl-skö rru-*mah*-nörr	engelske romaner
paper	puh-*peerr*	papir
pen (ballpoint)	pehn (*kü*-lö-pehn)	penn (kulepenn)
scissors	suhks	saks

NORWEGIAN

Photography

How much is it to process this film?
　　voor mü-yö *kos*-törr deh o　　*Hvor mye koster det å*
　　fruhm-kuhl-lö dehn-nö *fil*-mön?　*framkalle denne filmen?*
When will it be ready?
　　norr arr dehn *fa*-rdi?　　*Når er den ferdig?*
I'd like a film for this camera.
　　yay vil *ya*-rrnö hah ehn film　*Jeg vil gjerne ha en film*
　　til dehn-nö *kah*-mö-rruhn　*til denne kameraen.*

B&W (film)	svuhrt-vit	*svart-hvitt*
camera	*kah*-mö-rruh	*kamera*
colour (film)	*fuhrr*-gö(-film)	*farge(film)*
film	film	*film*
flash	blits	*blitz*
lens	*lin*-sö	*linse*
light meter	*lüs*-mor-lörr	*lysmåler*

Smoking

A packet of cigarettes, please.
　　ehn puhk-kö si-guh-*rreht*-törr　*En pakke sigaretter, takk.*
　　tuhk
Are these cigarettes strong/mild?
　　arr dis-sö si-guh-rreht-tö-neh　*Er disse sigarettene*
　　krruhf-ti-yö/*mil*-lö?　　*kraftige/milde?*
Do you have a light?
　　hah du *fürr*?　　*Har du fyr?*

cigarette papers	rrul-lö-puh-pee-rr	*rullepapir*
cigarettes	si-guh-rreht-törr	*sigaretter*
filtered	fil-törr	*filter*
lighter	lai-törr	*lighter*
matches	für-stik-körr	*fyrstikker*
menthol	mehn-tol	*mentol*
pipe	pee-pö	*pipe*
tobacco (pipe)	(pee-pö)-tu-buhk	*(pipe)tobakk*

NORWEGIAN

Colours

black	svuhrt	*svart*
blue	blor	*blå*
brown	brrun	*brun*
green	grrern	*grønn*
pink	rroo-suh	*rosa*
red	rrer	*rød*
white	veet	*hvit*
yellow	gul	*gul*

Sizes & Comparisons

small	lee-tn	*liten*
big	stoorr	*stor*
heavy	tung	*tung*
light	leht	*lett*
more	mehrr	*mer*
less	min-drrö	*mindre*
too much/many	forr mü-yö/muhng-ö	*for mye/mange*
many	muhng-ö	*mange*
enough	nok	*nok*
also	os-so	*også*
a little bit	lit	*litt*

HEALTH

Where is the ...?	*voor* arr ...?	*Hvor er ...?*
chemist	uh-pu-*tay*-kö	*apoteket*
dentist	*tuhn*-lay-gön	*tannlegen*
doctor	*lay*-gön	*legen*
hospital	sü-kö-hu-sö	*sykehuset*

I'm/My friend is sick.
   yay arr/*vehn*-n min arr *sük*   *Jeg er/Vennen min er syk.*
Could I see a female doctor?
   kuhn yay for *snuhk*-kö mayn   *Kan jeg få snakke med en*
   kvin-nö-li *lay*-gö?   *kvinnelig lege?*
What's the matter?
   vah arr i *vay*-ön?   *Hva er i veien?*
Where does it hurt?
   voor yer rdeh *vunt*?   *Hvor gjør det vondt?*
It hurts here.
   deh yer-rr *vunt harr*   *Dette gjør vondt.*
My ... hurts.
   deh yer-rr *vunt* i ...   *Det gjør vondt i ...*

Parts of the Body

ankle	*uhng*-kö-lön	*ankelen*
arm	*uhrr*-mön	*armen*
back	*rrüg*-gön	*ryggen*
chest	*brrüst*-kuhs-suh	*brystkassa*
ear	*ohrr*-rreh	*øret*
eye	*öy*-eh	*øyet*
finger	*fing*-ö-rrön	*fingeren*
foot	*foo*-tn	*foten*
hand	*hon*-nuh	*hånda*
head	*hoo*-deh	*hodet*
heart	*ya*-rteh	*hjertet*
leg	*bay*-neh	*beinet*
mouth	*mun*-n	*munnen*
nose	*nay*-suh	*nesa*
teeth	*tehn*-n-neh	*tennene*
throat	*strru*-pön	*strupen*

Ailments

I have (a/an) ...	yay hahr ...	Jeg har ...
allergy	ehn uhl-lehrr-*gee*	*en allergi*
anaemia	*bloo*-muhng-öl	*blodmangel*
burn	eht *brrehn*-sor-rr	*et brennsår*
cold	snu-ö	*snue*
constipation	fo-*shtop*-pölsö	*forstoppelse*
cough	*hoos*-tö	*hoste*
diarrhoea	*mah*-gö-show	*magesjau*
fever	*fay*-börr	*feber*
headache	*vunt* i *hoo*-dö	*vondt i hodet*
hepatitis	gul-sot	*gulsott*
indigestion	*dor*-rrli fo-*rdöy*-öl-sö	*dårlig fordøyelse*
infection	ehn beh-*tehn*-öl-sö	*en betennelse*
influenza	in-flu-*ehn*-suh	*influensa*
low/high blood	*lahft*/ *höyt*	*lavt*/*høyt*
pressure	*bloo*-trrük	*blodtrykk*
pain	sma-rtö	*smerte*
sore throat	*vunt* i *huhl*-sn	*vondt i halsen*
sprain	ehn *foshtu*-ing	*en forstuing*
sunburn	*sool*-brrehnt-hayt	*solbrenthet*
venereal disease	*chern*-sük-dom	*kjønnssykdom*
worms	*in*-vols-muhrrk	*innvollsmark*

NORWEGIAN

Some Useful Words & Phrases

I'm ...	yay hahr ...	Jeg har ...
asthmatic	*uhst*-muh	*astma*
diabetic	*suk*-kö-sük-eh	*sukkersyke*
epileptic	*fuhl*-lö-sük-eh	*fallesyke*

NORWEGIAN

I'm allergic to
antibiotics/penicillin.

yay arr uh-*lehrr*-gisk moot uhn-ti-bi-*yoo*-ti-kuh/ pehn-ni-si-*leen*	*Jeg er allergisk mot antibiotikal penicillin*

I'm pregnant.

yay arr gruh-*veed*	*Jeg er gravid.*

I'm on the pill.

yay tahrr *pay*-pil-lön	*Jeg tar P-pillen.*

I haven't had my
period for ... months.

yay hahrr *ik*-kö huht mehns por ... *mor*-ntörr	*Jeg har ikke hatt mens på ... måneder.*

I have been vaccinated.

yay arr vuhk-si-*nay*-rt	*Jeg er vaksinert.*

I have my own syringe.

yay hahrr min *eh*-gön *sprröy*-tö-spis	*Jeg har min egen sprøytespiss.*

I feel better/worse.

yay *fayrr*-lörr meh *bay*-drrö/*varr*-ö	*Jeg føler meg bedre/verre.*

accident	*oo*-lük-kö	*ulykke*
addiction	ahv-*hehng*-i-hayt	*avhengighet*
aspirin	dis-*prril*	*dispril*
bandage	buhn-*dah*-shö	*bandasje*
blood test	*bloo*-prrer-vö	*blodprøve*
contraceptive	prray-vehn-*shoons*-midl	*prevensjonsmiddel*
injection	*sprröy*-tö	*sprøyte*
menstruation	mehns-trroo-uh-*shoon*/ mens	*menstruasjon/ mens*

At the Chemist

I need medication for ...

yay trrehng-örr eht midl moot ...	*Jeg trenger et middel mot ...*

I have a prescription.

yay hahrr ehn rrö-sehpt	*Jeg har en resept.*

TIME & DATES

| What time is it? | vah arr *klok*-kuh? | *Hva er klokka?* |

It's ... (am/pm)	*klok*-kuh arr ...	*Klokka er ...*
in the morning	um *fo-rr-* mid-dah-gön	*om formiddagen*
in the afternoon	um *eht-törr-* mid-dah-gön	*om ettermiddagen*
in the evening	um *kvehl-*n	*om kvelden*

What date is it today?
vah *dah*-tu arr deh i-*dahg*?   *Hva dato er det i dag?*

Days of the Week

Monday	*muhm*-dah(g)	*mandag*
Tuesday	*teesh*-dah(g)	*tirsdag*
Wednesday	*uns*-dah(g)	*onsdag*
Thursday	*toosh*-dah(g)	*torsdag*
Friday	*frreh*-dah(g)	*fredag*
Saturday	*ler*-rdah(g)	*lørdag*
Sunday	*sern*-dah(g)	*søndag*

NORWEGIAN

NUTS ABOUT KNUT

Knut Hamsun is probably the best-known Norwegian writer since Henrik Ibsen. Often characterised as one of the most influential European writers of the 20th century, he is credited with inventing a new literary style. He was awarded the Nobel Prize for Literature in 1920 but is often shunned in Norway because of his support for Hitler and the Norwegian Nazi Party during WWII.

NORWEGIAN

Months

January	yuh-noo-*wahrr*	*januar*
February	feh-brroo-*wahrr*	*februar*
March	mahsh	*mars*
April	uh-*prril*	*april*
May	*mah*-i	*mai*
June	*yoo*-ni	*juni*
July	*yoo*-li	*juli*
August	ow-*gust*	*august*
September	sehp-*tehm*-börr	*september*
October	uk-*too*-börr	*oktober*
November	no-*vehm*-börr	*november*
December	deh-*sehm*-börr	*desember*

Seasons

summer	*som*-mörr	*sommer*
autumn	herst	*høst*
winter	*vin*-törr	*vinter*
spring	vor-rr	*vår*

Present

today	i-*dahg*	*i dag*
this morning	i-*morr*-ös	*i morges*
tonight (evening)	i-*kvehl*	*i kveld*
this week	dehn-nö *u*-kuh	*denne uka*
this year	i-*yor*-rr	*i år*
now	nor	*nå*

Past

yesterday	i-*gor*-rr	*i går*
day before yesterday	i *forr*-gor-sh	*i forgårs*
yesterday morning	i-*gor*-rr *forr*-mid-dahg	*i går formiddag*
last night	i-*nuht*	*i natt*
last week/month	*sis*-tö *u*-kö/*mor*-nt	*siste uke/måned*
last year	i-*fyoorr*	*i fjor*

Future

tomorrow (morning)	i-*mor-rrn*	*i morgen*
day after tomorrow	i-*or*-vörr-mor-rrn	*i overmorgen*
next week/year	*nehs*-tö u-köl/or-rr	*neste uke/år*

During the Day

afternoon	*eht*-törr-mid-dahg	*ettermiddag*
dawn, very early morning	*dahg*-grrü	*daggry*
day	dahg	*dag*
early	*tee*-li	*tidlig*
midnight	*mit*-nuht	*midtnatt*
morning	*forr*-mid-dahg	*formiddag*
night	nuht	*natt*
noon	klok-kuh *tol*	*klokka tolv*

NUMBERS & AMOUNTS

0	nul	*null*
1	ehn	*en*
2	too	*to*
3	trreh	*tre*
4	*fee*-rrö	*fire*
5	fehm	*fem*
6	sehks	*seks*
7	shu/süv	*sju/syv*
8	*ot*-tö	*åtte*
9	nee	*ni*
10	tee	*ti*

NORWEGIAN

NORWEGIAN

11	*el*-vö	elleve
12	tol	tolv
13	*trreh*-tehn	tretten
14	*fyor*-tehn	fjorten
15	*fehm*-tehn	femten
16	*sehks*-tehn	seksten
17	*sü*-tehn	sytten
18	*at*-tehn	atten
19	*ni*-tehn	nitten
20	*chu*-ö	tjue
21	*chu*-ehn	tjueen
30	*trreht*-te/*trrehd*-vö	trettil tredve
40	*fer*-rti	førti
50	*fem*-ti	femti
60	*sehks*-ti	seksti
70	*ser*-ti	sytti
80	*ot*-ti	åtti
90	*nit*-ti	nitti
100	*hun*-drrö	hundre
1000	*tus*-ön	tusen
one million	ehn mi-li-*yoon*	en million

1/4	ehn *kvuh*-rt	en kvart
1/3	ehn *trray*-dayl	en tredel
1/2	ehn *huhl*	en halv
3/4	*trreh*-kvuh-rt	trekvart
1st	*fersh*-tö	første
2nd	*ahn*-drreh	andre
3rd	*trreh*-dyö	tredje

Some Useful Words

Enough!	nok!	*Nok!*
a little (amount)	lit	*litt*
double	*dob*-bölt	*dobbelt*
a dozen	tol	*tolv*
few	for	*få*
less	*min*-drrö	*mindre*
many	*muhng*-ö	*mange*
more	may-rr/*flay*-rrö	*mer/flere*
once	ehn guhng	*en gang*
a pair	eht puhrr	*et par*
percent	prru-*sehnt*	*prosent*
some	*noo*-n	*noen*
too much	forr *mü*-yö	*for mye*
twice	*too* guhng-örr	*to ganger*

ABBREVIATIONS

AS	company
EF	EC
e.Kr./f.Kr.	AD/BC
FN	UN
f.o.m.	from (eg. today)
gt./vn.	St/Rd
hovudpostkontor	GPO
Herr/Fru	Mr/Mrs/MS
m.o.h.	metres above sea level
NAF	AA (Automobile Association)
nord/sør	Nth/Sth
NSB	Norwegian Railway Company
postnummer	ZIP-code
Storbritannia	UK

NORWEGIAN

NORWEGIAN

EMERGENCIES

Help!
   yehlp!   *Hjelp!*

It's an emergency!
   deht-tö arr eht uh-*kut*-til-fehl-lö!   *Dette er et akutt-tilfelle!*

There's been an accident!
   deh hah shehd ehn *oo*-lük-kö!   *Det har skjedd en ulykke!*

Call a doctor!
   rring ehn *lay*-gö!   *Ring en lege!*

Call an ambulance!
   rring eht-törr ehn *sü*-kö-beel!   *Ring etter en sykebil!*

I've been raped.
   yay arr *vol*-tuht   *Jeg er voldtatt.*

I've been robbed.
   yay arr *rrah*-nuh   *Jeg er rana.*

Call the police!
   rring pu-li-*tee*-ö!   *Ring politiet!*

Where is the police station?
   voor arr pu-li-*tee*-stuh-shoon-n?   *Hvor er politistasjonen?*

Go away!/Buzz off!
   fo-*shvin!!*/stik-*ahv!*   *Forsvinn!/Stikk av!*

I'll call the police!
   ya *til*-kuhl-lörr pu-li-*tee*-ö!   *Jeg tilkaller politiet!*

SIGNS

POLITI	**POLICE**
POLITISTASJON/	
LENSMANNSKONTOR	**POLICE STATION**

Thief!
  tiüv!   *Tyv!*

I'm ill.
  yay arr *sük*   *Jeg er syk.*

I'm lost.
  yay hahrr got meh *vil*   *Jeg har gått meg vill.*

Where are the toilets?
  voor arr too-uh-*leht-tö*-nö/veh-seh?   *Hvor er toalettene/wc?*

Could you help me please?
  kuhn du *yehl*-pö meh   *Kan du hjelpe meg*
  kuhn-shö?   *kanskje?*

Could I please
use the telephone?
  kuhn yay for *lor*-nö   *Kan jeg få låne*
  teh-leh-*foon*-n?   *telefonen?*

I'm sorry.
  yay arr *lay* fo *rdeh*   *Jeg er lei for det.*

I didn't realise I was doing
anything wrong.
  yay vahrr ik-kö *klahrr* or-vörr   *Jeg var ikke klar over*
  uht yay yoo-rrö noo-ö *gahlt*   *at jeg gjorde noe galt.*

I didn't do it.
  yay hahrr *ik*-kö yurt deh   *Jeg har ikke gjort det.*

I wish to contact my
embassy/consulate.
  va-sho-*snil* o lah meh for   *Vær så snill å la meg få*
  kon-*tuhk*-tö min   *kontakte min*
  uhm-buh-*sah*-dö/mit kon-su-*laht*   *ambassade/mitt konsulat.*

I speak English.
  yay snuh-körr *ehng*-ölsk   *Jeg snakker engelsk.*

I have medical insurance.
  yay hah *sü*-kö-fo-*shik*-rring   *Jeg har sykeforsikring.*

My possessions are insured.
  ay-ön-day-lö-nö mee-nö   *Eiendelene mine*
  arr fo-*shik*-rröt   *er forsikret.*

NORWEGIAN

My ... was stolen.	... arr styor-löt	... er stjålet.
I've lost my ...	yay hahrr *mis*-teht ...	*Jeg har mistet ...*
bags	buh-*gah*-shön min	*bagasjen min*
handbag	*vehs*-kuh mee	*vesken min*
money	*pehng*-eh-nö mee-nö	*pengene mine*
travellers cheques	*rray*-sö-shehk-	*reisesjekkene*
	kuh-neh mee-nö	*mine*
passport	*puhs*-sö mit	*passet mitt*

SWEDISH

QUICK REFERENCE

Hello.	hay	*Hej.*
Goodbye.	uh-*yer!*/ hay dor!	*Adjö!/Hej då!*
Yes./No.	yah/nay	*Ja./Nej.*
Excuse me.	ü-*shehk*-tuh *may*	*Ursäkta mig.*
Sorry.	fer-*lort*	*Förlåt.*
Please.	tuhk	*Tack.*
Thank you.	tuhk	*Tack.*
You're welcome.	vuh-sho-*goo*	*Varsågod.*
I'd like a...	yuh *skul*-leh	*Jag skulle*
	vil-yuh *hah* ehn ...	*vilja ha en ...*
one-way ticket	*ehn*-kehl-bil-*yeht*	*enkelbiljett*
return ticket	rreh-*türr*-bil-*yeht*	*returbiljett*

I (don't) understand.
 yuh fer-*shtor*-rr (*in*-teh)   *Jag förstår (inte).*
Do you speak English?
 tah-luhrr du *ehng*-ehls-kuh?   *Talar du engelska?*
Where is ...?
 vahrr *air/ lig*-gehrr ...?   *Var är/ligger ...?*
Go straight ahead.
 gor *rrahkt frruhm*   *Gå rakt fram.*
Turn left/right.
 svehng til *vehns*-tehrr/   *Sväng till vänster/*
 her-gehrr.   *höger.*
Do you have any rooms available?
 fins deh nor-*grruh*   *Finns det några*
 lea-di-guh *rrum*?   *lediga rum?*
I'm looking for a public toilet.
 yuh *lea*-tuhrr ehf-tehrr ehn   *Jag letar efter en*
 oo-*fehnt*-li too-uh-*leht*   *offentlig toalett.*

1	eht	*ett*		6	sehx	*sex*
2	tvor	*två*		7	fhü	*sju*
3	trrea	*tre*		8	ot-tuh	*åtta*
4	fü-rruh	*fyra*		9	nee-oo	*nio*
5	fehm	*fem*		10	tee-oo	*tio*

SWEDISH

SWEDISH

Swedish belongs to the Nordic branch of the Germanic languages. It's spoken by the Swedes, who number close to nine million, and by the Finnish-Swedish minority in southern Finland, including the island of Åland. The language is very closely related to Danish and Norwegian. In fact, Scandinavians can usually make themselves understood in their sister countries. Outside this northern outpost, however, it's a different matter, so most Swedes speak at least some English, which is a compulsory subject on school curriculums. Many Swedes actually enjoy practising their English on tourists.

Since English and Swedish have common roots in ancient Germanic, there are many similarities between the languages. Many words were also borrowed from Old Norse into the English language during the Viking period, which ended about a thousand years ago, making the language connection even stronger. In modern times the borrowing is going in the opposite direction, with Swedish borrowing mainly from American English.

There are also quite a few differences between English and Swedish. For a start, you will notice that there are three extra letters in Swedish: å, ä and ö. These are the last three letters of the alphabet, so if you want to look up Åkesson in the telephone directory, you have to look near the end.

Even though you won't have too much difficulty getting around with English, making the effort to learn a few common phrases in Swedish will definitely pay off, as it will be greatly appreciated by the Swedes, who are not used to foreign visitors speaking their language.

PRONUNCIATION

There's a great variety of dialects in Sweden. The pronunciation guide in this book reflects a neutral Swedish, rikssvenska, but don't be surprised if you're given a slightly different pronunciation from a Swede. It all depends on where they come from!

It's important to get the stress right in words. Swedish can have a single or a double accent on a word, giving it its sing-song quality, and sometimes the difference of meaning between two identical-looking words can be huge depending on which accent is used. A good example is anden '*uhn*-dehn' and anden '*uhn-dehn*' where the former is 'the duck' and the latter is 'the spirit/ghost'. In this guide we have used italic letters to denote stressed syllables.

Pronunciation is given in the pronunciation guide in the front of this book, with the following exceptions:

SWEDISH

Vowels

Most Swedish vowels have a long and a short variant. In a stressed syllable, a vowel is short if it's followed by two consonants and (generally) long when followed by only one consonant. The unstressed syllables have short vowel sounds.

The letter e is always pronounced in Swedish, even at the end of words, and the letter y is always a vowel.

The vowels are divided into two groups, the hard vowels are a, o, u, å and the soft vowels are e, i, y, ä, ö. They help determine the pronunciation of certain preceding consonants.

Diphthongs

SWEDISH	GUIDE	SOUNDS
e	ea	as in British English 'fear'

Consonants

Some consonants have different sounds depending on whether the following vowel is hard or soft (see *Vowels* above).

SWEDISH	GUIDE	SOUNDS
g	g	as in 'get' in front of hard vowels and consonants
	y	as in 'yet' in front of soft vowels
j	y	as in 'yet'. This sound can be spelled *dj*, *g*, *gj*, *hj*, *lj* at the beginning of words.
k	k	as 'c' in 'cap' in front of hard vowels and consonants
	ch	as *tj* in front of soft vowels
tj	ch	as the 'ch' in 'cheap' but without the slight 't' sound initially. Can also be spelled *ch*, *k*, *kj*.
sj	fh	not likely 'sh' in 'ship' but try touching the inside of your lower lip with your front teeth while saying it. Can be spelled *ch sch*, *skj*, *stj*.
sk	fh	in front of soft vowels as *sj*, in other positions each letter is pronounced separately

SWEDISH

PRONOUNS

SG		
I	yahg	jag
you	dü/nee	du/ni
he/she/it	huhn/hoon/dea	han/hon/det

PL		
we	vee	vi
you	nee	ni
they	dom	de

GREETINGS & CIVILITIES
Top Useful Phrases

Hello.	hay	*Hej.*
Goodbye.	uh-*yer*!/ hay dor!	*Adjö!/Hej då!*
Yes./No.	yah/nay	*Ja./Nej.*
Excuse me.	ü-*shehk*-tuh may	*Ursäkta mig.*
May I?	for yuh?	*Får jag?*
Do you mind?	*yer*-rr deh *nor*-got?	*Gör det något?*
Sorry.	fer-*lort*	*Förlåt.*
Please.	tuhk	*Tack.*
		(at the end of a request)
	snehl-luh!	*Snälla!* (when pleading)
Thank you.	tuhk	*Tack.*
Many thanks.	*tuhk* sor *mü*-keh	*Tack så mycket.*
That's fine.	dea air *brrah*	*Det är bra.*
You're welcome.	*vuh*-sho-*goo*	*Varsågod.*

Greetings

Good morning.	goo-*mo-rr-on*	*Godmorgon.*
Good afternoon.	goo-*mid*-duh	*Godmiddag.*
Good evening/	goo-*kvehl*/	*Godkväll*/
night.	goo-*nuht*	*Godnatt.*
How are you?	*hürr* stor rde *til*?	*Hur står det till?*
Well, thanks.	*brrah* tuhk	*Bra, tack.*

Forms of Address

you (sg)	dü	*du*
you	nee	*ni*
(pol sg & pl)		
Mrs	frrü	*fru*
Mr	harr	*herr*
Miss	*frrer*-kehn	*fröken*
companion	kuhm-*rraht*/kom-pis	*kamrat/kompis*
friend	veh-*nin-nuh*/vehn	*väninna/vän* (f/m)

SWEDISH

SMALL TALK
Meeting People

What is your name?
  vuh *hea*-tehrr du?

Vad heter du?

My name is ...
  yuh *hea*-tehrr ...

Jag heter ...

I'd like to introduce you to ...
  for-rr yuh prreh-sehn-*tea*-rra ...

Får jag presentera ...

I'm pleased to meet you.
  trreav-lit uht *trrehf*-fuhs/
  uhn-yeh-*nairmt*

*Trevligt att träffas./
Angenämt.* (pol)

Nationalities

Where are you from?
  vahrr-i-frrorn *kom*-mehrr doo?

Varifrån kommer du?

I'm from ...	yuh *kom*-mehrr frrorn ...	*Jag kommer från ...*
Australia	uh-u-*strrah*-lee-ehn	*Australien*
Canada	*kuh*-nuh-duh	*Kanada*
England	*ehng*-luhnd	*England*
Ireland	*eer*-luhnd	*Irland*
New Zealand	nü-uh *sea*-luhnd	*Nya Zealand*
Scotland	*skot*-luhnd	*Skottland*
Sweden	*svarr*-yeh	*Sverige*
the USA	*ü*-ehs-*ah*	*USA*
Wales	wayls	*Wales*

SWEDISH

Age

How old are you?
hürr *guh*-muhl *air* du?   *Hur gammal är du?*
I'm ... years old.
yuh air ... *or-rr guh*-mal   *Jag är ... år gammal.*

Occupations

What is your profession?
vuh *hahrr* du fer-rr *ürr-keh?*   *Vad har du för yrke?*

I'm (a/an) ...	yuh air ...	Jag är ...
artist	*konst-naer*	*konstnär*
business person	uh-*faesh-muhn*	*affärsman*
computer expert	*dah*-to-rr-ehks-*part*	*datorexpert*
doctor	*lair*-kuh-*rreh*	*läkare*
engineer	in-fhehn-*yer-rr*	*ingenjör*
farmer	*boon-deh*	*bonde*
handyman	*huhnt-varr*-kuh-rreh	*hantverkare*
journalist	fhoo-nuh-*list*	*journalist*
lawyer	uhd-voo-*kaht*	*advokat*
manual worker	*krrops-uhrr-bea-*tuh-rreh	*kroppsarbetare*
mechanic	meh-*kahn*-i-kehrr	*mekaniker*
nurse	*fhük-fher*-tehsh-kuh	*sjuksköterska*
office worker	kon-too-*rrist*	*kontorist*
scientist	nuh-*türr-vea*-tuh-rreh	*naturvetare*
student	stoo-*dea*-rruhn-deh	*studerande*
teacher	*laer*-uhrr-eh	*lärare*
waiter	sehrr-vi-*trrees*/ sehrr-vi-*ter-rr*	*servitris*/ *servitör* (f/m)
writer	fer-rr-*fuht*-tuh-rreh	*författare*

Religion

What is your religion?
vil-kehn rreh-li-*yoon*   *Vilken religion*
til-her-rr *du*?   *tillhör du?*

I'm not religious.
yuh air *in*-teh rreh-li-*fhers*   *Jag är inte religös.*

I'm ...	yuh air ...	*Jag är ...*
Buddhist	bu-*dist*	*buddist*
Catholic	kuh-too-*leek*	*katolik*
Christian	*krris-tehn*	*kristen*
Hindu	hin-*dü*	*hindu*
Jewish	*yü-deh*	*jude*
Muslim	mus-*leem*	*muslim*
Protestant	prroo-tehs-*tuhnt*	*protestant*

Family

Are you married?   air du *yift*?   *Är du gift?*

I'm ...	yuh air ...	*Jag är ...*
married	*yift*	*gift*
single	*ü-yift*	*ogift*

How many children do you have?
hürr mong-uh   *Hur många*
bahrn hahrr du?   *barn har du?*

I don't have any children.
yuh *hahrr* ing-uh *bahrn*   *Jag har inga barn.*

I have a daughter/son.
yuh hahrr ehn *dot-ehrr/sorn*   *Jag har en dotter/son.*

How many brothers/
sisters do you have?
hürr mong-uh *brrer-*dehrr/   *Hur många bröder/*
süs-trruhrr hahrr du?   *systrar har du?*

SWEDISH

Do you have a ...?	harr doo non ...?	*Har du någon ...?*
boyfriend	*poyk-vehn/kil-leh*	*pojkvän/kille* (col)
girlfriend	*flik-vehn/chehy*	*flickvän/tjej* (col)
brother/s	brroorr/*brrer*-dehrr	*bror/bröder*
children	bahrn	*barn*
daughter/s	*dot-tehrr/dert-rruhrr*	*dotter/döttrar*
de facto husband/wife	*suhm-boo*	*sambo*
family	fuh-*mily*	*familj*
father	fahrr/*puh-puh*	*far/pappa*
grandparents (maternal)	*moorr-moorr* o *moorr-fuhrr*	*mormor och morfar*
grandparents (paternal)	*fuhrr-moorr* o *fuhrr-fuhrr*	*farmor och farfar*
husband	muhn	*man*
mother	moorr/*muh-muh*	*mor/mamma*
sister/s	*süs-tehrr/süs-trruhrr*	*syster/systrar*
son/s	sorn/*ser-nehrr*	*son/söner*
wife	frrü	*fru*

Kids' Talk

How old are you?
  hürr *guh*-muhl *air* du? — *Hur gammal är du?*

When's your birthday?
  naer fül-ler du *or-rr?* — *När fyller du år?*

What do you do after school?
  vuh *yer-rr* du ehf-tehrr *skoo-luhn?* — *Vad gör du efter skolan?*

Do you have a pet at home?
  hahrr du nor-rruh *hüs-yürr?* — *Har du några husdjur?*

I have a ...	yuh hahrr ...	*Jag har ...*
bird	ehn *for*-gehl	*en fågel*
budgerigar	ehn un-du-*laht*	*en undulat*
canary	ehn kuh-*nah*-rree-eh-*for*-gehl	*en kanariefågel*
cat/pussycat	ehn *kuht/kis*-seh-*kuht*	*en katt/kissekatt*
dog/bow-wow	ehn *hund/voov-veh*	*en hund/vovve*
fish	*fis*-kuhrr	*fiskar*
frog	ehn *grroo-duh*	*en groda*
guinea pig	eht *mah-shveen*	*ett marsvin*
hamster	ehn *huhm*-stehrr	*en hamster*
horse	ehn *hehst*	*en häst*

Feelings

I (don't) like ...
yuh tük-kehrr (*in*-teh) om ...   *Jag tycker (inte) om ...*

I'm ...	yuh hahrr ...	*Jag har ...*
in a hurry	*brrot-tom*	*bråttom*
right/wrong	*rreht/feal*	*rätt/fel*

I'm ...	yuh air ...	*Jag är ...*
grateful	*tuhk-suhm*	*tacksam*
hot	vuhrrm	*varm*
hungry/thirsty	*hung-rri/ter-shti*	*hungrig/törstig*
angry	uhrry	*arg*
happy/sad	glahd/*leh-sehn*	*glad/ledsen*
tired	trrert	*trött*
worried	*oo-rroo*-li	*orolig*

I'm cold.	yuh *frrü*-sehrr	*Jag fryser.*
I'm well.	yuh mor-rr *brrah*	*Jag mår bra.*
I'm sorry. (condolence)	yuh beh-*klah*-guhrr	*Jag beklagar.*

SWEDISH

BREAKING THE LANGUAGE BARRIER

Do you speak English?
    tah-luhrr du *ehng*-ehls-kuh?   *Talar du engelska?*

Does anyone speak English?
    fins deh *non* hair som   *Finns det någon här som*
    tah-luhrr *ehng*-ehls-kuh?   *talar engelska?*

I speak a little ...
    yuh *tah*-luhrr *lee*-teh ...   *Jag talar lite ...*

I don't speak ...
    yuh *tah*-luhrr *in*-teh ...   *Jag talar inte ...*

I (don't) understand.
    yuh fer-*shtor-rr* (*in*-teh)   *Jag förstår (inte).*

Could you speak more
slowly please?
    kuhn du vuh *snehl* o *tah*-luh   *Kan du vara snäll och tala*
    lee-teh *long-suhm*-muh-rreh?   *lite långsammare?*

Could you repeat that?
    kuhn doo *up-rrea*-puh *deh*?   *Kan du upprepa det?*

How do you say ...?
    hürr *say*-ehrr muhn ...?   *Hur säger man ...?*

What does that mean?
    vuh beh-*tü*-dehrr *dea*?   *Vad betyder det?*

I speak ...	yuh *tah*-luhrr ...	*Jag talar ...*
Danish	*duhn*-skuh	*danska*
Dutch	*hol-lehn*-skuh	*holländska*
English	*ehng*-ehl-skuh	*engelska*
Finnish	*fin*-skuh	*finska*
French	*frruhn*-skuh	*franska*
German	*tüs*-kuh	*tyska*
Italian	i-*tuhl-yean*-skuh	*italienska*
Norwegian	*nosh*-kuh	*norska*
Swedish	*svehn*-skuh	*svenska*

Some Useful Phrases

Sure.	yuh-*vist*	*Javisst.*
Just a minute.	eht *er*-gon-*blik!*	*Ett ögonblick!*
It's (not) important.	deh air (*in*-teh) *vik*-tit	*Det är (inte) viktigt.*
It's (not) possible.	deh air (*oo*-)*mey*-lit	*Det är (o-)möjligt.*
Good luck!	*lük*-kuh *til!*	*Lycka till!*

BODY LANGUAGE

Swedes aren't very different from other westerners when it comes to body language. They nod their head for yes and shake it for no. An unarticulated little uhuh or umh always means 'yes' and is often accompanied by nodding. 'No' is nej or nähä or a plain shake of the head without a sound.

You'll find that the Swedes will want to shake hands with you every time you meet, men and women alike. Kissing on the cheek is becoming more common among close friends, but the old hand shake is still the most common form of greeting.

SIGNS

BAGAGEINLÄMNING	BAGGAGE COUNTER
DAMER/HERRAR	LADIES/GENTLEMEN
EJ INGÅNG	NO ENTRY
FÖRBJUDET	PROHIBITED
GRATIS INTRÄDE	FREE ADMISSION
INCHECKNING	CHECK-IN COUNTER
INFORMATION/UPPLYSNINGAR	INFORMATION
INGÅNG	ENTRANCE
NÖDUTGÅNG	EMERGENCY EXIT
RESERVERAD	RESERVED
RÖKNING FÖRBJUDEN	NO SMOKING
TELEFON	TELEPHONE
TOALETTER	TOILETS
TULL	CUSTOMS
UTGÅNG	EXIT
VARM/KALL	HOT/COLD
ÖPPET/STÄNGT	OPEN/CLOSED

SWEDISH

SWEDISH

PAPERWORK

address	uh-*drrehs*	*adress*
age	*ol*-dehrr	*ålder*
birth certificate	pa-*shoon*-beh-*vees*	*personbevis*
border	grrehns	*gräns*
date of birth	*fer*-dehl-seh-*dah*-tum	*födelsedatum*
driver's licence	*cher-rr-koort*	*körkort*
identification	leh-gi-ti-muh-*fhoon*	*legitimation*
immigration	*puhs*-kont-*rrol*	*passkontroll*
marital status	si-*veel*-stond	*civilstånd*
name	nuhmn	*namn*
nationality	nuht-fhoo-nuh-li-*teat*	*nationalitet*
passport (number)	*puhs*(-*num*-mehrr)	*pass(nummer)*
place of birth	*fer*-dehl-seh-*oort*	*födelseort*
profession	*ürr*-keh	*yrke*
reason for travel	*rrea*-suhns	*resans*
	ehm-duh-*morl*	*ändamål*
religion	rreh-li-*yoon*	*religon*
sex	chern	*kön*
tourist card	tu-*rrist-koort*	*turistkort*
visa	*vee*-sum	*visum*

GETTING AROUND

What time does the ... leave/arrive?	hürr duhks *gor-rr*/ *kom*-mehrr ...?	*Hur dags går/ kommer ...?*
(aero)plane	(*flüg-*)*plah*-neht	*(flyg)planet*
boat	*bor*-tehn	*båten*
bus	*bu*-sehn	*bussen*
ferry	*farr*-yuhn	*färjan*
train	*tor*-geht	*tåget*
tram	*spor-rr-vuhng*-nehn	*spårvagnen*

Directions

Where is ...?
vahrr *air*/*lig*-gehrr ...?   *Var är/ligger ...?*

How do I get to ...?
hürr *kom*-mehrr muhn til ...?   *Hur kommer man till ...?*

Is it near here?
air deh *longt* haer-i-*frrorn?*   *Är det långt härifrån?*

Can I walk there?
kuhn muhn *gor* deet?   *Kan man gå dit?*

Can you show me (on the map)?
kuhn du *vee*-suh may   *Kan du visa mig*
(po *kah*-rtuhn)?   *(på kartan)?*

Are there other means of
getting there?
kuhn muhn kom-muh   *Kan jag komma dit*
deet po *uhn*-nuht *seht?*   *på annat sätt?*

Go straight ahead.
gor *rrahkt frruhm*   *Gå rakt fram.*

SIGNS

ANKOMST	ARRIVALS
AVGÅNG	DEPARTURES
BAGAGEUTLÄMNING	LUGGAGE PICKUP
BILJETTKONTOR	TICKET OFFICE
BUSSHÅLLPLATS	BUS STOP
FLYGBUSS	AIRPORT BUS
GÅNGTUNNEL	SUBWAY (pedestrian)
JÄRNVÄGSSTATION	TRAIN STATION
PASSKONTROLL	IMMIGRATION
SPÅR	PLATFORM
SPÅRVAGNSHÅLLPLATS	TRAM STOP
TIDTABELL	TIMETABLE
TUNNELBANA	SUBWAY (metro)
VÄXEL	CHANGE (for coins)

SWEDISH

Turn left/	*svehng* til *vehns*-tehrr/	*Sväng till vänster/*
right at the ...	*her*-gehrr veed ...	*höger vid ...*
next	*nehst*-uh	*nästa*
corner	*her*-rn	*hörn*
traffic lights	trruh-*feek-yü*-seht	*trafikljuset*

behind	*bah-kom*	*bakom*
in front of	*frruhm-fer-rr*	*framför*
far	longt	*långt*
near	*nae-rruh*	*nära*
opposite	*mit eh-moot*	*mitt emot*

Booking Tickets

Where can I buy a ticket?
vahrr kuhn yuh *ker-puh*   *Var kan jag köpa*
ehn bil-*yeht*?   *en biljett?*

I want to go to ...
yuh vil *or-kuh* til ...   *Jag vill åka till ...*

Do I need to book?
mos-teh muhn *boo-kuh*?   *Måste man boka?*

I'd like to book a seat to ...
yuh *skul*-leh vil-yuh *boo*-kuh   *Jag skulle vilja boka*
ehn *pluhts* til ...   *en plats till ...*

I'd like (a) ...	yuh *skul*-leh	*Jag skulle*
	vil-yuh *hah* ...	*vilja ha ...*
one-way ticket	ehn *ehn*-kehl-bil-*yeht*	*en enkelbiljett*
return ticket	ehn rreh-*türr*-bil-*yeht*	*en returbiljett*
two tickets	tvor bil-*yeht*-ehrr	*två biljetter*
student's fare	ehn stu-*dehnt*-bil-*yeht*	*en studentbiljett*
child's fare	ehn *bahrn*-bil-*yeht*	*en barnbiljett*
pensioner's fare	puhn-*fhoo-naesh*-bil-*yeht*	*en pensionärs-biljett*

1st class	*fersh*-tuh kluhs	*första klass*
2nd class	*uhn*-drruh kluhs	*andra klass*

SWEDISH

Is it completely full?
    arr deat *uhl*-deh-lehs *fult?*   *Är det alldeles fullt?*
Can I get a stand-by ticket?
    fins deh non *vehn*-teh-*lis*-tuh?   *Finns det någon väntelista?*

Air

Is there a flight to ...?
    fins deh not *flüg* til ...?   *Finns det något flyg till ...?*
How long does the flight take?
    hürr long teed *tahrr flü*-geht?   *Hur lång tid tar flyget?*
What is the flight number?
    vil-keht *flight-num*-mehrr   *Vilket flightnummer*
    air deh?   *är det?*

airport tax	*flüg*-pluhts-*skuht*	*flygplatsskatt*
boarding pass	*boo*-rding-*kahrd*	*boardingcard*
customs	tul	*tull*

Bus

Where is the bus/tram stop?
    vahrr air *bus*-hol-*pluht*-sehn/   *Var är busshållplatsen/*
    spor-rr-vuhngns-hol-*pluht*-sehn?   *spårvagnshållplatsen?*
Which bus goes to ...?
    vil-kehn *bus* gor-rr til ...?   *Vilken buss går till ...?*
Could you let me know when
we get to ...?
    kuhn du seh-ya *til* naer   *Kan du säga till när*
    vi *kom*-mehrr til ...?   *vi kommer till ...?*
I want to get off!
    yuh vil gor *ahv!*   *Jag vill gå av!*

What time is	naer	*När*
the ... bus?	gor-rr ...?	*går ...?*
next	*nehs*-ta *bus*	*nästa buss*
first	*fersh*-tuh *bu*-sehn	*första bussen*
last	*sis*-tuh *bu*-sehn	*sista bussen*

SWEDISH

Metro

Which line takes me to ...?
    vil-kehn *leen*-yeh gor-rr til ...?   *Vilken linje går till ...?*
What is the next station?
    vil-kehn air *nehs*-tuh   *Vilken är nästa*
    stuh-*fhoon?*   *station?*

Train

Is this the right platform for
the train to/from ...?
    air deh *haer* rreht pa-rrong   *Är det här rätt perrong*
    fer-rr *tor*-geht til/frrorn ...?   *för tåget till/från ...?*
Passengers for ...
must change trains in ...
    rrea-suhn-deh moot ...   *Resande mot ...*
    mos-teh *bü*- tuh *torg* i ...   *måste byta tåg i ...*
The train leaves from platform ...
    torg-eht *ahv-gor-rr*   *Tåget avgår*
    frrorn *spor-rr* ...   *från spår ...*

dining car	rrehs-tu-*rruhng-vuhngn*	*resturangvagn*
express	ehx-*prrehs-torg*	*expresståg*
local	loo-*kahl-torg*	*lokaltåg*
sleeping car	*sorv-vuhngn*	*sovvagn*

Taxi

Can you take me to ...?
    kuhn doo *cher*-rruh may til ...?   *Kan du köra mig till ...?*
How much does it cost to go to ...?
    vuh *kos*-tuhrr deh til ...?   *Vad kostar det till ...?*
Here is fine, thank you.
    haer bleer *brrah* tuhk   *Här blir bra, tack.*
The next corner, please.
    nehs-tuh *her-rn* tuhk   *Nästa hörn, tack.*
Continue!
    foort-sheht!   *Fortsätt!*

SWEDISH

Stop here!
stuhn-uh *haer*!   *Stanna här!*

Please slow down.
kuhn du suhk-tuh *nearr*?   *Kan du sakta ner?*

Please wait here.
kuhn du *vehn*-tuh *haer*?   *Kan du vänta här?*

Some Useful Phrases

The train is delayed/cancelled.
tor-geht air fer-*shea*-nuht/   *Tåget är försenat/*
in-stehlt   *inställt.*

How long will it be delayed?
hurr *mük-keh* air deh   *Hur mycket är det*
fer-*shea*-nuht?   *försenat?*

How long does the trip take?
hurr long *teed tuhrr rrea*-suhn?   *Hur lång tid tar resan?*

Is it a direct route?
air deh ehn   *Är det en*
di-*rrehkt*-fer-rr-*bin*-dehl-seh?   *direktförbindelse?*

Is that seat taken?
air deh *up-tah*-geht *haer*?   *Är det upptaget här?*

I want to get off at ...
yuh vil gor *ahv* ee ...   *Jag vill gå av i ...*

Where can I hire a bicycle?
vahrr kuhn yuh *hü*-rruh   *Var kan jag hyra*
ehn *sük*-kehl?   *en cykel?*

SWEDISH

HOW FAR?

In Sweden, all road signs show distance in kilometres,
but the Swedes prefer to use the term mil (meel) for 10
km when they talk about how far away a place is, eg.
50 km is fem mil.

Car

Where can I rent a car?
vahrr kuhn yuh
hü-rruh ehn beel?

*Var kan jag
hyra en bil?*

How much is it daily/weekly?
hurr *mük*-keh kos-tuhrr
deh parr *dahg*/parr *vehk-kuh*?

*Hur mycket kostar
det per dag/per vecka?*

Does that include insurance/mileage?
in-gor-rr fer-*shaek*-rring/
free-uh meel?

*Ingår försäkring/
fria mil?*

Where's the next petrol station?
vahrr air *nehs*-tuh
behn-*seen*-stuh-*fhoon*?

*Var är nästa
bensinstation?*

How long can I park here?
hurr *lehng*-eh for-rr muhn
puhrr-*kea*-rruh haer?

*Hur länge får man
parkera här?*

Does this road lead to?
gor-rr dehn *haer*
vair-gehn til ...?

*Går den här
vägen till ...?*

SIGNS

BILMEKANIKER	MECHANIC
BILUTHYRNING	CAR RENTAL
BILVERKSTAD/GARAGE	GARAGE
BLYFRI BENSIN	UNLEADED
EJ INFART	NO ENTRY
ENKELRIKTAT	ONE WAY
FÖRBJUDET ATT STANNA	NO STANDING
MOTORVÄG	FREEWAY
PARKERING FÖRBJUDEN	NO PARKING
REPARATIONER	REPAIRS
SJÄLVBETJÄNING	SELF SERVICE
STOPP	STOP
SUPER/HÖGOKTANIG BENSIN	SUPER
VÄJNINGSPLIKT	GIVE WAY

SWEDISH

air (for tyres)	luft	*luft*
battery	buh-teh-*rree*	*batteri*
brakes	*brrom-suhrr*	*bromsar*
clutch	*kop-ling*	*koppling*
driver's licence	*cher-rr-koort*	*körkort*
engine	*moo-to-rr*	*motor*
fan belt	*flehkt-rrehm*	*fläktrem*
lights	*lü-seh*	*lyse*
oil	*ol-yuh*	*olja*
puncture	punk-*tea*-rring	*punktering*
radiator	*chü*-luh-rreh	*kylare*
road map	*vairg-kah*-rtuh	*vägkarta*
studded winter tyres	*dub-dehk*	*dubbdäck*
tyres	dehk	*däck*
windscreen	vind-rrü-tuh	*vindruta*
windscreen wipers	*vind*-rrü-teh-to-rr-kuh-rreh	*vindrutetorkare*
windscreen washer fluid	*spoo*-luhrr-*vehts*-kuh	*spolarvätska*

SWEDISH

I need a mechanic.
    yuh beh-*her*-vehrr ehn   *Jag behöver en*
    meh-*kah*-ni-kehrr   *mekaniker.*
The battery is flat.
    buh-teh-*rree*-eht air *slüt*   *Batteriet är slut.*
The radiator is leaking.
    chü-luh-rrehn *lehk*-kehrr   *Kylaren läcker.*
I have a flat tyre.
    yuh hahrr fot punk-*tea*-rring *Jag har fått punktering.*
It's overheating.
    moo-to-rn *koo-kuhrr*   *Motorn kokar.*
It's not working.
    dehn *gor-rr* in-teh   *Den går inte.*

ACCOMMODATION

Where is	vahrr *fins* deh	*Var finns det*
a ... hotel?	eht ... hoo-*tehl?*	*ett ... hotell?*
cheap	*bil*-lit	*billigt*
good	*brrah*	*bra*
nearby	*naer*-lig-guhn-deh	*närliggande*

What is the address?
vil-kehn uh-*drrehs air* deh?   *Vilken adress är det?*
Could you write the address, please?
kuhn du skrree-vuh   *Kan du skriva*
nearr uh-*drrehs*-sehn?   *ner adressen?*

At the Hotel

Do you have any rooms available?
    fins deh nor-grruh   *Finns det några*
    lea-di-guh *rrum?*   *lediga rum?*
I'd like to share a dorm.
    yuh *skul*-leh vil-yuh   *Jag skulle vilja*
    boo ee *sorv-sahl*   *bo i sovsal.*

I'd like a ...	yuh *skul*-leh	*Jag skulle*
	vil-yuh *hah* ...	*vilja ha ...*
single room	eht *ehn*-kehl-*rrum*	*ett enkelrum*
double room	eht *dub*-behl-*rrum*	*ett dubbelrum*
bed	ehn *sehng*	*en säng*

I want a room	yuh vil *hah*	*Jag vill ha*
with a ...	eht *rrum* meh ...	*ett rum med ...*
balcony	buhl-*kong*	*balkong*
bathroom	*bahd*	*bad*
shower	dufh	*dusch*
television	*tea-vea*	*teve*
window	*fern*-stehrr	*fönster*

SWEDISH

I'm going to	yuh tehn-kehrr	*Jag tänker*
stay for ...	*stuhn-nuh ...*	*stanna ...*
one day	*ehn dah*	*en dag*
two days	*tvor dah-guhrr*	*två dagar*
one week	*ehn veh-kuh*	*en vecka*

Do you have identification?
  hahrr du leh-gi-ti-muh-*fhoon*?　　*Har du legitimation?*
Your membership card, please.
  dit *mead*-lehms-*koort* tuhk　　*Ditt medlemskort, tack.*
Sorry, we're full.
  tü-*varr* air deh *ful*-beh-*luhkt*　　*Tyvärr är det fullbelagt.*
How long will you be staying?
  hurr lehng-eh *stuhn*-nuhrr *ni*?　　*Hur länge stannar ni?*
It's ... per day/per person.
  deh *kos-tuhrr* ... parr *dahg*/　　*Det kostar ... per dag/*
  parr pa-*shoon*　　*per person.*
How much is it per night/
per person?
  hurr mük-keh *kos*-tuhrr　　*Hur mycket kostar*
  deh parr *nuht*/parr pa-*shoon*?　　*det per natt/per person?*
Can I see the room?
  kuhn yuh for *sea rrum*-meht?　　*Kan jag få se rummet?*
Are there any other/cheaper rooms?
  fins deh nor-grruh *uhnd*-rruh/　　*Finns det några andra/*
  bil-li-guh-*rreh rrum*?　　*billigare rum?*
Is there a reduction for students/
children?
  fins deh stu-*dehnt*-rruh-*buht*/　　*Finns det studentrabatt/*
  bahrn-rruh-*buht*?　　*barnrabatt?*
Does it include breakfast?
  in-gor-rr frru-kost i *prree*-seht?　　*Ingår frukost i priset?*
It's fine, I'll take it.
  deht bleer *brrah* yuh *tahrr* deh　　*Det blir bra, jag tar det.*

SWEDISH

I'm not sure how long I'm staying.
yuh *veat* in-teh hurr *lehng*-eh
yuh *stuhn*-uhrr

*Jag vet inte hur länge
jag stannar.*

Is there a lift?
fins deh *his*?

Finns det hiss?

Where is the bathroom?
vahrr air *bahd*-rrum-meht?

Var är badrummet?

Do you have a safe where
I can leave my valuables?
hahrr ni non
fer-rr-*vah*-rrings-*boks* daer
yuh kuhn *lehm*-nuh mee-nuh
vaer-deh-*sah*-kehrr?

*Har ni någon
förvaringsbox där
jag kan lämna mina
värdesaker?*

Is there somewhere to wash clothes?
fins deh non *tveht-stü*-guh?

Finns det någon tvättstuga?

Can I use the kitchen?
kuhn yuh *uhn-vehn*-duh
ker-keht?

*Kan jag använda
köket?*

May I use the telephone?
for-rr yuh *lor*-nuh
teh-leh-*for*-nehn?

*Får jag låna
telefonen?*

Requests & Complaints

Please wake me up at ...
kuhn ni *vehk*-kuh may
klok-kuhn ...?

*Kan ni väcka mig
klockan ...?*

The room needs to be cleaned.
rrum-meht beh-her-vehrr
stair-duhs

*Rummet behöver
städas.*

I can't open/close the window.
yuh kuhn in-teh *erp-nuh*/
stehng-uh fernst-rreht

*Jag kan inte öppna/
stänga fönstret.*

I've locked myself out of my room.
yuh hahrr lorst may *ü-teh*

Jag har låst mig ute.

The toilet won't flush.
too-uh-*leht*-tehn
spoo-luhrr *in*-teh

*Toaletten
spolar inte.*

I (don't) like this room.
yuh tük-kehrr (in-teh) om   *Jag tycker inte om*
deh *haer* rrum-meht   *det här rummet.*

It's too ...   deh air fer-rr ...   *Det är för ...*
  dark   *mer-rrkt*   *mörkt*
  expensive   *dürt*   *dyrt*
  noisy   *bul-rrit*   *bullrigt*
  small   *lee-teht*   *litet*

Some Useful Words & Phrases

I'm/We're leaving now.
yah/vee skuh *or*-kuh *nü*   *Jag/Vi ska åka nu.*
I'd like to pay the bill.
yuh *skul*-leh vil-yuh   *Jag skulle vilja*
beh-*tah*-luh rrairk-ning-*ehn*   *betala räkningen.*

name	nuhmn	*namn*
surname	*ehf*-tehrr-*nuhmn*	*efternamn*
address	uh-*drrehs*	*adress*
room number	*rrums*-num-mehrr	*rumsnummer*
air-conditioning	*luft*-kon-di-fhoo-*nea*-rring	*luftkonditionering*
balcony	buhl-*kong*	*balkong*
bathroom	*bahd*-rrum	*badrum*
bed	sehng	*säng*
blanket	filt	*filt*
chair	stool	*stol*
clean (adj)	rreant	*rent*
cot	*bahrn*-sehng	*barnsäng*
cupboard	skorp	*skåp*
dirty	*smut*-sit	*smutsigt*
double bed	*dub*-behl-*sehng*	*dubbelsäng*
electricity	ehl-ehk-trri-si-*teat*	*elektricitet*
excluded	*in*-gor-rr *ay*	*ingår ej*
fan	flehkt	*fläkt*
heater	*varr*-meh-eh-leh-*mehnt*	*värmeelement*

SWEDISH

included	*in-beh-rraek-nuht/ in-gor-rr*	*inberäknat/ ingår*
key	*nük-kehl*	*nyckel*
lift (elevator)	hiss	hiss
light bulb	*glerd-luhm-puh*	*glödlampa*
a lock	lors	*lås*
mattress	*muh-drruhs*	*madrass*
mirror	*spea-gehl*	*spegel*
padlock	*hehng-lors*	*hänglås*
pillow	*kud-deh*	*kudde*
quiet	tüst	*tyst*
quilt	*teh-keh*	*täcke*
refrigerator	*chül-skorp*	*kylskåp*
room (in hotel)	rrum	*rum*
sauna	*buhs-tu*	*bastu*
sheet	*lah-kuhn*	*lakan*
shower	dufh	*dusch*
soap	tvorl	*tvål*
suitcase	*rreas-vehs-kuh*	*resväska*
swimming pool	*sim-buh-sehng*	*simbassäng*
table	boord	*bord*
toilet (paper)	*too-uh-leht(-puhp-pehrr)*	*toalett(papper)*
towel	*huhn-dook*	*handduk*
(hot/cold) water	*(vuhrrm-/kuhl-)vuht-ehn*	*(varm/kall)vatten*
window	*fern-stehrr*	*fönster*

SIGNS

CAMPINGPLATS	CAMPING GROUND
FULLBELAGT/ INGA LEDIGA RUM	FULL/ NO VACANCIES
GÄSTGIVERI/PENSIONAT	GUESTHOUSE
HOTELL	HOTEL
MOTELL	MOTEL
LEDIGA RUM/RUM ATT HYRA	ROOMS AVAILABLE
VANDRARHEM	YOUTH HOSTEL

SWEDISH

AROUND TOWN

I'm looking for (the/a) ...	yuh *lea*-tuhrr ehf-tehrr ...	*Jag letar efter ...*
art gallery	*konst*-mu-*sea*-eht	*konstmuséet*
bank	ehn *buhnk*	*en bank*
cathedral	*doom-chürr*-kuhn	*domkyrkan*
church	*chürr-kuhn*	*kyrkan*
city centre	*sehnt*-rrum	*centrum*
... embassy	... uhm-buh-*sah*-dehn	*... ambassaden*
hotel	mit hoo-*tehl*	*mitt hotell*
market (outdoor)	sah-lu-to-rr-yeht	*salutorget*
market (indoor)	sah-lu-*huhl*-lehn	*saluhallen*
museum	mu-*sea*-eht	*muséet*
police	poo-*lee*-sehn	*polisen*
post office	*pos*-tehn	*posten*
public toilet	ehn oo-*fehnt*-li too-uh-*leht*	*en offentlig toalett*
public telephone	ehn teh-leh-*forn-chosk*	*en telefonkiosk*
tourist information office	tu-*rrist*-in-for-muh-*fhoon*-ehn	*turist-informationen*

What time does it open/close?
  narr *erp*-nuhrr/
  stehng-ehrr dom?   *När öppnar/
                                       stänger de?*

What ... is this?	vuh air deh *haer* fer-rr ...	*Vad är det här för ...?*
road	*vairg*	*väg*
street	*gah-tuh*	*gata*
suburb	*stuhts-deal*/ *fer-rr-oort*	*stadsdel/ förort*

For directions, see the Getting Around section, page 319.

SWEDISH

At the Post Office

I'd like to send a ...	yuh *skul*-leh vil-yuh *fhik*-kuh eht ...	*Jag skulle vilja skicka ett ...*
letter	*brreav*	*brev*
postcard	*vü-koort*	*vykort*
parcel	puh-*keat*	*paket*
telegram	teh-leh-*grruhm*	*telegram*

I'd like some stamps.
  yuh skul-leh vil-yuh *hah*   *Jag skulle vilja ha*
  nor-grruh *free-marr*-kehn   *några frimärken.*

How much does it cost to
send this to ...?
  hurr mük-keh *kos*-tuhrr deh   *Hur mycket kostar det*
  uht *fhik*-uh deh *haer* til ...?   *att skicka det här till ...?*

an aerogram	eht ae-rroo-*grruhm*	*ett aerogram*
airmail	*flüg-post*	*flygpost*
envelope	ku-*vaer*	*kuvert*
mailbox	*brreav-lor*-duh	*brevlåda*
registered mail	rreh-kom-mehn-*dea*-rruht *brreav*	*rekommenderat brev*
surface mail	*üt-post*	*ytpost*

Telephone & Internet

Can I use the telephone, please?
  kuhn *yah* fo *lor*-nuh   *Kan jag få låna*
  teh-leh-*for*-nehn?   *telefonen?*
I want to ring ...
  yuh vil *rring*-uh til ...   *Jag vill ringa till ...*
The number is ...
  num-rreht air ...   *Numret är ...*

How much does a
three-minute call cost?
>   hurr *mük-keh kos*-tuhrr eht
>   *trrea*-mi-*nü*-tehsh-suhm-*tahl?*

*Hur mycket kostar ett
treminuterssamtal?*

How much does each extra
minute cost?
>   hurr *mük-keh kos*-tuhrr
>   *vuhrr*-yeh *ehks*-trruh mi-*nüt?*

*Hur mycket kostar
varje extra minut?*

I'd like to speak to
(Göran Persson).
>   yuh *skul*-leh vil-yuh *tah*-luh
>   meh (yer-rruhn *pae*-shon)

*Jag skulle vilja tala
med (Göran Persson).*

I want to make a reverse-charges
phone call.
>   yuh *skul*-leh vil-yuh *yer*-rruh
>   eht *bea-ah*-suhm-*tahl*

*Jag skulle vilja göra
ett ba-samtal.*

What is the area code for ...?
>   vuh air *rrikt-num*-rreht til ...?

Vad är riktnumret till ...?

It's engaged.
>   deh air *up-tah*-geht

Det är upptaget.

I've been cut off.
>   *suhm-tahl*-eht *brrerts*

Samtalet bröts.

Is there an Internet cafe nearby?
>   *fihns* deh not *in*-tehrr-neht-
>   kuh-*fea* i *naer-hea*-tehn?

*Finns det något Internet-
kafé i närheten?*

Can I access the Internet from here?
>   *kuhn* yuh kop-luh *up* may por
>   *in*-tehrr-neht *haer-i-frrorn?*

*Kan jag koppla upp mig på
Internet härifrån?*

I'd like to check my e-mail.
>   yuh *skul*-leh vil-yuh-*kol*-luh
>   min *ea-mail*

*Jag skulle vilja kolla
min e-mail.*

computer	*dah-to*-rr	*dator*
public telephone	teh-leh-*forn-chosk*	*telefonkiosk*
telephone directory	teh-leh-*forn*-kuh-tuh-*lorg*	*telefonkatalog*

At the Bank

I want to exchange some money/
travellers cheques.

yuh *skul*-leh vil-yuh *vehks*-luh *pehng*-uhrr/ *rrea*-seh-*chehk*-kuhrr	*Jag skulle vilja växla pengar/resecheckar.*

What is the exchange rate?

vuh air *vehks*-ehl-*ku*-shehn?	*Vad är växelkursen?*

How many kronor per dollar?

hurr mong-uh *krroo*-ner parr *dol*-luhrr?	*Hur många kronor per dollar?*

automatic teller machine	buhn-koo-*maht*	bankomat
bank draft	post-*vehk*-sehl	postväxel
bank notes	sead-luhrr	sedlar
cashier	*kuhs-suh*/kuh-ser	kassa/kassör
coins	münt	mynt
credit card	krreh-*deet*-koort	kreditkort
to exchange	vehks-luh	växla
foreign exchange	üt-*lehnsk* vuh-*lü-tuh*	utländsk valuta
loose change	smor-*pehng*-uhrr	småpengar
signature	un-dehrr-*skrrift*	underskrift

INTERESTS & ENTERTAINMENT
Sightseeing

Do you have a guidebook/map of ...?

hahrr ni ehn *rrea*-seh-huhnd-*book*/ kah-rtuh er-vehrr ...?	*Har ni en resehandbok/ karta över ...?*

What are the main attractions?

vilk-uh air hü-vud-uht-rruhk-*fhoon*-ehrr-nuh?	*Vilka är huvudattraktionerna?*

What is that?

vuh air *dea*?	*Vad är det?*

How old is it?

hurr *guhm*-muhl air dehn?	*Hur gammal är den?*

May I take photographs?
for-rr yuh foo-too-grruh-*fea*-rruh?   *Får jag fotografera?*
What time does it open/close?
hurr *duhks erp*-nuhrr/   *Hur dags öppnar/*
stehng-ehrr dom?   *stänger de?*

ancient	*foo-rn-tee*-duh	*forntida*
archaeological	uhrr-keh-o-*lor*-gisk	*arkeologisk*
beach	strruhnd	*strand*
bridge	brroo	*bro*
building	*büg-nuhd*	*byggnad*
castle	slot	*slott*
cathedral	*doom-chürr*-kuh	*domkyrka*
church	*chürr-kuh*	*kyrka*
concert hall	kon-*saer-hüs*	*konserthus*
island	er	*ö*
lake	fher	*sjö*
library	bib-lee-oo-*teak*	*bibliotek*
the main square	*stoorr-to-rr*-yeht	*stortorget*
market (outdoor)	*to-rry-huhn*-dehl	*torghandel*
market (indoor)	*sah*-lu-*huhl*	*saluhall*
monastery	*klos*-tehrr	*kloster*
monument	mo-nu-*mehnt*	*monument*
mosque	mos-*kea*	*moské*
the old city	guhm-luh *stahn*	*gamla stan*
palace	puh-*luhts*/slot	*palats/slott*
opera house	*oo-peh-rruh-hüs*	*operahus*
river	or/ehlv	*å/älv*
ruins	rru-*ee*-nehrr	*ruiner*
the sea	*hah*-veht	*havet*
square	*to*-rry	*torg*
stadium	ee-drrots-*pluhts*	*idrottsplats*
statues	stuh-*tü*-ehrr	*statyer*
synagogue	*sü*-nuh-*goo*-guh	*synagoga*
temple	*tehm*-pehl	*tempel*
university	u-ni-va-shi-*teat*	*universitet*

SWEDISH

Going Out

What's there to do in the evenings?

> vuh fins deh uht *yer*-rruh
> po *kvehl*-luhrr-*nuh*?

Vad finns det att göra
på kvällarna?

Are there places where you can
hear Swedish folk music?

> *fins* deh not *stehl-leh* daer
> muhn kuhn *her*-rruh
> svehnsk *folk*-mu-*seek*?

Finns det något ställe där
man kan höra
svensk folkmusik?

How much does it cost to get in?

> hurr *mük-keh* kos-tuhrr
> deh ee *in-trrair*-deh?

Hur mycket kostar
det i inträde?

cinema	*bee*-oo	*bio*
concert	kon-*saer*	*konsert*
discotheque	dis-koo-*teak*	*diskotek*
nightclub	*nuht*-klub	*nattklubb*
theatre	teh-*ah*-tehrr	*teater*

Sports & Interests

What sports do you play?

> vil-kuh *spo-rtehrr*
> *üt*-er-vuhrr du?

Vilka sporter
utövar du?

What are your interests?

> vuh hahrr du fer-rr
> in-*trrehs-sehn*?

Vad har du för
intressen?

art	konst	konst
bandy (team sport on ice)	*buhn*-dü	bandy
basketball	*bahs*-keht	basket
canoeing	uht *puh*-dluh kuh-*noot*	att paddla kanot
chess	fhuhk	schack
collecting ...	yuh *suhm*-luhrr ...	Jag samlar ...
computer games	*dah*-to-rr-*speal*	datorspel
dancing	duhns	dans
fishing	uht *fis-kuh*	att fiska
football	*foot-boll*	fotboll
hiking/trekking	uht *vuhn-drruh*	att vandra
horse riding	uht *rree-duh*	att rida
icehockey	*ees-hok-*kü	ishockey
martial arts	*kuhmp-spo-*rtehrr	kampsporter
meeting (new) friends	uht *trrehf-fuh* (*nü-uh*) *vehn-nehrr*	att träffa (nya) vänner
movies	film	film
music	mu-*seek*	musik
photography	foo-too-grruh-*fea-*rring	fotografering
reading	uht *lair-suh*	att läsa
running	uht *sprring-uh/yog-guh*	att springa/jogga
sailing	uht *seag-luh*	att segla
shopping	uht *shop-puh*	att shoppa
skating	uht or-kuh *skrri-*sker	att åka skridskor
skiing (downhill)	uht or-kuh (*slah-*lom)/*fhee-*der	att åka (slalom)/skidor
swimming	uht *sim-muh/bah-duh*	att simma/bada
tennis	*tehn*-nis	tennis
travelling	uht *rrea-suh*	att resa
visiting friends	uht gor *hehm* til *kom*-pi-suhrr	att gå hem till kompisar
walking	uht gor *üt* o *gor*	att gå ut och gå

SWEDISH

Festivals

Lucia is celebrated 13 December, which was the longest night in the old calendar. During the dark ages it was vital to make sure the evil forces of darkness didn't get a foothold, so people feasted with lots of food and bright lights. These days, Lucia, a young woman wearing a crown of candles, and her followers all dressed in white and carrying candles, sing traditional songs and serve golden saffron buns in the early morning hours.

On the first Sunday of Advent the first of four candles, one for every Sunday of Advent, is lit in every home. The big Christmas celebrations take place on julafton, the evening of 24 December. The tree, julgranen, is decorated with candles, tinsel, home-made crackers, hearts and a star on top and the Christmas table is laden with food.

On Christmas Day morning, the churches are lit with candles for the pre-dawn service, Julottan. In central Sweden you may see people arrive at church in a horse drawn sleigh. To wish someone a merry Christmas, you say God Jul!

In some cultures Lent (Fastan) is observed as a time of fasting, but not in Sweden! Instead the Swedes indulge in traditional Shrove Tuesday fare of delicious fastlagsbullar or semlor (sweet buns with almond paste and cream) after a meal of bruna bönor och fläsk (brown beans and pork). The home is decorated with fastlagsris, small birch or willow branches with coloured feathers tied to them.

Easter, Påsk, is in the beginning of spring – daffodils are called påskliljor (Easter lilies) in Swedish. Eggs are painted in delicate patterns before being served and some are blown empty and hung in the påskris, small birch branches decorated with fluffy chickens, eggs and feathers.

The påskkärringar, Easter hags, are said to fly off to Blåkulla (the Blue Hill) on Maundy Thursday to party with the devil and on påskafton, Easter Saturday, they return home. To prevent the witches landing in their community, people light bonfires and shoot firecrackers to scare them off. Children dress up as påskkärringar and go around with Easter letters to their neighbours calling out Glad Påsk!

SWEDISH

On 30 April, Valborgsmässoafton (Walpurgis Night), Sweden celebrates the coming of spring with predominantly male choirs singing traditional songs by huge bonfires.

Perhaps the most exotic of all Swedish festivals, Midsommar (Midsummer) is celebrated all over the country. The maypole, majstången, decorated with leaves and flowers, is erected in an open space. People who have a traditional costume wear it, and girls wear wreaths of flowers in their hair. Everyone dances around the maypole and sings traditional songs until late into the night that never really goes beyond dusk.

Throughout the year there are also many local cultural festivals and events all over Sweden. To mention but a few:

Jokkmokk Winter Market in Lapland since 1602. Meet the Same people and their reindeer at this unique cultural event.

Vasaloppet is 85 km of skiing from Sälen to Mora in Dalecarlia, following the tracks of King Gustav Vasa in the 1520s.

Himlaspelet in Leksand, Dalecarlia is an open air theatre performance in traditional costumes which has been on stage since 1941.

Stockholm Water Festival is a huge event with all sorts of activities including sports, music and fireworks.

Medieval Week, Visby, Gotland. The medieval city goes back to the 1300s with historical re-enactments, markets and a medieval banquet.

IN THE COUNTRY
Sweden offers unique possibilities for trekking, canoeing and camping as Allemansrätten 'Everyman's right' allows you to use all land, regardless of ownership, as long as you are careful and don't cause any damage or bother the owner. You can even pitch a tent for one night without permission, but for a caravan or a longer stay, ask the land owner first. And remember to clean up before you leave!

Weather
What's the weather like?

	hürr air *vaird*-rreht?	*Hur är vädret?*
It's ...	deh air ...	*Det är ...*
cloudy	*mol-nit*	*molnigt*
cold	*kuhlt*	*kallt*
foggy	*dim-mit*	*dimmigt*
frosty	*frrost ü-*teh	*frost ute*
warm	*vuhrrmt*	*varmt*
It's raining.	deh *rrehng-nuhrr*	*Det regnar.*
It's snowing.	deh *sner-uhrr*	*Det snöar.*
It's sunny.	*soo-*lehn *fhee-*nehrr	*Solen skiner.*
It's windy.	deh *blor-*sehrr	*Det blåser.*

Camping
Am I allowed to camp here?

for-rr yuh *kuhm-*puh *haer?*   *Får jag campa här?*

Is there a campsite nearby?

fins deh non *kuhm-*ping-*pluhts*   *Finns det någon campingplats*
ee *naer-hea-*tehn?   *i närheten?*

backpack	*rrüg-sehk*	*ryggsäck*
can opener	kon-*sehrrv-*erp-nuh-rreh	*konservöppnare*
compass	kom-*puhs*	*kompass*
crampons	*ees-brrod-*duhrr	*isbroddar*
firewood	vead	*ved*
gas cartridge	guh-*sorl-fluhs-*kuh	*gasolflaska*

SWEDISH

gas cylinder	guh-*sol-tüb*	*gasoltub*
hammock	*hehng-muht*-tuh	*hängmatta*
ice axe	*ees-ük*-suh	*isyxa*
mattress	muh-*drruhs*	*madrass*
mosquito repellent	*müg-ol*-yuh	*myggolja*
padlock	*hehng-lors*	*hänglås*
penknife	*fik-kneev*	*fickkniv*
rope	rreap	*rep*
tent (pegs)	*tehlt(-pin*-nuhrr)	*tält(pinnar)*
torch/flashlight	*fik-luhm*-puh	*ficklampa*
sleeping bag	*sorv-sehk*	*sovsäck*
stove (for camping)	guh-*sorl-cherk*	*gasolkök*
water bottle	*vuht*-ehn-*fluhs*-kuh	*vattenflaska*

FOOD

The Swedish smörgåsbord is famous throughout the world for its great variety of cold and hot dishes, but there's more to Swedish food than that. Many dishes are associated with different seasons and may be difficult to find at other times.

SPRING

The first sign of spring is the semla, a sweet bun filled with almond paste and whipped cream, traditionally served on Tuesdays during Lent. Some prefer it in a bowl with hot milk and then it's called hetvägg. Following Lent is Easter with its tradition of brightly painted Easter eggs which are eaten with ham or fish dishes like gravad lax (cured salmon).

SUMMER

During summer the Swedes eat light food, with many cold meals like salads and smoked ham, lots of fish and for dessert a variety of berries (bär) with cream (grädde) or ice cream (glass).

During the Midsummer celebrations, inlagd sill (pickled herring) with sour cream and chives and new potatoes boiled with dill is a must and it's accompanied by a cold beer and a snaps (shot of akvavit) or two. Jordgubbar (strawberries) are most likely served as dessert. Ideally, this meal should be eaten outdoors.

SWEDISH

SWEDISH

AUTUMN

Towards the end of August the crayfish season is in full swing with kräftskivor (crayfish parties) all over the country. People wearing bibs and party hats, get together to eat kräftor (crayfish) boiled with dill, and drink quite a few glasses of snaps in between singing well-known drinking songs, snapsvisor.

If you're in the north, you might try their autumn specialty, surströmming (fermented herring), which tastes somewhat better than it smells. It's eaten with raw onion on tunnbröd (thin bread) or knäckebröd (crisp bread), and quite a few snapsar.

Autumn also sees an abundance of funghi, svamp, in the woods. Try kantareller, which should be available at markets and well-stocked grocery stores throughout the season.

More berries appear in autumn such as lingon (lingonberries) and the northern delicacy hjortron (cloudberries), and apples, pears and plums are ripe on the trees.

WINTER

The cold weather requires substantial meals. The traditional Thursday dinner is ärter med fläsk (yellow peasoup with pork) and for dessert pannkakor med lingonsylt (pancakes with lingonberry jam).

December 13 is Lucia when lussekatter (saffron-flavoured sweet buns), pepparkakor (ginger snaps) and glögg (mulled wine) are served by Lucia, and her followers.

At Christmas, a special smörgåsbord called julbord is the tradition. On the julbord you will find ham, different sorts of pickled herring, sausages, kalvsylta (brawn), patés, red cabbage, vörtbröd (rye bread flavoured with wort, a kind of herb) lutfisk (dried ling soaked in lye before being boiled), mustard, cheese, risgrynsgröt (sweet rice pudding) and more. A special Christmas beer, julöl, is served and the children get julmust, a sweet dark-brown soft drink which forms a head like beer when poured.

Some Useful Words & Phrases

breakfast	*frroo*-kost	*frukost*
lunch	lunfh	*lunch*
dinner	*mid*-duh	*middag*
supper	su-*peal kvehls-morl*	*supé/kvällsmål*

Table for ..., please.
eht *boord* fer-rr ... tuhk   *Ett bord för ..., tack!*

Can I see the menu, please?
kuhn yuh for *sea* meh-*nün*?   *Kan jag få se menyn?*

What does it include?
vuh *in-gor-rr* i *dea*?   *Vad ingår i det?*

Is service included in the bill?
air sehrr-*vea*-rrings-ahv-*yif-tehn*   *Är serveringsavgiften*
in-rraek-nuhd?   *inräknad?*

ashtray	eht *uhsk-faht*	*ett askfat*
the bill	*noo-tuhn*	*notan*
a cup	ehn *kop*	*en kopp*
dessert	dehs-*saer*	*dessert*
a drink	nor-got uht *drrik-kuh*	*något att dricka*
a fork	ehn *guhf*-fehl	*en gaffel*
fresh	faeshk	*färsk*
a glass	eht *glahs*	*ett glas*
a knife	ehn *kneev*	*en kniv*
a plate	ehn *tuhl-rrik*	*en tallrik*
spicy	vairl-*krrüd*-duht	*välkryddat*
a spoon	ehn *fhead*	*en sked*
stale (bread)	tort	*torrt*
sweet	sert	*söt*
teaspoon	ehn *tea-fhead*	*en tesked*
toothpick	ehn *tuhnd-pea*-tuh-rreh	*en tandpetare*

Vegetarian Meals

I'm a vegetarian.

yuh air veh-geh-tuh-rri-*ahn*   *Jag är vegetarian.*

I don't eat meat.

yuh *ae*-tehrr *in*-teh *chert*   *Jag äter inte kött.*

I don't eat chicken, or fish, or ham.

yuh *ae*-tehrr *vuhrr*-kehn *chük*-ling   *Jag äter varken kyckling*
ehl-lehrr *fisk* ehl-lehrr *fhing*-kuh   *eller fisk eller skinka*

Spices, Herbs & Condiments

allspice	*krrüd-pehp-*puhrr	*kryddpeppar*
chives	*grraes-lerk*	*gräslök*
dill	dil	*dill*
garlic	*veet-lerk*	*vitlök*
herbs	*errt-krrü-*der	*örtkryddor*
mustard	*sea-nuhp*	*senap*
parsley	*pa-shil-yuh*	*persilja*
pepper	*pehp-puhrr*	*peppar*
salt	suhlt	*salt*
soy sauce	*soh-yuh*	*soja*
spices	*krrüd-*der	*kryddor*
sugar	*sok-*kehrr	*socker*
tomato sauce	*keht*-chup	*ketchup*
vinegar	vi-*nae*-gehrr/	*vinäger/*
	veen-eh-ti-kuh	*vinättika*

Vegetables

asparagus	*spuhrr*-rris	*sparris*
beans	*ber-ner*; huh-rri-koo-*vaer*	*bönor; haricot vert*
beetroot	*rrerd-beht-*ter	*rödbetor*
Brussels sprouts	*brrüs-*sehl-*korl*	*brysselkål*
cabbage	*veet-korl*	*vitkål*
capsicum	*puhp*-rri-*kuh*	*paprika*
carrot	*moo-rroot*	*morot*
cauliflower	*bloom-korl*	*blomkål*
cucumber	*gurr-kuh*	*gurka*
leek	*purr*-yoo-*lerk*	*purjolök*

lettuce	*suhl*-luhd	sallad
mushrooms	svuhmp/	svamp/
	fham-pin-*yoo*-nehrr	champinjoner
onion	lerk	lök
parsnip	*puhls*-tehrr-*nuhk*-kuh	palsternacka
peas	a-rtehrr	ärter
potato	poo-*tah*-tis	potatis
spinach	speh-*naht*	spenat
tomato	too-*maht*	tomat
turnip	korl-rroot	kålrot

Fruit & Berries

apple	*ehp-leh*	äpple
banana	buh-*nahn*	banan
blackberries	*bjer-rn*-baer	björnbär
black/red currants	*svuh*-rtuh/	svarta/
	rrer-duh *veen*-baer	röda vinbär
blueberries	*blor*-baer	blåbär
cherries	*chersh*-baer/	körsbär/
	bi-guh-*rror*-ehrr	bigarråer
cloudberries	*yoort*-rron	hjortron
cranberries	*trrahn*-baer	tranbär
gooseberries	*krrüs*-baer	krusbär
grapefruit	*grreyp*-frrukt	grapefrukt
grapes	*veen-drrü*-ver	vindruvor
lemon	sit-*rroon*	citron
lingonberries	*ling-on*	lingon
orange	uh-pehl-*seen*	apelsin
peach	*pa*-shi-*kuh*	persika
pear	*pae*-rron	päron
pineapple	*uh*-nuh-nuhs	ananas
plum	*ploo-mon*	plommon
raspberries	*huhl*-lon	hallon
rhubarb	rruh-*buhrr*-behrr	rabarber
strawberries	*yoord-gub*-buhrr	jordgubbar
wild strawberries	*smult*-rron	smultron

SWEDISH

Breakfast

bread	brrerd	*bröd*
bread roll	*smor-frruhns*-kuh/ *frru*-kost-*bul*-leh	*småfranska/ frukostbulle*
butter	smer-rr	*smör*
boiled egg	*kookt ehg*	*kokt ägg*
cereal	*fling-er/müs*-li	*flingor/müsli*
cheese	oost	*ost*
coffee	*kuh-feh*	*kaffe*
fried egg	*steakt ehg*	*stekt ägg*
jam/marmalade	sült/muhrr-meh-*lahd*	*sylt/marmelad*
milk	mjerlk	*mjölk*
orange juice	uh-pehl-*seen*-yoos	*apelsinjuice*
scrambled eggs	oo-meh-*leht*	*omelett*
sugar	sok-kehrr	*socker*
tea	tea	*te*
toast	rros-tuht *brrerd*	*rostat bröd*
yoghurt	*yorg*-urt	*yoghurt*

Soup

broth	bul-*yong*	*buljong*
chicken soup	herns-*sop*-puh	*hönssoppa*
fish soup	fisk-*sop*-puh	*fisksoppa*
mushroom soup	svuhmp-*sop*-puh	*svampsoppa*
vegetable soup	grrern-sahks-*sop*-puh	*grönsakssoppa*

Meat

beef	*nert-chert*	*nötkött*
casserole	*grrü-tuh*	*gryta*
chicken	*chük-ling*	*kyckling/broiler*
fillet of beef	*ooks-fi-lea*	*oxfilé*
ham	*fhing-kuh*	*skinka*
lamb chops	*luhm-kot-leht-tehrr*	*lammkotletter*
liver paté	*lea*-vehrr-puhs-*tehy*	*leverpastej*
meatballs	*chert-bul-luhrr*	*köttbullar*
minced beef	*chert-fash*	*köttfärs*
minced beef and pork	*bluhnd-fash*	*blandfärs*

pork (lean)	*grrees-chert*	*griskött*
pork (with fat)	*flehsk*	*fläsk*
pork chops	*flehsk*-kot-*leht*-tehrr	*fläskkotletter*
roast beef	*ooks*-steak/*rrost*-bif	*oxstek/rostbiff*
roast lamb	*luhm*-steak	*lammstek*
sausage/salami	ko-rrv/suh-*lah*-mi	*korv/salami*
spare ribs	*rreav*-beans-*spyehl*	*revbensspjäll*
steak	bif/uhn-trreh-*kor*	*bifflentrecote*
turkey	kuhl-*koon*	*kalkon*
veal	*kuhlv*-chert	*kalvkött*

Fish & Seafood

baltic herring	*strrer-ming*	*strömming*
caviar	*rrüsk kuhv*-yuhrr	*rysk kaviar*
cod (roe)	*toshk*(-*rrom*)	*torsk(rom)*
cod roe cream	*kuhv*-yuhrr	*kaviar*
crab	*krruhb-buh*	*krabba*
crayfish	*krrehf*-ter	*kräftor*
eel	orl	*ål*
fish	*fisk*	*fisk*
haddock	*kol-yuh*	*kolja*
halibut	*hehl*-leh-*flund*-rruh	*hälleflundra/ helgeflundra*
herring	sil	*sill*
lobster	*hum*-mehrr	*hummer*
mackerel	*muhk-rril*	*makrill*
mussels	*mus-ler*	*musslor*
oysters	*oost-rron*	*ostron*
perch	*uhb-bor*-rreh	*abborre*
pike	*yehd-duh*	*gädda*
plaice	*rrerd-speht*-tuh	*rödspätta*
prawns	*huhfs-krrehf*-ter	*havskräftor*
salmon	luhks	*lax*
shrimps	*rrair-ker*	*räkor*
sole	*fher-tung*-uh	*sjötunga*
trout	fo-*rrehl*	*forell*
whiting	*vit-ling*	*vitling*

SWEDISH

Desserts & Pastries

apple pie	*ehp*-pehl-*puhy*	*äppelpaj*
cake (with cream)	*tor-rtuh*	*tårta*
cake (no cream)	*myük kah*-kuh	*mjuk kaka*
cheese cake	*oost-kah*-kuh	*ostkaka*
mousse	*frroo-mahsh*	*fromage*
custard	vuh-*nily-krrairm*/	*vaniljkräm*/
	muhy-*sea-nuh*	*maizena*
fruit salad	*frrukt-suhl*-luhd	*fruktsallad*
ginger snaps	*pehp*-puhrr-*kah*-ker	*pepparkakor*
ice cream	gluhs	*glass*
pancakes	*puhn-kah*-ker/	*pannkakor*/
	pleht-tuhrr	*plättar*
whipped cream	*visp-grrehd*-deh	*vispgrädde*

Non-Alcoholic Drinks

apple juice	*ehp*-pehl-*must*	*äppelmust*
coffee	*kuhf-feh*	*kaffe*
herbal tea	*errt-tea*	*örtte*
hot chocolate	*vuhrrm* fhook-*lahd*	*varm choklad*
milk	myerlk	*mjölk*
orange juice	uh-pehl-*seen-yoos*	*apelsinjuice*
punch	*frrukt-borl*	*fruktbål*
soft drink	lehsk	*läsk*
(carbonated)		
cordial	suhft	*safi*
tea	tea	*te*
water	*vuht*-tehn	*vatten*

Alcoholic Drinks

beer	erl/*pils*-nehrr	*öl/pilsner*
fortified wine	*stuhrrk-veen*	*starkvin*
liqueur	li-*ker-rr*	*likör*
red/white wine	*rrerd-veen*; *vit veen*	*rödvin; vitt vin*

SWEDISH

Menu Decoder 349

MENU DECODER

Breakfast

filmjölk	*feel-myerlk*	cultured milk, similar to buttermilk, eaten with cereal and a sprinkle of sugar
gröt	*grrert*	porridge made of rolled oats
knäckebröd	*knehk-keh-brrerd*	crisp bread, usually rye
välling	*vehl-ling*	gruel (Try it, you'll like it!)

Breads and Sandwiches

tunnbröd   *tun-brrerd*
  very thin crisp or soft bread made from barley
vörtbröd   *verrt-brrerd*
  rye bread flavoured with wort (a kind of herb)

franskbröd	*frruhnsk-brrerd*	white French loaf
fullkornsbröd	*ful-koonsh-brrerd*	whole grain loaf
grahamsbulle	*grrah-huhms-bul-leh*	brown bread roll
kavring	*kahv-rring*	dark sweetened rye bread
limpa	*lim-puh*	loaf of bread
rågbröd	*rrorg-brrerd*	rye bread
sötlimpa	*sert-lim-puh*	sweetened brown loaf

Swedish sandwiches are always open and if they're very elaborate you eat them with a knife and fork. In winter you may be served grilled open sandwiches, varma smörgåsar, for an evening snack. You can make a smörgås with any sort of bread, a thin spread of butter and some pålägg (any kind of sandwich topping).

landgång	'gangplank' – long gourmet sandwich with a variety of pålägg
räksmörgås	shrimps on lettuce, hardboiled egg, mayonnaise and lemon
sillsmörgås	pickled herring on cold boiled potato
smörgåstårta	a large layered sandwich with lots of different fillings, cut like a cake

Soup

kålsoppa	*korl-sohp*-puh
med frikadeller	meh frri-kuh-*dehl*-lehrr

    cabbage soup with boiled meatballs (usually pork)

köttsoppa	*chert-sop*-puh

    beef broth with meat and vegetables

nässelsoppa	neh-sehl-*sop*-puh

    nettle soup with a hardboiled egg (spring only)

ärtsoppa	*art-sop*-puh

    yellow pea soup with pork

Meat

Meat is quite expensive in Sweden and the Swedes have come up with a host of different ways of making a little meat go a long way. Casseroles are common, as are dishes made with minced meat like köttbullar (Swedish meatballs), but perhaps the most famous Swedish meat product is the sausage, korv, which comes in all shapes and forms.

biff á la Lindström	*bif* uh-luh *lin-strrerm*

    patties of minced meat mixed with beetroot and served
    with a fried egg

blodpudding med lingon	*blood-pud*-ding meh *ling-on*

    black pudding with lingonberry jam

bruna bönor och fläsk	brrü-nuh *ber*-ner o *flehsk*

    brown beans in a sweet sauce with bacon

falukorv	*fah*-lu-*ko-rrv*

    a lean sausage cut in thick slices and fried

isterband is-tehrr-*buhnd*
  sausage of pork, beef and barley grains
kalops kuh-*lops*
  meat casserole with onions and allspice
pannbiff med lök puhn-*bif* meh *lerk*
  minced beef patties with lots of fried onion
pytt i panna püt-i-*puhn-nuh*
  diced meat, boiled potatoes and onion fried and served with
  beetroot and a fried egg
rotmos och fläskkorv rroot-*moos* o flehsk-ko-rrv
  boiled pork sausage with mashed turnips
varm korv vuhrrm ko-rrv
  hot dog on a breadroll, the special comes with mashed
  potatoes – Swedish fast food!
viltgryta vilt-*grrü*-tuh
  game casserole – try älg, elk, in October

kåldolmar	korl-*dol*-muhrr	stuffed cabbage leaves
lövbiff	lerv-*bif*	very thinly sliced beef
renskav	rrean-skahv	thinly sliced reindeer meat

Fish & Seafood
Sweden has an enormous coastline and thousands of lakes and
fish is an important part of the diet. Kräftor (crayfish) are caught
in creeks and lakes from late August and many other types of
seafood are brought ashore all year round.

inlagd sill in-luhgd *sil*
  pickled herring which comes in a great number of varieties
lutfisk lüt-fisk
  dried ling soaked in lye before being boiled. Served with a
  white sauce with allspice. (Christmas only)
sotare soo-tuh-rreh
  'chimney sweep' – lightly salted herring grilled over an open fire

böckling	berk-ling	smoked herring
gravad lax	grrah-vuhd *luhks*	cured salmon

SWEDISH

Potatoes

Swedes eat potatoes with just about everything and there's a great number of ways to prepare them for the table.

Janssons frestelse   *yahn*-sons *frrehs*-tehl-*seh*
  'Jansson's Temptation' – potato, onion and anchovy, oven-baked with lots of cream
raggmunkar/rårakor   *rruhg-mung*-kuhrr/*rror-rrah*-ker
  pancakes made from grated potatoes
råstekt potatis   *rror-steakt* poo-*tah*-tis
  raw potato slices fried in oil
skalpotatis   *skahl*-poo-*tah*-tis
  potatoes boiled in their jackets
stekt potatis   *steakt* poo-*tah*-tis
  fried pre-boiled potatoes
stuvad potatis   *stü*-vuhd poo-*tah*-tis
  potatoes in white sauce

potatismos	poo-*tah*-tis-*moos*	mashed potatoes
potatissallad	poo-*tah*-tis-*suhl*-luhd	potato salad
färskpotatis	*fashk*-poo-*tah*-tis	new potatoes

Desserts & Pastries
chokladpudding   fhook-*lahd-pud*-ding
  chocolate mousse
kanelbulle   kuh-*neal-bul*-leh
  sweet roll with cinnamon and cardamon
kräm och mjölk   krrairm-o-*myerlk*
  thickened berry juice with milk
mazarin   muh-suh-*rreen*
  pastry with almond paste filling

nyponsoppa   *nü*-pon-*sop*-puh
  rose hip soup, eaten with a dollop of cream
prinsesstårta   prrin-*sehs*-*tor*-rtuh
  layered sponge cake with jam, cream and custard filling
  covered with green marzipan
ris á la malta   rrees uh-luh *muhl*-*tuh*
  rice with whipped cream and orange
schwartzwaldstårta   shvuhrtsh-vuhlds-*tor*-rtuh
  meringue, cream and chocolate cake
småländsk ostkaka   smor-lehnsk *oost*-*kah*-kuh
  baked curd cake with almonds
sockerkaka   sok-kehrr-*kah*-kuh
  sponge cake, usually flavoured with lemon

skorpor	*skohrr*-per	rusks
småkakor	smor-*kah*-ker	biscuits/cookies
wienerbröd	vee-nehrr-*brrerd*	Danish pastries

Alcoholic Drinks

Alcohol can only be purchased by those over 20 at special shops called Systembolaget. If a Swede asks you if you would like 'a drink', they probably have alcohol in mind as the word drink in Swedish denotes an alcoholic drink, usually a cocktail.

brännvin   brrehn-*veen*
  spirit distilled from potatoes, may be flavoured with herbs
  and berries or plain
glögg   glerg
  mulled wine with raisins and almonds, served in winter
punsch   punfh
  a sweet liqueur flavoured with arrack
snaps   snuhps
  a shot of *brännvin*. With the word Skål! a shot glass is
  emptied in one go.
vinbål   veen-*borl*
  a punch based on wine

SWEDISH

SHOPPING

English	Pronunciation	Swedish
bookshop	book-huhn-dehl	bokhandel
camera shop	foo-too-uh-faer	fotoaffär
clothing store	moo-deh-bu-teek	modebutik
delicatessen	deh-li-kuh-tehs-uh-faer	delikatessaffär
general store	di-veh-sheh-huhn-dehl	diversehandel
laundry/laundrette	tveht/tveh-too-maht	tvätt/tvättomat
market (indoor)	sah-lu-huhl	saluhall
market (outdoor)	to-rry-huhn-dehl	torghandel
newsagency	prrehs-bü-rro/	pressbyrå/
	too-buhks-uh-faer	tobaksaffär
pharmacy	uh-poo-teak	apotek
shoeshop	skoo-uh-faer	skoaffär
shop	uh-faer	affär
souvenir shop	soo-veh-neer-uh-faer	souveniraffär
stationers	puhp-pehsh-huhn-dehl	pappershandel
supermarket	snuhb-cherp	snabbköp
vegetable shop	grrern-sahks-uh-faer	grönsaksaffär

I'd like to buy ...
yuh *sku*-leh vil-yuh *hah* ...   *Jag skulle vilja ha ...*

Do you have others?
hahrr ni nor-rruh *uhn-drruh*?   *Har ni några andra andra?*

I (don't) like it.
yuh tük-kehrr (*in*-teh)   *Jag tycker (inte)*
om dehn/deh   *om den/det.*

I'm just looking.
yuh *tit*-tuhrr *bah*-rruh   *Jag tittar bara.*

How much is it?
hurr *mük*-keh *kos*-tuhrr deh?   *Hur mycket kostar det?*

Can you write down the price?
kuhn doo skrree-vuh   *Kan du skriva*
nearr prree-seht?   *ner priset?*

Do you accept credit cards?
tahrr ni krreh-*deet*-koort?   *Tar ni kreditkort?*

Could you lower the price?
kuhn du gor *nearr* i *prrees*?   *Kan du gå ner i pris?*

Can I help you?
    kuhn yuh *yehl*-puh *day?*   *Kan jag hjälpa dig?*
Will that be all?
    vahrr deh *uhlt?*   *Var det allt?*
Sorry, this is the only one.
    tü-*varr* deh *haer* air   *Tyvärr, det här är*
    dehn *ehn-duh*   *den enda.*
How much/many do you want?
    hurr *mük*-keh/   *Hur mycket/*
    mong-uh vil du *hah?*   *många vill du ha?*

Essential Groceries

batteries	buh-teh-rree-ehrr	batterier
bread	brrerd	bröd
butter	smer-rr	smör
cheese	oost	ost
chocolate	fhook-*lahd*	choklad
cooking oil	*maht-ol*-yuh	matolja
dishwashing liquid	disk-*mea*-dehl	diskmedel
eggs	ehg	ägg
flour (plain)	vea-teh-*myerl*	vetemjöl
ham	*fhing-kuh*	skinka
honey	*hor-nung*	honung
marmalade	muhrr-meh-*lahd*	marmelad
matches	*tehnd-stik*-korr	tändstickor
milk	myerlk	mjölk
pepper	*pehp-puhrr*	peppar
rice	rrees	ris
salt	suhlt	salt
shampoo	*fham*-poo	schampo
soap	tvorl	tvål
sugar	*sok*-kehrr	socker
toilet paper	too-uh-*leht-puhp*-pehrr	toalettpapper
toothpaste	*tuhn-krrairm*	tandkräm
washing powder	*tveht-mea*-dehl	tvättmedel

SWEDISH

SWEDISH

AT THE MARKET

Basics

bread	brrerd	bröd
butter	smer-rr	smör
cereal	*fling-er/müs*-li	flingor/müsli
cheese	oost	ost
chocolate	fhook-*lahd*	choklad
cooking oil	*maht-ol*-yuh	matolja
eggs	ehg	ägg
flour (plain)	*vea*-teh-*myerl*	vetemjöl
marmalade	muhrr-meh-*lahd*	marmelad
milk	myerlk	mjölk
pasta	*pahs*-tah/ *nood*-lahr	pasta/nudlar
rice	rrees	ris
sugar	*sok*-kehrr	socker
water	*vuht*-tehn	vatten
yoghurt	*yorg*-urt	yoghurt

Meat & Poultry

beef	*nert*-chert	nötkött
chicken	*chük*-ling	kyckling/broiler
ham	*fhing*-kuh	skinka
lamb	luhm	lamm
meat	chert	kött
pork	*grees-chert*/	griskött (lean)/
(with fat)	*flehsk*	fläsk
sausage/salami	ko-rrv/suh-*lah*-mi	korv/salami
turkey	kuhl-*koon*	kalkon
veal	*kuhlv*-chert	kalvkött

Vegetables

beans	*ber-ner*; huh-rri-koo-*vaer*	bönor; haricot vert
beetroot	*rrerd-beht*-ter	rödbetor
cabbage	*veet-korl*	vitkål
capsicum	*puhp*-rri-*kuh*	paprika

carrot	*moo-rroot*	morot
cauliflower	*bloom-korl*	blomkål
cucumber	*gurr-kuh*	gurka
lettuce	*suhl-luhd*	sallad
mushrooms	svuhmp/	svamp/
	fham-pin-*yoo*-nehrr	champinjoner
onion	lerk	lök
peas	*a-rtehrr*	ärter
potato	poo-*tah*-tis	potatis
spinach	speh-*naht*	spenat
tomato	too-*maht*	tomat
vegetables	*grrern*-sahk-ehrr	grönsaker

Seafood

cod	toshk	torsk
crayfish	*krrehf-ter*	kräftor
fish	*fisk*	fisk
herring	sil	sill
lobster	*hum*-mehrr	hummer
mussels	*mus-ler*	musslor
oysters	*oost-rron*	ostron
salmon	luhks	lax

Fruit

apple	*ehp-leh*	äpple
banana	buh-*nahn*	banan
fruit	frrukt	frukt
grapes	veen-*drrü*-ver	vindruvor
lemon	sit-*rroon*	citron
orange	uh-pehl-*seen*	apelsin
peach	*pa*-shi-*kuh*	persika
pear	*pae-rron*	päron
plum	*ploo-mon*	plommon
strawberries	*yoord-gub*-buhrr	jordgubbar

Souvenirs

earrings	*er-rr-hehng-ehn*	*örhängen*
glassware	glahs	*glas*
handicraft	*hehm-sleyd*	*hemslöjd*
necklace	*huhls-buhnd*	*halsband*
pottery	cheh-rruh-*meek*	*keramik*
ring	*rring*	*ring*

Clothing

bathers	*bahd-drrehkt/*	*baddräkt/*
	bahd-bük-sorr	*badbyxor* (f/m)
clothing	*klae-dehrr*	*kläder*
coat	*kuhp-puh/rrok*	*kappa/rock* (f/m)
dress	*klehn-ning*	*klänning*
jacket	*yak-kuh*	*jacka*
jumper (sweater)	*trrer-yuh*	*tröja*
shirt	*fhoo-rtuh*	*skjorta*
shoes	skoorr	*skor*
skirt	chool	*kjol*
trousers/pants	*bük-ser*	*byxor*

It doesn't fit.

dehn *puhs*-uhrr *in*-teh	*Den passar inte.*

It's too ...	dehn air fer-rr ...	*Den är för ...*
big/small	*stoorr/lee-tehn*	*stor/liten*
long/short	*long/kort*	*lång/kort*
loose/tight	*veed/trrong*	*vid/trång*

Materials

brass	*mehs-sing*	*mässing*
cotton	*boom-ul*	*bomull*
fabric	tüg	*tyg*
flax	leen	*lin*
gold	guld	*guld*
handmade	*huhnd-yoord*	*handgjord*
hand woven	*hehm-vairvd*	*hemvävd*

leather	*lair*-dehrr	*läder*
linen	*lin-neh*	*linne*
silk	*sil-keh/see-dehn*	*silke/siden*
silver	*sil*-vehrr	*silver*
wood	trrair	*trä*
wool	*ül-leh*	*ylle*

Colours

black	svuhrt	*svart*
blue	blor	*blå*
brown	brrün	*brun*
green	grrern	*grön*
orange	o-*rruhnsh*	*orange*
pink	*rror*-suh/fhaer	*rosa/skär*
purple	*lee*-luh	*lila*
red	rrerd	*röd*
white	veet	*vit*
yellow	gül	*gul*

Toiletries

comb	kuhm	*kam*
condoms	kon-*dor*-mehrr	*kondomer*
deodorant	dea-oo-doo-*rruhnt*	*deodorant*
hairbrush	*hor-rr-bosh*-teh	*hårborste*
moisturising cream	*hüd-krrairm*	*hudkräm*
mosquito repellent	*müg-ohl*-yuh	*myggolja*
razor	*rrahk-hü-vehl*	*rakhyvel*
razor blades	*rrahk-blahd*	*rakblad*
sanitary napkins	*dahm-bin*-der	*dambindor*
shampoo	*fham*-poo	*schampo*
shaving cream	*rrahk-tvorl*	*raktvål*
soap	tvorl	*tvål*
sunblock cream	*sool-krrairm*	*solkräm*
tampons	tuhm-*pong*-ehrr	*tamponger*
tissues	*nairs-dü*-kuhrr	*näsdukar*
toilet paper	too-uh-*leht-puh*-pehrr	*toalettpapper*
toothbrush	*tuhn-bosh*-teh	*tandborste*

SWEDISH

Stationery & Publications

envelope	ku-*vaer*	*kuvert*
map	*kah-rtuh*	*karta*
newspaper (in English)	(*ehng*-ehlsk) *tee*-ning	(*engelsk*) *tidning*
novels in English	*ber*-kehrr po *ehng*-ehls-kuh	*böcker på engelska*
paper	*puh-pehrr*	*papper*
pen	*pehn-nuh*	*penna*
scissors	suhks	*sax*

Photography

How much is it to process this film?
hurr mük-eht *kost*-uhrr deh uht *fruhm*-kuhl-luh dehn *haer fil*-mehn?
Hur mycket kostar det att framkalla den här filmen?

When will it be ready?
naer air dehn *klahrr*?
När är den klar?

I'd like a film for this camera.
yuh skool-leh vil-yuh *hah* ehn *film* til dehn *haer kahm*-rruhn.
Jag skulle vilja ha en film till den här kameran.

B&W (film)	*svuhrt-veet* film	*svart-vit film*
battery	buh-teh-*rree*	*batteri*
camera	*kahm*-rruh	*kamera*
colour (film)	*farry-film*	*färgfilm*
copy	ko-*pee-uh*	*kopia*
film	film	*film*
flash	blikst	*blixt*
lens	ob-yehk-*teev*	*objektiv*
light meter	*yüs-mair*-tuh-rreh	*ljusmätare*

Smoking

A packet of cigarettes, please.
	eht puh-*keat*	*Ett paket*
	si-guh-*rreht*-tehrr *tuhk*	*cigarretter, tack.*

Are these cigarettes strong/mild?
	air dom *haer*	*Är de här*
	si-guh-*rreht*-tehrr-nuh	*cigarretterna*
	stuhrr-kuh/*mil-duh?*	*starka/milda?*

Do you have a light?
	hahrr du *ehld?*	*Har du eld?*

May I smoke here?
	for-rr yuh *rrer*-kuh *haer?*	*Får jag röka här?*

cigarette papers	si-guh-*rreht*-*puhp*-pehrr	*cigarrettpapper*
cigarettes	si-guh-*rreht*-tehrr	*cigarretter*
filtered	*fil*-tehrr	*filter*
lighter	*tehn*-duh-*rreh*	*tändare*
matches	*tehnd-stik*-korr	*tändstickor*
menthol	mehn-*torl*	*mentol*
pipe	*pee*-puh	*pipa*
tobacco (pipe)	(*peep*-)*too*-buhk	*(pip)tobak*

Sizes & Comparisons

small	*lee-tehn*	*liten*
big	stoorr	*stor*
heavy	tung	*tung*
just right	*lah-gom*	*lagom*
light (not heavy)	leht	*lätt*
more	mearr	*mer*
less	*min*-drreh	*mindre*
too much/many	fer-rr *mük-keh*/ *mong-uh*	*för mycket*/ *många*
many	*mong-uh*	*många*
enough	*til-rrehk*-lit	*tillräckligt*
also	*ok*-so	*också*
a little bit	*lee*-teh *grruhn*	*lite grand*

SWEDISH

HEALTH

Where is the ...?	vahrr air ...?	*Var är ...?*
chemist	uh-poo-*tea*-keht	*apoteket*
dentist	*tuhnd*-*lair*-kuh-rrehn	*tandläkaren*
doctor	*dok*-to-rn	*doktorn*
hospital	*fhük*-hü-seht	*sjukhuset*

I'm/My friend is sick.
  yuh air/min *vehn* air *fhük*   *Jag är/Min vän är sjuk.*
Could I see a female doctor?
  kuhn yuh for *trrehf*-fuh   *Kan jag få träffa*
  ehn *kvin*-li *lair*-kuh-rreh?   *en kvinnlig läkare?*
What's the matter?
  vuh air deh fer-rr *feal* po *day*?   *Vad är det för fel på dig?*
Where does it hurt?
  vahrr yer-rr deh *oont*?   *Var gör det ont?*

I have ...	yuh hahrr ...	*Jag har ...*
It hurts here.	deht yer-rr *oont haer*	*Det gör ont här.*

Parts of the Body

ankle	*vrris*-tehn	*vristen*
arm	*uhrr*-men	*armen*
back	*rrüg*-gehn	*ryggen*
chest	*brrerst*-eht	*bröstet*
ear	*er*-rruht	*örat*
eye	*er*-guht	*ögat*
finger	*fing*-rreht	*fingret*
foot	*foo*-tehn	*foten*
hand	*huhn*-dehn	*handen*
head	*hü*-veht	*huvudet*
heart	*yarr*-tuht	*hjärtat*
leg	*bea*-neht	*benet*
mouth	*mun*-nehn	*munnen*
nose	*nair*-suhn	*näsan*
ribs	*rreav*-*bea*-nehn	*revbenen*
skin	*hü*-dehn	*huden*

spine	rrüg-rrah-dehn	ryggraden
stomach	mah-gehn	magen
teeth	tehn-dehrr-nuh	tänderna
throat	huhl-sehn	halsen
wrist	huhnd-lea-dehn	handleden

Ailments

an allergy	ehn uh-lehrr-gee	en allergi
anaemia	blood-brrist	blodbrist
a blister	ehn blor-suh	en blåsa
a burn	eht brrehn-sor-rr	ett brännsår
a cold	ehn fer-chül-ning	en förkylning
constipation	fer-shtop-ning	förstoppning
a cough	hoos-tuh	hosta
diarrhoea	dee-uh-rrea	diarré
fever	fea-behrr	feber
glandular fever	ker-rtehl-fea-behrr	körtelfeber
headache	hü-vud-varrk	huvudvärk
hepatitis	heh-puh-teet/gül-soot	hepatit/gulsot
indigestion	dor-li	dålig
	maht-smehlt-ning	matsmältning
an infection	ehn in-fehk-fhoon	en infektion
influenza	in-flu-ehn-suh	influensa
lice	lers	löss
low/high	lorgt/hergt	lågt/högt
blood pressure	blood-trrük	blodtryck
motion sickness	ork-fhü-kuh	åksjuka
a pain	oont	ont
sore throat	oont i huhl-sehn	ont i halsen
sprain	stük-ning	stukning
a stomachache	oont i mah-gehn	ont i magen
sunburn	sool-brrehn-nuh	solbränna
urinary tract	blors-kuh-tuhrr	blåskatarr
infection		
venereal disease	cherns-fhük -doom	könssjukdom
worms	muhsk i mah-gehn	mask i magen

SWEDISH

Some Useful Words & Phrases

I'm ...	yuh air ...	*Jag är ...*
asthmatic	uhst-*mah*-ti-kehrr	*astmatiker*
diabetic	dee-uh-*bea*-ti-kehrr	*diabetiker*
epileptic	eh-pi-*lehp*-ti-kehrr	*epileptiker*

I'm allergic to antibiotics/penicillin.
    yuh air uh-*lehrr*-gisk moot   *Jag är allergisk mot*
    uhn-ti-bi-*or*-ti-kuh/pehn-i-si-*leen*   *antibiotika/penicillin.*
I'm pregnant.
    yuh air grruh-*veed*   *Jag är gravid.*
I'm on the pill.
    yuh air-tehrr *pea-pil*-lehrr   *Jag äter p-piller.*
I haven't had my period for ... months.
    yuh hahrr *in*-teh huhft   *Jag har inte haft*
    mehns por ... *mor*-nuh-dehrr   *mens på ... månader.*
I have been vaccinated.
    yuh air vuhk-si-*nea*-rruhd   *Jag är vaccinerad.*
I have my own syringe.
    yuh hahrr min *ea*-gehn   *Jag har min egen*
    sprrü-*tuh*   *spruta.*
I feel better/worse.
    yuh mor-rr *beht*-rreh/*sehm*-rreh   *Jag mår bättre/sämre.*

accident	*oo-lük*-kuh	*olycka*
addiction	*mis-brrük*	*missbruk*
antiseptic	uhn-ti-*sehp*-tisk	*antiseptisk*
aspirin	mang-neh-*sül*	*magnecyl*
bandage	fer-rr-*buhnd*	*förband*
band-aid	*plos*-tehrr	*plåster*
a bite	eht *beht*	*ett bett*
blood pressure	blood-*trrük*	*blodtryck*
blood test	*blood-prroov*	*blodprov*
contraceptive	prreh-vehn-*teev-mea*-dehl	*preventivmedel*
injection	*sprrü-tuh*	*spruta*
injury	*skah-duh*	*skada*
itch	*klor-duh*	*klåda*

medicine	meh-di-*seen*	*medicin*
menstruation	mehns	*mens*
nausea	*il*-luh-*mor*-ehn-deh	*illamående*
oxygen	*sü*-rreh	*syre*
panadol	puh-noo-*deel*	*panodil*
vitamins	vi-tuh-*mee*-nehrr	*vitaminer*
wound	sor-rr	*sår*

At the Chemist

I need medication for ...
  yuh beh-*her*-vehrr eht
  mea-dehl moot ...
I have a prescription.
  yuh *hahrr* eht rreh-*sehpt*

*Jag behöver ett
medel mot ...*

Jag har ett recept.

At the Dentist

I have a toothache.
  yuh hahrr *tuhnd-varrk*
I've lost a filling.
  yuh hahrr *tuhp*-puht
  ehn *plomb*
I've broken a tooth.
  yuh hahrr slah-git *ahv*
  ehn *tuhnd*
My gums hurt.
  yuh hahrr *oont* i
  tuhnd-cher-teht
I don't want it extracted.
  yuh vil *in*-teh hah dehn
  üt-drrah-gehn
Please give me an anaesthetic.
  yuh vil hah be-*derv*-ning

Jag har tandvärk.

*Jag har tappat
en plomb.*

*Jag har slagit av
en tand.*

*Jag har ont i
tandköttet.*

*Jag vill inte ha den
utdragen.*

Jag vill ha bedövning.

TIME & DATES

What date is it today?

    vil-keht *dah*-tum air deh i-*dah*?   *Vilket datum är det idag?*

What time is it?

    hürr *mük*-keh air *klok*-kuhn?   *Hur mycket är klockan?*

It's ...	hun air ...	*Hon är ...*
in the morning (early)	por *mo*-rro-*nehn*	*på morgonen*
in the morning (later on)	por *fer-rr-mid*-duhn	*på förmiddagen*
in the afternoon	por *ehf*-tehrr-*mid*-duhn	*på eftermiddagen*
in the evening	por *kvehl*-lehn	*på kvällen*
at night	por *nuht*-tehn	*på natten*

Days of the Week

Monday	*mon*-duh	*måndag*
Tuesday	*tees*-duh	*tisdag*
Wednesday	*oons*-duh	*onsdag*
Thursday	*toosh*-rduh	*torsdag*
Friday	*frrea*-duh	*fredag*
Saturday	*ler*-rduh	*lördag*
Sunday	*sern*-duh	*söndag*

Months

January	yuh-nu-*ah*-rri	*januari*
February	feb-rru-*ah*-rri	*februari*
March	muhsh	*mars*
April	uhp-*rril*	*april*
May	muhy	*maj*
June	*yü*-ni	*juni*
July	*yü*-li	*juli*
August	uh-*gus*-ti	*augusti*
September	sehp-*tehm*-behrr	*september*
October	ok-*too*-behrr	*oktober*
November	noo-*vehm*-behrr	*november*
December	deh-*sehm*-behrr	*december*

Seasons
summer	*som-muhrr*	*sommar*
autumn	herst	*höst*
winter	*vin*-tehrr	*vinter*
spring	vor-rr	*vår*

Present
today	i-*dah*	*idag*
this morning	i-*dah* po *mo*-rro-*nehn*	*idag på morgonen*
tonight (evening)	i-*kvehl*	*i kväll*
tonight (very late)	i-*nuht*	*i natt*
this week	dehn *haer* vehk-*kuhn*	*den här veckan*
this year	i *or*-rr	*i år*
now	nü	*nu*

Past
yesterday	i-*gor*-rr	*igår*
day before yesterday	i-*fer*-rr-*gor*-rr	*i förrgår*
this morning	i-*mo*-sheh	*i morse*
yesterday morning	i-gor-rr *mosh-eh*	*igår morse*
last night	i-gor-rr *kvehl*	*igår kväll*
last week	i fer-rruh *vehk*-kuhn	*förra veckan*
last year	fer-rruh *or*-rreht	*förra året*

Future
tomorrow (morning)	i-*mo*-rron (*bit-ti*)	*i morgon (bitti)*
day after tomorrow	i *er*-vehrr-*mo*-rron	*i övermorgon*
tomorrow	i *mo*-rron	*i morgon*
afternoon/	*ehf*-tehrr-*mid*-duh/	*eftermiddag/*
evening	*kvehl*	*kväll*
next week/year	*nehs*-tuh veh-*kuh*/or-rr	*nästa vecka/år*

SWEDISH

WHAT TIME IS IT?
Swedes often use the 24-hour system for telling the time.

SWEDISH

During the Day

afternoon	*ehf*-tehrr-*mid*-duh	*eftermiddag*
dawn	*grrü-ning*	*gryning*
day	dahg	*dag*
dusk	*fhüm-ning*	*skymning*
early	*tee-dit*	*tidigt*
evening	kvehl	*kväll*
late	seant	*sent*
late morning	*fer-rr-mid*-duh	*förmiddag*
midnight	*meed-nuht*	*midnatt*
morning	*mo-rron*	*morgon*
night	nuht	*natt*
noon	mit po *dahn*;	*mitt på dagen*;
	klo-kuhn *tolv*	*klockan tolv*

NUMBERS & AMOUNTS

0	nol	*noll*
1	eht	*ett*
2	tvor	*två*
3	trrea	*tre*
4	*fü-rruh*	*fyra*
5	fehm	*fem*
6	sehx	*sex*
7	fhü	*sju*
8	*ot-tuh*	*åtta*
9	*nee-oo*	*nio*
10	*tee-oo*	*tio*
11	*ehl-vuh*	*elva*
12	tolv	*tolv*
13	*trreh-ton*	*tretton*
14	*fyoo-rton*	*fjorton*
15	*fehm-ton*	*femton*
16	*sehx-ton*	*sexton*
17	*fhu-ton*	*sjutton*
18	*ah-rton*	*arton*
19	*ni-ton*	*nitton*

20	*chü*-goo	tjugo
21	chü-goo-*eht*	tjugoett
30	*trreh*-ti	trettio
40	*fer*-rti	fyrtio
50	*fehm*-ti	femtio
60	*sehx*-ti	sextio
70	*fhu*-ti	sjuttio
80	*ot*-ti	åttio
90	*ni*-ti	nittio
100	eht *hun*-drruh	ett hundra
101	hun-drruh-*eht*	hundraett
1000	eht *tü*-sehn	ett tusen
one million	ehn mil-*yoon*	en miljon
one billion	ehn mil-*yahrd*	en miljard
1st	*fersh*-rtuh	första
2nd	*uhnd*-rruh	andra
3rd	*trread*-yeh	tredje
1/4	ehn *fyae*-rdeh-*deal*/ehn *kvartsh*	en fjärdedel/en kvarts
1/3	ehn *trrea*-dyeh-*deal*	en tredjedel
1/2	ehn *huhlv*	en halv
3/4	*trrea fyae*-rdeh-*dea*-luhrr/ *trrea kvartsh*	tre fjärdedelar/ tre kvarts

Some Useful Words

Enough!	deh *rrehk*-kehrr!	Det räcker!
a little (amount)	lee-teh *grruhn*	lite grand
double	*dub*-behl	dubbel
a dozen	eht *dus*-sin	ett dussin
few	nor-grruh *for*	några få
just right	*lah*-gom	lagom
less	*min*-drreh	mindre
many	*mong*-uh	många
more	*mea*-rruh	mera
once	ehn gong	en gång
a pair	eht *pahrr*	ett par

SWEDISH

percent	prroo-*sehnt*	*procent*
some	*nor-grruh*	*några*
too much	fer-rr *mük-keh*	*för mycket*
twice	*tvor gong-ehrr*	*två gånger*

ABBREVIATIONS

AB	limited corporation
avd	department
dl	decilitre (100 ml)
e Kr/f Kr	AD/BC
EU	European Union
exkl	excluded
FN	United Nations
fr o m	from and including
Gbg	Göteborg (Gothenburg)
hg	hecto (100 grams)
Hr/Fr/Frk	Mr/Mrs/Miss
inkl	included
jvgstn	railway station
kg	kilogram
kl	at (about time)
km	kilometre
kr	kronor (Swedish currency)
M	Motorists' National Organisation
moms	VAT/GST – sales tax
N/S/Ö/V	north/south/east/west
Obs!	Important
osv	and so on
Rea	Sale
SAS	Scandinavian Airlines System
SJ	Swedish railways
STF	Swedish Tourism Organisation
Sthlm	Stockholm
T-bana	underground, metro
t o m	until and including
tr	stairs (in an address)

SWEDISH

EMERGENCIES

Help!	*yehlp!*	*Hjälp!*
Fire!	ehl-dehn air *lers!*	*Elden är lös!*
Thief!	tuh *fuhst* chü-vehn!	*Ta fast tjuven!*
Call the police!	rring poo-*lee*-sehn!	*Ring polisen!*
I'm lost.	yuh hahrr got *vil*-seh	*Jag har gått vilse.*

It's an emergency!
   deh air ehn
   nerd-si-tu-uh-*fhoon!*
Det är ett
nödsituation!

There's been an accident!
   deh hahrr *hehnt* ehn oo-*lük*-kuh!
Det har hänt en olycka!

Call a doctor/an ambulance!
   rring ehf-tehrr ehn *dok*-to-rr/
   ehn uhm-boo-*luhns!*
Ring efter en doktor/
en ambulans!

I've been raped.
   yuh hahrr blee-vit *vold-tah*-gehn
Jag har blivit våldtagen.

I've been robbed!
   yuh hahrr blee-vit *rror-nuhd!*
Jag har blivit rånad!

Where is the police station?
   vahrr air poo-*lees*-stuh-*fhoo*-nehn?
Var är polisstationen?

Go away!
   fer-*shvin!*; gor din *vairg!*
Försvinn!; Gå din väg!

I'll call the police!
   yuh *kuhl*-luhrr po poo-*lees!*
Jag kallar på polis!

I'm/My friend is ill.
   yuh air/min vehn air *fhook*
Jag är/Min vän är sjuk.

Where are the toilets?
   vahrr air too-uh-*leht*-tehn?
Var är toaletten?

Could you help me please?
   kuhn du *yehl*-puh *may*?
Kan du hjälpa mig?

Could I please use the telephone?
   kuhn yuh for *lor*-nuh
   teh-leh-*for*-nehn?
Kan jag få låna
telefonen?

I'm sorry. I apologise.
   fer-*lort*. yuh bearr om *ü-shehkt*
Förlåt. Jag ber om ursäkt.

SWEDISH

I didn't realise I was doing
anything wrong.

    yuh fer-*shtood* in-teh uht   *Jag förstod inte att*
    yuh yoo-rdeh *feal*   *jag gjorde fel.*

I didn't do it.

    yuh *yoo*-rdeh deh *in-teh*   *Jag gjorde det inte.*

I wish to contact my embassy/
consulate.

    yuh vil kon-*tuhk*-tuh min   *Jag vill kontakta min*
    uhm-buh-*sahd*/mit kon-su-*laht*   *ambassad/mitt konsulat.*

I speak English.

    yuh tah-luhrr *ehng*-ehl-skuh   *Jag talar engelska.*

I have medical insurance.

    yuh hahrr *fhük*-fer-*shairk*-rring   *Jag har sjukförsäkring.*

My possessions are insured.

    yuh hahrr fer-*shairk*-rring   *Jag har försäkring.*

My ...	min ... hahrr	*Min ... har*
was stolen.	blee-vit *stü-lehn*	*blivit stulen.*
I've lost my ...	yuh hahrr	*Jag har*
	fer-*loo*-rruht ...	*förlorat...*
bags	mee-nuh *vehs-korr*	*mina väskor*
handbag	min *huhnd-vehs*-kuh	*min handväska*
money	mee-nuh *pehng*-uhrr	*mina pengar*
travellers	mee-nuh	*mina*
cheques	rrea-seh-*chehk*-kuhrr	*resecheckar*
passport	mit *puhs*	*mitt pass*

ICELANDIC 197

INTRODUCTION 9

NORWEGIAN 243

NOTES

Phrasebooks

Lonely Planet phrasebooks are packed with essential words and phrases to help travellers communicate with the locals. With colour tabs for quick reference, an extensive vocabulary and use of script, these handy pocket-sized language guides cover day-to-day travel situations.

- handy pocket-sized books
- easy to understand Pronunciation chapter
- clear & comprehensive Grammar chapter
- romanisation alongside script to allow ease of pronunciation
- script throughout so users can point to phrases for every situation
- full of cultural information and tips for the traveller

'... vital for a real DIY spirit and attitude in language learning'
– Backpacker

'the phrasebooks have good cultural backgrounders and offer solid advice for challenging situations in remote locations'
– San Francisco Examiner

Australian *(Australian English, Aboriginal & Torres Strait languages)* • Baltic *(Estonian, Latvian, Lithuanian)* • Bengali • Brazilian • British *(English, dialects, Scottish Gaelic, Welsh)* • Burmese • Cantonese • Central Asia *(Kazakh, Kyrgyz, Pashto, Tajik, Tashkorghani, Turkmen, Uyghur, Uzbek & others)* • Central Europe *(Czech, German, Hungarian, Polish, Slovak, Slovene)* • Costa Rica Spanish • Czech • Eastern Europe *(Albanian, Bulgarian, Croatian, Czech, Hungarian, Macedonian, Polish, Romanian, Serbian, Slovak, Slovene)* • East Timor *(Tetun, Portuguese)* • Egyptian Arabic • Ethiopian *(Amharic)* • Europe *(Basque, Catalan, Dutch, French, German, Greek, Irish, Italian, Maltese, Portuguese, Scottish Gaelic, Spanish, Turkish, Welsh)* • Farsi *(Persian)* • Fijian • French • German • Greek • Hebrew • Hill Tribes *(Lahu, Akha, Lisu, Mong, Mien & others)* • Hindi & Urdu • Indonesian • Italian • Japanese • Korean • Lao • Latin American Spanish • Malay • Mandarin • Mongolian • Moroccan Arabic • Nepali • Pidgin • Pilipino (Tagalog) • Polish • Portuguese • Quechua • Russian • Scandinavian *(Danish, Faroese, Finnish, Icelandic, Norwegian, Swedish)* • South-East Asia *(Burmese, Indonesian, Khmer, Lao, Malay, Pilipino (Tagalog), Thai, Vietnamese)* • South Pacific *(Fijian, Hawaiian, Kanak languages, Maori, Niuean, Rapanui, Rarotongan Maori, Samoan, Tahitian, Tongan & others)* • Spanish *(Castilian, also includes Catalan, Galician & Basque)* • Sinhala • Swahili • Thai • Tibetan • Turkish • Ukrainian • USA *(US English, vernacular, Native American, Hawaiian)* • Vietnamese

COMPLETE LIST OF LONELY PLANET BOOKS

AFRICA Africa on a shoestring • Cairo • Cape Town • East Africa • Egypt • Ethiopia, Eritrea & Djibouti • The Gambia & Senegal • Healthy Travel Africa • Kenya • Malawi • Morocco • Mozambique • Read This First: Africa • South Africa, Lesotho & Swaziland • Southern Africa • Southern Africa Road Atlas • Tanzania, Zanzibar & Pemba • Trekking in East Africa • Tunisia • Watching Wildlife East Africa • Watching Wildlife Southern Africa • West Africa • World Food Morocco • Zimbabwe, Botswana & Namibia

AUSTRALIA & THE PACIFIC Aboriginal Australia & the Torres Strait Islands • Auckland • Australia • Australia Road Atlas • Bushwalking in Australia • Cycling Australia • Cycling New Zealand • Fiji • Healthy Travel Australia, NZ and the Pacific • Islands of Australia's Great Barrier Reef • Melbourne • Micronesia • New Caledonia • New South Wales & the ACT • New Zealand • Northern Territory • Outback Australia • Out to Eat – Melbourne • Out to Eat – Sydney • Papua New Guinea • Queensland • Rarotonga & the Cook Islands • Samoa • Solomon Islands • South Australia • South Pacific • Sydney • Sydney Condensed • Tahiti & French Polynesia • Tasmania • Tonga • Tramping in New Zealand • Vanuatu • Victoria • Walking in Australia • Watching Wildlife Australia • Western Australia

CENTRAL AMERICA & THE CARIBBEAN Bahamas, Turks & Caicos • Baja California • Bermuda • Central America on a shoestring • Costa Rica • Cuba • Dominican Republic & Haiti • Eastern Caribbean • Guatemala • Guatemala, Belize & Yucatán: La Ruta Maya • Havana • Healthy Travel Central & South America • Jamaica • Mexico • Mexico City • Panama • Puerto Rico • Read This First: Central & South America • World Food Mexico • Yucatán

EUROPE Amsterdam • Amsterdam Condensed • Andalucía • Austria • Barcelona • Belgium & Luxembourg • Berlin • Britain • Brussels, Bruges & Antwerp • Budapest • Canary Islands • Central Europe • Copenhagen • Corfu & the Ionians • Corsica • Crete • Crete Condensed • Croatia • Cycling Britain • Cycling France • Cyprus • Czech & Slovak Republics • Denmark • Dublin • Eastern Europe • Edinburgh • England • Estonia, Latvia & Lithuania • Europe on a shoestring • Finland • Florence • France • Frankfurt Condensed • Georgia, Armenia & Azerbaijan • Germany • Greece • Greek Islands • Hungary • Iceland, Greenland & the Faroe Islands • Ireland • Istanbul • Italy • Krakow • Lisbon • The Loire • London • London Condensed • Madrid • Malta • Mediterranean Europe • Milan, Turin & Genoa • Moscow • Mozambique • Munich • The Netherlands • Normandy • Norway • Out to Eat – London • Paris • Paris Condensed • Poland • Portugal • Prague • Provence & the Côte d'Azur • Read This First: Europe • Rhodes & the Dodecanese • Romania & Moldova • Rome • Rome Condensed • Russia, Ukraine & Belarus • Scandinavian & Baltic Europe • Scotland • Sicily • Slovenia • South-West France • Spain • St Petersburg • Sweden • Switzerland • Trekking in Spain • Tuscany • Venice • Vienna • Walking in Britain • Walking in France • Walking in Ireland • Walking in Italy • Walking in Spain • Walking in Switzerland • Western Europe • World Food France • World Food Ireland • World Food Italy • World Food Spain